UN/FAMILIAR THEOLOGY:
RECONCEIVING SEX, REPRODUCTION
AND GENERATIVITY

Rethinking Theologies: Constructing Alternatives in History and Doctrine

Edited by

Marion Grau
Susannah Cornwall
Hyo-Dong Lee
Steed Davidson

VOLUME 1

UN/FAMILIAR THEOLOGY

Reconceiving Sex, Reproduction and Generativity

Susannah Cornwall

t&tclark

LONDON • NEW YORK • OXFORD • NEW DELHI • SYDNEY

T&T CLARK
Bloomsbury Publishing Plc
50 Bedford Square, London, WC1B 3DP, UK
1385 Broadway, New York, NY 10018, USA

BLOOMSBURY, T&T CLARK and the T&T Clark logo are
trademarks of Bloomsbury Publishing Plc

First published 2017
Paperback edition first published in 2018

Library of Congress Cataloging-in-Publication Data
Names: Cornwall, Susannah, author.
Title: Un-familiar theology : reconceiving sex, reproduction, and
generativity /by Susannah Cornwall.
Description: New York : Bloomsbury Publishing, 2017. |Series: Rethinking
theologies: constructing alternatives in history and doctrine ; Volume 1
Identifiers: LCCN 2016055559| ISBN 9780567673251 (hb) |ISBN 9780567673268 (epub)
Subjects: LCSH: Queer theology. | Sex–Religious aspects–Christianity. |
Human reproduction–Religious aspects–Christianity.
Classification: LCC BT83.65 .C67 2017 | DDC 261.8/35–dc23
LC record available at https://lccn.loc.gov/2016055559

ISBN: HB: 978-0-5676-7325-1
PB: 978-0-5676-8584-1
ePDF: 978-0-5676-7327-5
ePub: 978-0-5676-7326-8

Series: Rethinking Theologies, volume 1

Typeset by Deanta Global Publishing Services, Chennai, India

To find out more about our authors and books visit
www.bloomsbury.com and sign up for our newsletters.

For Lars: not a happy ending, but a new beginning

Contents

ACKNOWLEDGEMENTS

I'm grateful to the group of scholars with whom I've spent the most time over the last few years discussing marriage, sex and family, especially the fellow-contributors to *Thinking Again about Marriage: Key Theological Questions* (SCM, 2016): John Bradbury, Raphael Cadenhead, Frances Clemson, Ben Fulford, Julie Gittoes, Brett Gray, Mike Higton, Charlotte Methuen, Rachel Muers and Augur Pearce. Brett Gray started the original conversation to which most of us pitched in and which eventually led to that book, and, more indirectly, to this one. My discussions with members of the Centre for the Study of Christianity and Sexuality's theological educators' group, including Sharon Ferguson, Jane Fraser, Carla Grosch-Miller, Martin Pendergast, Nicola Slee and Terry Weldon, have also sharpened my thinking on many of these issues.

I'm grateful to my colleagues, who make the University of Exeter Department of Theology and Religion such a convivial research environment. They include Siam Bhayro, Grace Davie, Brandon Gallaher, Tim Gorringe, Jonathan Hill, Katy Hockey, David Horrell, Louise Lawrence, Emma Loosley, Morwenna Ludlow, Esther Reed, Christopher Southgate, Francesca Stavrakopoulou, Adrian Thatcher, David Tollerton and Susan Margetts, who keeps the ship afloat. Excellent postgraduate students with whom I've also been privileged to think and talk on these and other themes, at Exeter and Manchester, have included Hannah Barr, Penny Cowell Doe, Rohan Gideon, Cherryl Hunt, Scott Midson, Karen O'Donnell, Charlie Pemberton, Catherine Matlock, Wei-Hsien Wan and Farah Zeb. They all have bright futures ahead.

Thanks also to colleagues elsewhere who keep the academy humane, including Hannah Bacon, Christina Beardsley, Rebecca Catto, David Clough, Rob Clucas, Ash Cocksworth, Anna Collar, Mat Collins, Andy Crome, Wendy Dossett, Marion Grau, Deryn Guest, Peter Hegarty, Nina Hoel, Jess Keady, Katharina Keim, Dawn Llewellyn, Esther McIntosh, Chris Meredith, Paul Middleton, David Nixon, Suzanne Owen, Katrina Roen, Peter Scott, Katja Stuerzenhofecker, Mitch Travis, Adriaan Van Klinken, Alana Vincent, Andy Williams and Alexandra Wörn.

To those who have read and commented on draft chapters of this book, including Julie Gittoes, Louise Lawrence, Jacqui Stewart, Katja Stuerzenhofecker, Adrian Thatcher and (most tirelessly, in this and so much more, as ever) Jon Morgan: thank you for being appropriately critical and constructive, and for helping me see how my ideas fit together better than I could by myself. To my readers: the mistakes are mine, not theirs.

My fellow series editor Marion Grau, and Anna Turton at Bloomsbury T&T Clark were instrumental in bringing the project into being, and I'm grateful to the whole team. Parts of Chapter 6 were presented at the University of Chichester's public theology research seminar in October 2014, and my thanks are due to Ruth Mantin, Stephen Roberts, Graeme Smith and others who contributed questions and comments on that occasion. Parts of this chapter were also presented at the annual conference of the Society for the Study of Theology at the University of Durham in April 2016. Ideas underlying (in particular) Chapter 7 were first given an outing at the Sexual Futures colloquium at Exeter in April 2014: very many thanks go to Kate Fisher, Jana Funke, Michael Hauskeller, Rebecca Langlands, Laura Salisbury and the others who were part of that conversation.

John Hughes, my first ever Reverend Doctor friend, also makes it into these pages. His life on earth ended as the book's began, and I miss him very much.

I'm surrounded by people who have generous, expansive notions of family. To those of you who include me in yours, you know who you are. Thank you.

Chapter 1

Introducing Un/familiar Theology

> The Church is not an ordinary family. It is an ark full of strange beasts, who
> nevertheless are brothers and sisters.
>
> (Mason 1996: 57)

This book is not about the ethics of reproductive interventions – such as IVF,[1] ICSI[2]
and embryo screening – or related technologies for aiding conception. Rather, it
is about the ways in which Christian *theological* conceptions of institutions such
as marriage, family, parenting and reproduction have changed and are changing,
and about what resources exist within and beyond the tradition to understand
these changes not as a raging tide to be turned back, but as in continuity with
goods deeply embedded in the collection of theologies concerned with the
Christian faith. I will be arguing that how communities order themselves, and (in
particular) how Christians speak about and out of institutions such as marriage,
family and parenting, may endorse and promote – or otherwise compromise and
elide – the full humanity and flourishing of all involved, and may give more or
less acknowledgement of the diversity within the historical and contemporary
traditions. I will also argue that our changing institutions are in dynamic
relationship with us: we shape them as they shape us, such that they are not to be
artificially fixed in a particular manifestation, but recognized as living.

In this book, I'll attempt to show that forms of marriage and family understood
as non-traditional – or somehow a departure from those the tradition has tended
to endorse – may stand as signs of the hope of the possibility of change. I will
show that generativity is about far more than biology, and that the transmission
of values and culture, and the creation of legacies that transcend ourselves, does
not exist only in those who survive us and share our genes. One of the key themes
is natality. This is well-attested in the work of Grace Jantzen, following Hannah
Arendt, and I will not attempt to reinvent their wheel (though I do draw on what
they argue). The crux of what natality means for each of these writers is that
every single human being is both a new *beginning* and a new *beginner*. Each new
person represents a pause, a shift, a caesura in the lives of those who welcome

---

1. In vitro fertilization.
2. Intra-cytoplasmic sperm injection.

them. Each person, too, has the capacity and the potential to be a fresh start. I will argue that this is particularly significant for reflections on adoption, since it means that knowing where a child comes from biologically does not, cannot, tell us everything they are or everything they will become. Even biological children are initiated into their families and cultures.

I will also suggest, going well beyond Jantzen's and Arendt's purviews, that adoption and same-sex marriage, as two examples, are themselves 'natal children': new beginnings with the potential to be fruitful and generative in their own right. If same-sex marriage, for example, somewhat changes marriage, and adoptive parenting by same-sex couples or single people, for example, somewhat alters what we understand family and parenthood to be, this is not a departure to be mourned, but a shift to be critically engaged. There will be both continuity and discontinuity with more familiar versions of these institutions: continuity because of their shared genealogy and the fact that at least some same-sex couples seeking marriage are doing so precisely because they want equality of rights with other married couples; discontinuity because they are expansions of the definitions of our terms. I admire much of John Milbank's work, but I am left uncomfortable by the implications of some of his assertions about same-sex marriage and parenting. I will argue that Milbank's contestation that the legalization of same-sex marriage changes the institution of marriage per se is accurate, but that this should not be a cause for reactionary alarm or shoring up the boundaries. I will take greater issue with Milbank's argument that the adoption of children by same-sex couples tends to commodify children, and will note in passing that the use of reproductive technologies does not (or need not) in itself entail commodification.

Many of the themes in this book chime with those explored by Rachel Muers in her 2008 book *Living for the Future: Theological Ethics for Coming Generations*. That book, however, specifically considered the future through the lenses of climate change and the future of humans alongside other creatures in the world. Here I wish to focus rather on the implications for theological accounts of generativity and, in particular, to examine the implications for accounts of marriage and parenthood which assume the male–female biologist model to be key. It is my assertion that, in this way, theologies of non-biological generativity may be developed which do not disparage either non-biologically procreative bodies or non-biologically formed families. Parts of the book also resonate with the ideas explored by Michael Banner in his 2013 Bampton Lectures, subsequently published as *The Ethics of Everyday Life: Moral Theology, Social Anthropology and the Imagination of the Human* (2014). Too often, holds Banner, Christian moral theology and ethics have concerned themselves with perceived 'border cases' such as reproductive technologies, abortion, euthanasia and other beginning and end-of-life issues, rather than the more commonly shared life experiences of conception, birth and death which give rise to 'everyday ethics'. Like Banner, in this book I engage in an exercise of troubling the apotheosization of biological kinship relationships. However, I also fear that Banner relativizes kinship *so* far that he risks diminishing human animality and the common urge many people – including, as I will show later, those who could not reproduce biologically with their partners – have to create a child who is recognizably 'one of them'. I have noted that, unlike Banner, my focus is not on assisted reproductive technologies; furthermore, I will show later that Banner's characterization of the 'desperation' of childlessness as solvable by greater attention to the 'spiritual kinship' available via formalized non-biological relationships such as those between godparent and godchild may give too little weight to the desires for the specific experiences of pregnancy and birth experienced by many people.

'Non-biological' is an ugly term. It characterizes what I am getting at by lack: what it is not, rather than what it is. The 'non-biological' therefore always invokes, repeats and (to some extent) reinforces the biological. But I am sticking with it here, rather than coming up with another more affirmative term, precisely because I want to draw attention to our collective linguistic and conceptual failure to figure generativity otherwise. 'Creativity' gets somewhere near the mark, but not quite near enough; I want to argue that even those of us who refuse any suggestion that we are creative ('I can't draw! My cooking's hopeless! Don't put me in charge of coming up with a colour scheme!') yet still generate. The non-biological is non-*bio-logical*. It does not follow a biological logic. It does not assume that the bios, the living, the genetic relationship, is all. It assumes that the logic of the bios has actually served to shut down as well as to promote life. It argues that the logic of the bios has denied multiplicity and variety of relationship.[3]

This is, also, why it may be understood as queer, and why another conversation-partner here, especially in the final chapters, is the queer literary theorist Lee Edelman. I will suggest that Edelman (2004) is both correct and limited in his account of the invocation of the mythic Child-as-innocent, and its propensity to bring about quietism and quash political change. But I will argue that Edelman has not taken sufficient account of the fact that all of us (however old, however

---

3. Theorists such as Giorgio Agamben (1998: 75) note the distinction drawn in ancient Greek thought between 'natural' life, 'the pure fact of birth' – the Greek ζωή (*zoē*) – and qualified life, life already subject to political control, βίος (*bios*). Here I follow Agamben in his assumption that even apparently 'natural' life – that involving reproduction and the domestic sphere – is already so politicized (10), such that it is possible (if undesirable) to conceive of some lives as less than fully morally considerable (cf. 75, 80ff). Furthermore, as Agamben also notes, for Michel Foucault (1990: 143) such politicizations and qualifications are not only externally imposed, but come – through mechanisms of the naturalization of biopower – to be inscribed by individuals on themselves. Through a series of complex economic and epistemological relations, politics came to inform biological discourse as much as biological discourse informed politics, for biology 'passed into knowledge's field of control and power's sphere of intervention' (142). Just as the management of sex becomes the management of life itself for Foucault, so the management of biological norms continues to influence and be influenced by external notions of what does and does not entail life well governed. Although Foucault identifies biopower as concerning itself with and being disseminated through discourses of sex specifically (146), it is also possible to trace the effects of biopower streaming through embodied life far more broadly. What Agamben seeks to explore in *Homo Sacer* is *how* such institutional and biopolitical power intersects.

damaged and bleak and no-longer-innocent) are still children, and that futurity is for each of us, the real ones here and now, not just the ones whose existence is invoked to write out of signification the reality of others.

A theme which recurs throughout the book is generativity. This specific term is probably a neologism original to the psychologist Erik Erikson in the 1950s, as I discuss further in Chapter 2. But its etymological roots are far older. 'Generate' comes from the Latin *generare*, meaning to produce, beget, create, engender or arouse. The Old French *générer*, in instances from around 1200, implies, more specifically, regeneration via the life-giving force of baptism: a metaphor well-attested in the New Testament texts. The Oxford English Dictionary's entries for 'generate' make clear its (at least) dual senses: one denotation clearly implies bringing into being for the first time (with the implication of doing something new); another's gist is more along the lines of reproduction, repeating something old. As I will show in Chapters 4, 5 and 6 (on natality, adoption and the reproductive futurism of the Quiverfull movement), reproduction is never quite as simple as that: nothing reproduced is an exact facsimile or clone of its original, and, as I will show, there are good theological reasons for being glad that this is so. It is appropriate that the etymology is doubled; to generate always, I will argue, implies a commingling of originality and repetition, new and old.

Generativity and generation also, unsurprisingly, have their origins in *genesis*, the first origin of all. The Greek γένεσις, source or creation, is the root of γίγνεσθαι, to come into being, to be born. From here, we get the Greek γένημα, fruit or offspring, and γεννάω, the verb of begetting or bringing forth. So, in English, to be generative is to cause, to create, to produce; to engender is to bring about or bring into existence, which may or may not manifest in actual literal offspring or progeny. To be degenerate, however, does not imply a failure to generate; the root there is, rather, genre or genus, so degeneracy is the loss of qualities proper to one's kind – or having deviated from the bounds of one's genre. Generosity has this same history: to be generous is, in Middle French, to be of good spirit or good stock, that is, of good genus.[4]

Genre or genus is what levels us all. It is what says we are of a kind; that we are all in it together. Kindness, being of a kind, is also kin-ness, and Janet Martin Soskice reminds us that this kin-ness and kindness are at the heart of the interrelationships of the Triune God as frequently symbolized with human familial language such as Father and Son. As such, she notes, God in Christ is human kin, and human beings are veritably Christ's mother and brothers (Mt. 12.48) (Soskice 2007: 5). The Latin *genus* (race, stock, kind) is cognate with Greek γένος, and closely similar to the Sanskrit *gana* (which implies flock, tribe, class, number, multitude or series) and the Persian *jins* (again: kind, stock, sort, mode, type – and commonly used in present-day Iran to mean sex or gender; Najmabadi 2013). But being of a kind might also be read, negatively, as lacking individuality:

4. In the Italian of the late thirteenth century, the term *generoso* also implies fertility specifically.

it is, from this same root, generic. (There is nothing complimentary about the term 'genre fiction' as applied to murder mysteries and hospital romances: such works are often dismissed as interchangeable, lacking in any character beyond the conventions of the subcategory and repeating tired old tropes.) Here I will be holding that, while human beings and their creations may be of a common kind, they are far from generic. Each human is a distinctive, non-interchangeable locus of being, and combines their biological, social and cultural history with something novel, something new. No person is entirely distinct from their background, but nor is any person entirely a product of it. So while accounts of what it is to be human – including theological anthropologies – may speak in general rules (i.e. rules applicable to every individual instance of the genus or genre), and trace genealogies (stories of descent), they will also transcend them. Humans push the bounds of our genres; we resist genericism. We push back at the limits within which we seem to find ourselves, and create new imaginaries which more fully acknowledge the interactive nature of our relationships with the world (and the divine). So while there will remain things that are true about all humans, it is also true that human worlds are malleable. We shape our societies and our institutions, and, in so doing, we shape ourselves.

This is significant because, I will argue, it means that we are both 'parents' and 'children' of our social institutions. We are born of them and influenced by them, but we also shape their transmission and continuation. In Jacqui Stewart's (2008: 93) words:

> A human being is spoken of in the narratives of his or her mother, father, family, friends and carers, when a physical or biological presence has been established to allow those narratives to be meaningfully created. ... The interpretation of narratives both of the self and of others is inherently ethical because it is always responsible to something over and against itself.

As Stewart notes, this relationship between self and other is expressed variously by twentieth-century philosophers, as in Paul Ricoeur, for whom ethics necessitates attention to and respect for the otherness of the other alongside attention to and respect for the self, and in Emmanuel Levinas, for whom selfhood is almost submerged by the ontological priority of the other having been constructed *by* the other. Key is locatedness: the fact that *this* person exists *here* in *this* community and *this* body. But locatedness does not mean never changing; rather, 'as a human being develops, becomes able to act and respond, able to communicate and able to tell his or her own story, so the human person grows and a reflexive self emerges. *The identity of the human person is an identity of continuity, not a static essence, that is, the person is historical*' (93, my emphasis).[5]

___

5. For Ricoeur, narrative leads to meaning; the free and original is the point at which the narrative begins and ends. Plot, character, promise and witness are all inherent in language. Thus humans can act creatively in undertaking moral evaluation via language: 'The narrative

Likewise, I will be arguing, human institutions and the cultural phenomena along the lines of which humans organize their societies – families, marriages and so on – are not static but dynamic. This is why animality and culture indeed exist in creative tension, neither reducible to the other.

This seems an obvious and an undevastating thing to say, except that much of the rhetoric underlying theological accounts of family, sex and marriage in the debates of the past several decades seems to want to claim that these phenomena are (or should be) somehow unchanging and immaculate; that to acknowledge (and celebrate and accelerate) their shifting and developing natures is to reject them as good gifts of God. We see this keenly, for example, in reports and statements on marriage and human sexuality from several Christian denominations. In what follows in the remainder of this Introduction I will draw attention, in particular, to texts from the Church of England and the Roman Catholic Church.

Finally, I will be mindful throughout the volume that generativity in human terms is one aspect of a broader and more universal creaturehood. Humans have a special propensity to shape and develop our social and technological worlds, but we are less unique in this respect than the moderns often wished to admit. Creatureliness is, fundamentally, social and relational, for creatures are related to, in the first instance, by God, their sustainer. Furthermore, life in an ecosystem means that each of us, whether consciously or not, relies on the life, death and work of millions of other organisms in order to sustain our own existence. All creaturely activity has implications for (known and unknown) others. We are often unaware of many of the other inhabitants of this ecosystem, but responsibility is about exercising answerable choice in how we relate to those of whom we can reasonably be aware. While death and predation may be inescapable this side of the eschaton, conscious exploitation and violence are more avoidable and thereby less excusable. Wherever our activity compromises the full flourishing of others, it is *a priori* unjust. There must be an excellent, exceptional reason for it if it is to happen; it cannot be allowed to occur lightly or unremarked, and no given individual is casually sacrificable for the 'greater good' of the community.

Church of England

For the Church of England Faith and Order Commission in its 2013 document *Men and Women in Marriage*, marriage is a creation ordinance (Archbishops' Council 2013: 1, following the bishops' 2005 statement on civil partnerships). The document does acknowledge that marriage is not unchanging: 'Calling it

---

of action also involves allocation of responsibility, and narrative itself implies evaluation of action' (Stewart 2010: 396). Personhood arises in the dialectic between consciousness of the continuity of identity and consciousness of the possibility of being an agent of change. Change always assumes and involves relationship with the world. See further, Ricoeur (1992) and Stewart (2010).

a gift of God, we mean that it is not simply a cultural development (though it has undergone much cultural development) nor simply a political or economic institution (though often embedded in political and economic arrangements)' (2); indeed, it is an 'aspect of human society' (3). However, the document still gives a sense that it is what it is because this is how *God* has ordained it as a 'structure of life' (3). Indeed, it is, in some sense, foundational: 'Marriage is a paradigm of society, facilitating other social forms' (5). The report is fairly dismissive of differences in expressions of marriage across times and cultures: 'It is possible to exaggerate the cultural relativity of marriage-forms. Many differences there have been, but they hardly amount to a significant challenge to these structural foundations' (6). The 'structural foundations' in question are the three elements found in Christian and Jewish accounts of marriage but also, they argue, across most 'developed traditions': that marriage be exogamous, permanent and between partners of different sexes (6).

But there is an interesting tension here surrounding where marriage actually comes from and about its existence or otherwise as an *a priori*, incontrovertible fact. On the one hand, 'Neither the state nor the Church can claim a prior right over marriage, nor does either of them "make" marriages, which is done by God's providence working through the public promises of the couples themselves' (13). On the other hand, the document implies that the church precisely *can* define what marriage is, and does so: 'The reality of marriage between one man and one woman will not disappear as the result of any legislative change, for God has given this gift, and it will remain part of our created human endowment' (16). Given that many people and jurisdictions patently do *not* believe that part of the 'reality' of marriage is its exclusively heterosexual character, or that marriage is a creation of God, what else is the church doing here but claiming a prerogative on marriage, seizing the right to define it on behalf of others? Marriage is therefore simultaneously being figured in the document as something unchangeable and unshakeable, which will not be changed in 'fact' by changing legal definitions of it, *and* as something oddly vulnerable which must be protected and shored up: the report warns gloomily: 'When marriage is spoken of unclearly or misleadingly, it distorts the way couples try to conduct their relationship and makes for frustration and disappointment. ... The disciplines of living in it may become more difficult to acquire, and the path to fulfilment, in marriage and in other relationships, more difficult to find' (16).

The rhetoric of marriage as being somehow immovable and unchanging is even more evident in the earlier short statement from the Church of England made in response to the UK government's consultation on same-sex marriage in 2012. This refers to 'the intrinsic nature of marriage as the union of a man and a woman, as enshrined in human institutions throughout history' (Church of England 2012: 1). Here, it is culture (i.e. human institutions) which 'enshrines' (i.e. preserves and protects) marriage – which is therefore, again, simultaneously something with an 'intrinsic nature' prior to culture and something vulnerable and in need of defence. The statement speaks out against changing, for 'essentially ideological reasons', a term 'as familiar and fundamental as marriage' (1). Marriage's nature as exclusively heterosexual is 'intrinsic' and has been understood this way 'throughout history' (1); it (purportedly) precedes definition and recognition by either church or state; yet here, again, is the church defining, defending and upholding what it wants to say simply *is* self-evident and *a priori*. For the Church of England, even more is at stake than challenging state power: marriage is the context in which the very fact of what it means to be a gendered human being is worked out (4). This has been convincingly challenged by Mike Higton (2016) among others, but the sense throughout the 2012 statement is that, like the children scared into obedience by Hilaire Belloc's 'Jim', who ran away from his nurse and was eaten by a lion, the Church of England is urging adherence to an incontrovertible (yet vulnerable) 'truth' about marriage, 'for fear of finding something worse' (Belloc 1998 [1907]: 22). Might we, in fact, counter that if marriage has a 'stable' character at all, it is precisely its capacity to respond to social and theological change?

The Church of England's *Marriage: A Teaching Document* (1999) reads as far less reactionary, perhaps because the possibility of the legal recognition of same-sex marriage was not, at that time, such a live issue in England and Wales, and the discussions which would lead to the passage of the Civil Partnership Act 2004 were in their early stages. Although the document recommends marriage without prior cohabitation as a less risky route for couples because of the 'uncertainties and tensions' of living together, it acknowledges the frequency of marriage following cohabitation earlier in history (3–4).[6] Marriage is described as a 'natural endowment' given by God, but this is grounded more in affirmation of security and continuity than in rhetoric about gender and orders of creation. Throughout, the tone of the 1999 document is far more pastoral than the more recent ones. It does not shy away from recognizing the diversity of opinion within the Church of England on divorce and remarriage, as well as on living together before marriage, and it is more irenic than heavy handedly didactic in its pastoral recommendations. Indeed, the picture of marriage here is rather cosy in its pragmatism: it reads as though marriage is more fundamentally about the general stability of society and good of children than about the relationship of specific spouses. There is even a hint that, while remarriage after divorce might sometimes be licit, especially if there are young children to be cared for, this should not take place between formerly adulterous partners: 'A new relationship is needed, avoiding suspicion that the new marriage consecrates an old infidelity' (7). In other words, James might divorce from Anna following his extramarital relationship with Liv, but if he wants to remarry for the good of his children, Liv is not the one to choose, and he would do better starting afresh with Cassie. There is not much space here for Liv to prove to have been the true passion of James's life; or, at least, if she is, this has little to do with whom he should marry.

---

6. The page numbers given here refer to the PDF version of the document available at: https://www.churchofengland.org/media/45645/marriage.pdf.

Roman Catholic Church

In the Catechism of the Catholic Church, marriage is presented, again, as instituted by God (para 1602); as a more than 'purely human' institution, with 'common and permanent characteristics' (1603); and as an institution 'prior to any recognition by public authority, which has an obligation to recognize it' (2202). The 1965 document *Gaudium et Spes*, published under Pope Paul VI and reflecting the mind of the Second Vatican Council, holds, despite its generally progressive attitude towards human culture, that the nature of marriage is as 'an unbreakable compact between persons ... a whole manner and communion of life' (para 50). The unchanging nature of the situation is expressed even more strongly in *Persona Humana* (1975): there are 'immutable laws inscribed in the constitutive elements of human nature and which are revealed to be identical in all beings endowed with reason' (Congregation for the Doctrine of the Faith 1975, para 4). Any shifts may only occur within predetermined limits:

> Of course, in the history of civilization many of the concrete conditions and needs of human life have changed and will continue to change. But all evolution of morals and every type of life must be kept within the limits imposed by the immutable principles based upon every human person's constitutive elements and essential relations – elements and relations which transcend historical contingency. (Para 3)

Specifically, on matters of sex and marriage,

> There exist principles and norms which the Church has always unhesitatingly transmitted as part of her teaching, however much the opinions and morals of the world may have been opposed to them. These principles and norms in no way owe their origin to a certain type of culture, but rather to knowledge of the Divine Law and of human nature. (Para 5)

In some respects, *Familiaris Consortio* (1981) and *Veritatis Splendor* (1993) try to shut down the more expansive moral theologies that had emerged during and since Vatican II which, their critics felt, had gone too far down the road of moral relativism and informed uncertainty; even *Gaudium et Spes* came to be considered dangerously liberal in its endorsement of the diverse judgement of human conscience on issues such as birth control. It is, therefore, perhaps unsurprising that, in *Familiaris Consortio*, Pope John Paul II affirms marriage as having been 'willed by God in the very act of creation', but now in need of being 'restored' to its 'beginning' because of the wounding effects of sin (John Paul 1981, para 3). Here, because it is willed by God, 'the institution of marriage is not an undue interference by society or authority, nor the extrinsic imposition of a form' (para 11).

A 2003 statement of the Congregation for the Doctrine of the Faith co-signed by Cardinal Joseph Ratzinger, who would go on to become Pope Benedict XVI two years later, contains perhaps some of the strongest official Roman Catholic declarations of the solely heterosexual nature of marriage (possibly because, as with the 2012 Church of England statement, it was prepared specifically in light of questions about the possibility of recognizing same-sex relationships). Marriage has 'inalienable' characteristics:

> The Church's teaching on marriage and on the complementarity of the sexes reiterates *a truth that is evident to right reason* and *recognized as such by all the major cultures of the world*. Marriage is not just any relationship between human beings. It was *established by the Creator with its own nature, essential properties and purpose*. No ideology can erase from the human spirit the certainty that marriage exists solely between a man and a woman, who by mutual personal gift, proper and exclusive to themselves, tend toward the communion of their persons. ... The *natural truth* about marriage was confirmed by the Revelation contained in the biblical accounts of creation, an expression also of the original human wisdom, in which *the voice of nature itself* is heard. (Congregation for the Doctrine of the Faith 2003, para 2–3; my emphasis)

For states and other legal jurisdictions to recognize same-sex marriages would specifically be a failure to 'promote and defend marriage [that is, exclusively heterosexual marriage] as an institution essential to the common good' (para 6). In other words, here the issue is about the *institutionalization* of same-sex marriage, which would, suggests the document, endow same-sex marriage with greater reach and influence 'and would result in changes to the entire organization of society, contrary to the common good' (para 6); specifically, 'The inevitable consequence of legal recognition of homosexual unions would be the redefinition of marriage, which would become, in its legal status, an institution devoid of essential reference to factors linked to heterosexuality; for example, procreation and raising children' (para 8). For, of course, the context here is that 'changing' marriage would entail disrupting the association between spousehood and parenthood, between sex, marrying and having children. Francis has been depicted as a liberal, reformist pope in many respects, yet throughout his papacy thus far he has repeated the position (as in a homily of June 2014) that marriage is *for* children and that couples who choose not to have children are refusing 'fruitfulness' and choosing instead, selfishly, to be 'carefree' (Wooden 2014). In this, Francis is in closer continuity with his immediate predecessor than the latter's critics might want to acknowledge. The strong natural law rhetoric of the 2003 statement recurs in a 2010 letter of Benedict XVI (2010, para 85), wherein Jesus is said – borrowing terminology from the Council of Trent – to have elevated 'to the dignity of a sacrament what was described in human nature from the beginning'.

There is a similar tension in evidence here as in the Church of England documents: marriage is simultaneously so self-evident, so incontrovertible, so certain and so readily decipherable via natural law that no one could possibly doubt, question or erode it; and yet also, apparently, so threatened and vulnerable that the Congregation must trumpet it aloud and make quite clear what marriage is and is not. *Everyone* – at least, everyone belonging to a 'major culture' – *knows*, apparently, that marriage is self-evidently and inherently heterosexual, and it is this very self-evidence that is part of the argument for its 'naturalness' and certainty; yet here is a reminder anyway, just in case we have forgotten – and a suggestion that even something apparently so unassailable and indubitable *could* be obscured (Congregation for the Doctrine of the Faith 2003, para 11). Apart from anything else, this seems to point to possible flaws in strong natural law-based reasoning.

Appeals to origins as a basis for authority are a mixed blessing. On the one hand, as they seems to be designed to do in these churches' statements and documents, they guard against accepting any innovation as progressive or superior just because it is new. On the other, however, there is something less self-evident than we might suppose about appealing to the good of 'in the beginning'. It is no coincidence that the kinds of texts we have been discussing appeal so heavily to the early chapters of Genesis, or to concepts such as 'orders of creation' which are, similarly, given ontological primacy. There is more than a hint of prescriptive doxology about them: 'As it was in the beginning, is now, and ever shall be, world without end'. But as Hugh Pyper has shown, beginnings are not unambiguous or unambivalent, and the placing of discussions of questions such as sex and reproduction early on in what has come to be accepted as the biblical canon does not necessarily mean we should assume a clear primacy of them.[7] (In any case, argues Ken Stone (2005: 43), texts which today's readers interpret as being self-evidently about questions of sex and reproduction have also been understood in quite other ways, as pertaining to mortality, or correct food and farming practices.) For Pyper (2012: 40), 'Far from presenting beginnings as "natural", the poetics of the Hebrew Bible are characterized by an evasion of beginnings. … Indeed, … far from being natural, "beginning" in the Bible is the antithesis of the "natural"'. The Hebrew Bible, he continues, actually begins in the *middle* of God's action, not at the outset (43). Christian obsessions with origins and beginnings owe more to Plato and Augustine than to the biblical canon itself (42). The Hebrew *bereshit* is usually translated as 'beginning' – but this might be understood in terms of priority rather than chronology (and rather than the priority being given on the *grounds* of the putative chronology) – and reading Genesis via the lens of 'nature' is far from its 'plain' sense. Pyper says,

> What is clear is that creation in Genesis is emphatically *not* natural. Things did not come about through some natural process, but through the unmotivated speech and action of an unexplained God. In fact, one could argue that the whole point of the text is to declare that there is nothing natural about this beginning. There is no process that could [be] traced back to a further origin, no intrinsic quality in matter or in space/time that explicably gave rise to whatever is. (43)

So, we might add, it is ironic that it is to just such texts that proponents of natural law often appeal to argue that the goodness of marriage and family life are revealed

---

7. I am grateful to Jon Morgan for alerting me to Pyper's discussion of this theme.

in Scripture as written into nature from the beginning. Original sin is a sin of origins, hence having become linked in the theological imagination with sex, the phenomenon from which we (in one sense) originate. But another sin of origins is, I want to suggest, the apotheosizing of origins: so originalism is also, itself, a kind of original sin. I develop this point in more detail later in the book.

ECUSA: Some Alternative Approaches

Not all recent church statements on marriage have made the same kind of appeals, or have assumed that marriage must always be open to procreation (thereby making same-sex marriage impossible). The Task Force on the Study of Marriage appointed to report to the Episcopal Church in the United States of America (ECUSA) in 2015, indeed, explicitly appeals to generativity in a broader sense as a good of marriage:

> Ideally, the spouses find in each other an appropriate end, rather than the means to some other end or objective, however good. Procreation does have virtue, in the bringing to be of human life, and it is a good toward which human endeavor in marriage is well intended when possible, growing out of the love of the couple for each other, rather than simply as an intended (or unintended) consequence. But it is also important to note that the love of a couple for each other can result in other goods for the benefit both of the couple and the society of which they form a part, even when procreation either cannot or does not take place. There is a generativity that comes with the 'mutual society' of marriage and which spills over to the larger society in which the couple lives and participates. It is perhaps good to note that the water jars at Cana were filled to the brim, and that the very act of dipping out the wine must have caused some overflow. (25)

So the Task Force holds that the primary task of the spouses in marriage is to become 'an enacted parable for the community of the Church, as it "preaches Christ" to a wider world' (27). This is not contingent on the spouses' respective sexes, or capacity to procreate, but on their mutual comforting and joy-taking. There is therefore no inherent barrier to same-sex marriage. This is the kind of logic on which I expand in Chapters 2 and 3 of this book.

However, Episcopalian critics of the Task Force's report hold that changing the church's liturgy and canons to this effect (such that the necessarily different sexes of the spouses, and the nature of marriage as intended for procreation, were not written in) 'would obscure the nature of marriage as a mysterious icon of the union between "Christ and the Church" (Eph. 5:32), present in creation itself' (Bauerschmidt et al. 2015: 2). More specifically, they hold that the appeal to generativity does too little to set out what makes marriage distinctive from other kinds of spiritual, familial or communitarian relationships (7), and that it excludes *eros* from the equation (8). Like the documents discussed earlier, the critics hold that marriage is 'a divine reality, to which the created social form bears witness: a covenanted union between Christ and the Church' (11). When, later in 2015, ECUSA did approve liturgies for blessing same-sex marriages, some of the responses drew on even stronger originalist rhetoric in protest; Most Reverend Stanley Ntagali (2015), archbishop of the Church of Uganda, held:

> The definition and meaning of marriage is not something that can be defined by voting. It is something that is given by God in general revelation and in special revelation, and it is for us as human beings and, especially, the Church, to simply receive and follow. The fact that 2+2 equals 4 cannot be changed by a vote or decree. Neither can the meaning of marriage between a man and a woman be changed by a vote.

Indeed, it was on the grounds that it was not possible to move away from a 'traditional' account of marriage as between a man and a woman (as well as faithful and lifelong) that ECUSA was disciplined by the Primates of the Anglican Communion in January 2016.

But I will be arguing in this book that, whatever the reality of the relationship between God and humanity (as represented by Christ and the church), marriage can only be a metaphor for it, not the other way around. Marriage begins in human interactions. My criticism therefore chimes with Scott MacDougall's rejoinder to Bauerschmidt et al. and his observation that they 'invert' the marriage metaphor of Eph. 5.32. MacDougall (2015: 3) says,

> I want to emphasize that, in verse 32, Paul is analogizing from the unitive love between spouses in marriage to the unitive love between Christ and his church: 'This [the spousal love through which two people become one flesh] is a great mystery, *and I am applying it to* Christ and the church.' ... Against the plain sense of the text and scholarly exegesis, [Bauerschmidt et al. invert] the direction of the analogy, starting with a claim about the Christ-church relationship that is then used to determine the significance of marriage. Moreover, while doing this, the analogy is inflated from a (now-reversed) metaphor into an ontological claim: the oneness of Christ and church, upon which the entire order of creation is founded and toward which it is heading, is not merely analogized to spousal unity but becomes the metaphysical basis of marriage itself.

Finally, throughout the book I am working with the assumption that the Christian tradition is a dynamic one whose adherents are called to be responsive to changing times and circumstances as they work out what it means to be faithful to their tradition. Faithfulness to the tradition means, for those of us in it, as I have suggested elsewhere, remaining in conversation with our theological forebears; it does not mean holding earlier norms or positions as untouchable, especially where these have had a damaging ongoing legacy. Faithfulness to the tradition means calling out its failings and its injustices, just as we can expect and hope that those who come after us will do to us in the light of the wisdom of the unfolding revelation of their own age (Cornwall 2014a: 77–8). The life and story of Christ are the centre for all Christians; but, as Ben Fulford (2016: 52–3) notes,

> We cannot always simply repeat the ways in which these writers and their contemporaries set forth faithful living in conformity with Christ. ... Yet in responding to this Lord, we are afforded in these texts, under the Spirit's guidance, a sort of education. It is a training in the 'transformation of the mind' (Rom. 12:2) and life in accordance with the way God and Christ are identified in the story and with the way all people are identified in relation to them. Acknowledging the authority of this literature, then, means learning to think with it in dependence upon the Spirit of God. Such a model of scriptural authority also allows us, where appropriate, to bring our own knowledge to bear, where the texts make room for an appeal to such knowledge, and to relate it to what Scripture discloses about the identities of God, Jesus Christ and creatures.

The tradition, then, *both* shapes and forms us, *and* continues to be shaped (redacted, interpreted, disseminated, sometimes disowned) by us.

Un/familiar Theology

My thesis is that un/familiar theology is, then, theology which acknowledges its genealogy, its 'family history', but which is also well aware that genealogy is an arbitrary and constructed science. Family trees usually trace only a few of the possible strands: by four generations back, each of us had sixteen direct ancestors. If we sought to trace each of them, and each of *their* great-grandparents, we would soon be consumed by the task, even assuming that evidence and documentation for each of them was available. But most of our family histories focus on only two or three of the best-attested branches, those with the best (or most notorious) stories attached. We might say the Christian tradition is less complex than this, since we share fewer 'ancestors' between all of us: I might claim Augustine of Hippo or Julian of Norwich as my own, but so might you, even if we are of entirely different ethnicities and denominational allegiances and have grown up on opposite sides of the world. But this selectivity is also an important part of the story: the Christian tradition has just as many silent, forgotten and embarrassing progenitors as any biological family does, yet it is too often the same old stories of the same old great-great-great-grandfathers and aunts and cousins sixteen times removed that get trotted out on every occasion. Queer, postcolonial, feminist, womanist and other hermeneutics of retrieval have done well at highlighting some of the voices which are missing, even if they can never adequately be reconstructed. Nonetheless, the tradition will always remain more various and more disputed than the scrapbooks of its most celebrated stories can acknowledge. When the Primates of the Churches of the Anglican Communion met in Canterbury at a meeting convened by archbishop of Canterbury Justin Welby in January 2016, they stated in a communiqué, 'The traditional doctrine of the church in view of the teaching of Scripture, upholds marriage as between a man and a woman in faithful, lifelong union'. Yet the concomitant implication – that those Anglican provinces which celebrated same-sex marriages were somehow breaking with tradition (leading to the exclusion of ECUSA from decision-making on doctrine or policy for the Anglican Communion, or representing the Anglican Communion in ecumenical and interfaith work, for a period of three years) – gave too little acknowledgement of tradition's shifting and dynamic nature. After all, even those member churches which refused to recognize same-sex marriage were pragmatic about the acknowledgement that many marriages were *not* in fact either faithful or lifelong, and that there therefore needed to be mechanisms for dealing with divorce and remarriage.

Un/familiar theology, then, is about acknowledging that both the familiar and the unfamiliar – and both the familial, and what we might prefer were *not* the familial – are part of the tradition. More specifically, it acknowledges that this is the case for the traditions *about* families – about marriage, and parenting and reproduction – that have come down to us. And, furthermore, it holds that what now seems unfamiliar is precisely part of what the tradition may be yet to embrace. The unfamiliar is therefore both already a part of the tradition, and part of what the tradition might become.[8] I cannot claim to have settled disputed accounts of the centrality of family and reproduction across the tradition, but I do seek to identify a new set of questions which bring to the fore the tensions between exhorting animality and refusing to relegate non-biological kinship relationships to being second best.

Un/familiar theology is also theology which is circumspect about the apotheosizations of some forms of family which have taken place within parts of Christianity, and this is the other strand which I explore throughout this book. As theologian and historian Rosemary Radford Ruether (2000: 9, 60–82, 107–55) notes, Christian endorsements of particular models of family have not arisen in distinction from matters of economic and political power. Certain types of family structures have proven themselves useful in reinforcing certain modes of authority. That said, the Christian tradition does already attest that families come in different shapes and sizes. This has often taken place in an inclusive and non-pathologizing way. For example, the 1995 Church of England document *Something to Celebrate* (Central Board of Finance 1995) acknowledges the ubiquity (even greater now than then) of stepfamilies, families where the parents are unmarried and those led by a lone parent – and emphasizes, in particular, the long history of blended and otherwise 'non-typical' family structures (39). It also emphasizes as positive changes the increase in the number of fathers directly involved in their children's care, and the possibility of more children knowing their grandparents and great-grandparents because of increased life expectancies (204). It specifically recommends, 'The Church needs to recognize and value the different ways in which people live in families. ... We recommend that the life of local churches

8. I'm grateful to Adrian Thatcher for helping me to clarify my thinking on this point.

be ordered in ways which help everyone feel welcome, whatever their family circumstances' (210; original emphasis).[9]

Nonetheless, some of the time, and in much Christian rhetoric surrounding marriage and parenthood, only certain types of families are apotheosized and held to be ideal. Even *Something to Celebrate* holds:

> The Christian practice of lifelong, monogamous marriage lies at the heart of the Church's understanding of how the love of God is made manifest in the sexual companionship of a man and a woman. The increasing popularity of cohabitation, among Christians and non-Christians, is no reason to modify this belief. On the contrary, it is an opportunity and a challenge to the Church to articulate its doctrine of marriage in ways so compelling, and to engage in a practice of marriage so life-enhancing, that the institution of marriage regains its centrality. (Central Board of Finance 1995: 188)

In Chapter 6, therefore, I reflect in detail on the particular multi-child families, led by fathers who are conceptualized as their authority, 'covering' and protecting from the wider world, and mothers who are charged with keeping the home, which have been associated with the pro-natalist Quiverfull movement. While, as I will show, proponents of Quiverfull theology are concerned more with disseminating ideology than with actually conceiving large numbers of children, there are some authors prominent within the movement who specifically hold that large family sizes align more closely with God's plan for Christians than small ones do. The Quiverfull movement has had a particularly interesting relationship with adoption, especially from overseas, and several figures prominent in the movement thereby demonstrate a conviction that families are always already about more than biological relationships. Nonetheless, there has also been circumspection elsewhere about adoption, particularly by same-sex couples, and the ways in which this may be seen as disrupting associations between marriage, sexual activity, procreation and parenthood. It is on these grounds that, for example, John Milbank holds that same-sex adoptive parents are not *really* parents ontologically, but have simply been 'allowed' by the state to function as though they were. Along less vociferous lines, Robert Song holds that the willingness for openness to procreation is what marks out marriages from relationships (whether between heterosexual or same-sex partners) where the couple is not open to procreating and should therefore, according to Song, be defined differently.

9. Members of the working party which produced the report included liberal Christian scholars such as New Testament biblical scholar Stephen Barton (2001), author of texts including *Life Together: Family, Sexuality and Community in the New Testament and Today*; Anne Borrowdale (1989), whose theological research until that date had focused on the negative effects of Christian gendered idealizations of work, service and self-denial on women; and Alison Webster (1995), author of the groundbreaking study of women's sexuality and Christianity, *Found Wanting?*

I engage with these positions in Chapters 2 and 5 in particular, and conclude that the emphasis on biological relationship (perhaps unwittingly) at once devalues the reality of familial relationships where kinship exceeds biology, detracts from the significance of broader forms of generativity and sets up an assumption that same-sex couples do *not* value procreativity in the way that many heterosexual couples do. In this way I challenge the close association between procreativity and heterosexuality from a new angle – not to diminish the desire for procreation in heterosexual relationships but to acknowledge and emphasize its existence in many same-sex ones.

Elsewhere in the book, I ask questions about what kinds of iterations of family, marriage and parenting might be *so* unfamiliar that they lack all continuity with what has been understood as good and life-affirming in these institutions. As an example, in Chapter 3, I take the case of polyamory, and reflect on the extent to which the exclusive 'twoness' of marriage is an unbreachable theological barrier even where the sex and gender of the spouses is not. I hold that aspects of polyamorous constructions of relationship may be understood to mediate grace as effectively – or even more so – than monogamous relationships do, and that reflection on what polyamory does best (including close attention to dynamics of consent and power, and disruption of the dyads which have become petrified in some mainstream theologies) may prompt useful self-critical reflection on the parts of apologists for 'traditional' marriage; but that there are still aspects of monogamous marriages (such as the principles of mutuality, reciprocity and the holding-together of recreation and responsibility) which seem difficult to replicate in polyamorous structures. Polyamory remains undertheologized and is seldom acknowledged beyond specifically queer theological contexts except as an instantly dismissed bogey. Here I hope to prompt serious engagement with the possibility that the existence of faithfulness across a context of more-than-two is worthy of further consideration, not least because it sheds light back on the often unreflexive assumption that twoness itself equals licitness and fullness of life within Christian accounts of marriage.

The book ends with closer reflection on the principles of repetition and difference. Here in Chapter 7 as throughout, I hold that un/familiar theology necessitates genuine disruption of and resistance to aspects of the Christian inheritance, alongside a conscious refusal to break off conversation or discourse with even those 'ancestors' whose legacy appears particularly damaging. I refuse the idea that institutions appear as immaculate and unchangeable forms. Rather, I hold, they develop over time, and it is in and through mutual relationship between the people formed by institutions and the institutions formed by people that Christians create and recreate their faith. Just as a sacrament such as Eucharist involves initiation of the veritably new as well as invocation of a past event, so rendering institutions such as marriage, parenting and family somehow immaculate and ideally unchanging detracts from their capacity to mediate unexpected grace and exceed what we expect of them. Despite my engagement throughout the book with Edelman's circumspection about the sacrifice of the present for the sake of a putative future and its mythic innocents, I conclude that the primacy of the eschatological in Christian theology necessitates attention to ends rather than origins, and a resistance to the cult of originalism. This does not entail an ahistoricist refusal of what has come before, but, rather, an acknowledgement that recognition entails *re-cognizing*, thinking again, knowing anew. It is far more than just an apprehension of what has been.

Un/familiar theology acknowledges its family history without being hidebound by it. It refuses to apotheosize a monolithic or univocal version of the story. For this reason, I might rightfully be held to account for all those voices and traditions to which I myself have failed to do justice throughout the book. On this I can only say mea culpa, beg forgiveness, and invite others to speak back to me and show me how things look from where they are. This is one version of an un/familiar theology, but doubtless not the only possible one. Some readers will find me too much of an apologist for Western constructive and systematic theologies; others will find me so unsystematic (though, I hope, not unconstructive) that they cannot see how to make sense of my approach at all. But at least some of my readers belong to my various families – academic, theological, religious, cultural, social, political, philosophical and, yes, even biological – and, when families operate well, their members do their best to give one another a fair hearing.

Chapter 2

GENERATIVITY: THE DISRUPTION OF BIOLOGICAL ORIGINS

Introduction

From its earliest days, the Christian tradition has contained a stream which figures reproduction and generativity as more than biological, and which queries normative and hegemonic constructions of masculinity, femininity and interpersonal relationship.[1] In this book, I suggest that patterns of bodily and gendered givenness may legitimately be reinterpreted and reframed in light of Christianity's own tradition. I argue that accounts of marriage and sexuality which demand exclusively heterosexual groundings do too little to embrace the rich Christian traditions of generation as more than biological and identity as more than fixed and unmalleable. As Margaret Farley (2006: 227–8) comments:

> Beyond the kind of fruitfulness that brings forth biological children, there is a kind of fruitfulness that is a measure, perhaps, of all interpersonal love. … Without fruitfulness of some kind, any significant interpersonal love (not only sexual love) becomes an *égoisme à deux*. If it is completely sterile in every way, it threatens the love and the relationship itself. But love brings new life to those who love.

In this chapter, I begin with the tradition of fictive reproduction evident from Christianity's earliest days, and note that appeals to the significance of reproduction within marriage continue to recur in theologies of marriage up to the present – to the extent that in some instances, such as the recent work of Robert Song, it is whether a couple is open to having children that signals whether their relationship may be understood as being in continuity with marriage as

---

1. There are, of course, also strands which seem far more uncritically to endorse normative patterns of gender and power, going right back to the earliest days of the Jesus movement; see, for example, Colleen Conway's (2008) discussion of the gospel writers' constructions of the masculine figure of Jesus and the extent to which these were influenced by idealized Greco-Roman norms of manliness and strength.

'traditionally' understood. I will argue that Song's account goes too far in hiving off parenting-as-normative from other types of generativity, and that, while there may indeed be a case for endorsing the values of responsibility and care, these need not supervene only on child-rearing. If children and the possibility of conceiving them are gifts of God, there must be a real possibility to decline the gift or its 'giftness' is negated and it becomes merely a manipulative obligation. When patterns of care are embedded too exclusively in patterns of nuclear family life, there is an elision of the other possibilities for responsibility and generativity which deserve richer theological conceptualization than they have often received.

Fictive Reproduction

Augustine used concepts such as fruitfulness metaphorically, and can, notes Jana Bennett, figure those who are *virgo intacta* as still nonetheless veritably 'fecund' because their ministry and witness may 'birth' many more people to faith in Christ than they could have birthed natural children. For Augustine, love is itself a 'fertile power', which, when outworked in the lives of believers, continues to bring Christ to birth in each of them (*De Virginitate* 5; cf. Bennett 2008: 106). For the church, as for Mary, virginity does not hinder fruitfulness (just as, conversely, fruitfulness does not compromise virginity) (*De Virginitate* 2). Furthermore, the fact that Mary physically bore and gave birth to Christ is less significant than the fact that she received the faith of Christ: 'Thus also her nearness as a Mother would have been of no profit to Mary, had she not borne Christ in her heart after a more blessed manner than in her flesh' (3). Those who are not 'mothers in the flesh' should not, therefore, mourn their lack, urges Augustine (5). Their symbolic Christ-bearing in faith and love is a greater work than the bearing of actual children (7), and 'no fruitfulness of the flesh can be compared to holy virginity even of the flesh' (8).

This is attractive in many ways, in that it interrupts the inevitable associations between femaleness and biological motherhood. Generativity in Christ is not limited to those who are generative in the flesh. Elsewhere, the relativization of procreation is expanded further: in *On the Good of Marriage* (para 17), Augustine notes that, while, in the past, having children was an act of piety, by his own time the truly holy seek to have only spiritual 'children'. A husband and wife together, he believes, constitute a family even if they have been unable to have children; furthermore, knowing that one is infertile with one's spouse does not give one a licit reason to try to reproduce with someone else. While this might have been licit in more ancient times – Augustine seems to be thinking of the concubines taken by the patriarchs of the Hebrew Bible – because at the time it was necessary to ensure the perpetuation of the species, by Augustine's own time this is no longer an imperative. (I will return to this discussion in the next chapter, with reference to the issue of polygamous and polyamorous relationships.) Similarly, in John Chrysostom's *Sermon on Marriage* (in Roth and Anderson 1986: 81–6), believers are told that the 'children' they can now birth spiritually are better than the actual children that were the only possibility of posterity before there was hope for a resurrection – even down to the potential benefits for the believer's old age.

Yet the close conceptual and cultural association between Christianity and the family has often obscured the tradition's at best ambivalent relationship with the begetting of children and the ties of kin. The tradition has not always kept this stream at the forefront of its constructions of marriage and sexuality. Ruth Mazo Karras argues that, despite the widespread exhortation of virginity in the Christian tradition in the medieval era, the expectation was still that most of the population would marry and reproduce. Indeed, Karras holds the high value placed on reproductivity as the reason that even clergy and other religious, such as abbots and abbesses, who could not have their own biological children (or at least not licitly), came to be known as 'father' and 'mother'. The role of abbots was 'fatherly' in the sense that they provided spiritual nurture and education for those in their care, and often ensured they were provided for economically too. Later, of course, priests also came to be known by the title 'father'. This adoption of parental titles by and for celibates (or purported celibates) may be understood as a denigration of biological parenthood – with the sense that an abbot could be an *even better* 'father' or 'mother' than an actual layperson who was a parent could, because the abbot more closely imaged the ultimate 'parent', God (and this chimes, too, with claims, as in John Chrysostom's 'Against Opponents of the Monastic Life', that the spiritual 'children' of vowed religious are *even more* fulfilling than actual children would have been (in Rogers 2002: 93–5)). Karras (2014: 281) refers to this notion as 'fictive reproduction'.

It is not always clear whether these fictive familial relationships subverted or apotheosized the actual familial relationships they invoked. Indeed, the account of 'fictive reproduction' is not without its problems. One might be that it undermines the specificity and legitimacy of relationships between actual parents (whether adoptive or not) and their children. Heather Walton (2014: 69) comments on the rite of baptism, 'Here we say in words and symbols that the birth of blood and water from the mother is not enough. Something is lacking. It is not real birth. Let her be born by the priest and by the Father, then she will be truly a child of God'. This might be understood as just another kind of Christian colonialism which says that a *real* parent is whatever the church says it is, and *real* parental care and oversight are whatever it is that a priest or other religious authority does – which risks writing everything into a reductive singularity. Another problem might be that it detracts from the specificity of *female* reproductivity – and is, conceivably, a way to wrest conceptual control of generation away from women and under the authority of a patriarchal church and its ancestry. Yvonne Sherwood (2015), for example, has suggested that the Hebrew Bible's narrative depiction of the almost-sacrifice of Isaac is a way to transfer reproductive power from mothers onto father–son relationships. Isaac's sacrificing, as a gateway to further blessings for Abraham (and, in the narrative, subsequently, for Israel), equals a kind of hyper-birth, a birth done better, a super-generation wherein the entire future is 'incubated' in Isaac.

I want to suggest, however, that 'fictive reproduction' is a broader concept existing within Christian discourses, right up to the present day. I want to suggest, further, that it need not be seen as an inevitably sinister trope, or one which elevates familial relationships above all others, but may rather be figured as one which itself begins to disturb and relativize the centrality of appeals to family and reproductivity in some (both Protestant and Roman Catholic) present-day Christian subcultures.

Fictive reproduction might be identified in some of the earliest texts associated with the Christian faith. Even if some of the Pauline epistles are relatively conservative about family, the Jesus of the Gospels is more circumspect about its value. Many commentators have noted and attributed significance to depictions of Jesus's generous and non-biological approaches to family (such as in Lk. 8.21 and Jn 19.25–27); his apparently casual attitude towards his own blood relations (Mt. 12.47–49; Lk. 8.19–21; 14.26); his superseding of existing familial ties and commitments in favour of commitments to the new community (Lk. 9.60–62; 18.29–30); his disruption of the assumption that childlessness is a curse (Lk. 23.29); and his querying of Roman imperial and Jewish patriarchal norms of male supremacy which tended to disadvantage children, women and slaves (Mt. 19–20) in favour of the elevation of the latter groups (see Bohache 2006: 508–9; Goss 2006: 535–7; Moxnes 2003; Jennings 2003; Isasi-Díaz 2003; and Carter 2000 for further discussion of these texts and themes). We should perhaps not be surprised that Jesus appears to sit light to norms of family given that, on some readings of the gospel accounts, he himself likely grew up without the presence of a human father figure (Van Aarde 2001). We should note shifting constructions of family and kinship, given Halvor Moxnes' (2003: 29) reminder that 'terms like family, household, and kinship are not objective facts; they are cultural constructions', and that 'families' in the gospels are not 'families' as Christian rhetoric often understands them today, but are associations more of common place than common blood. For John Dunnill (2013), the eschatological nature of the Christian promise means that biological generation (and its concomitant activity, such as patterns of marriage and child-rearing) are relativized. For example, he characterizes the story of the wedding at Cana as 'the one final feast, which fulfils all the "marrying and giving in marriage" which constitutes the old age. ... From this point on, the balance between mortality and eternity is fundamentally altered' (120). In other words, from this point onward, at the instigation of Jesus's earthly ministry, the social and cosmic significance of marriage and regeneration have changed (as Barth also holds in *Church Dogmatics* III/4, and as I explore more fully in Chapter 6 – which is why, as we shall see there, parenting is a grace but not an obligation under the new dispensation in Christ). So given that the socially radical message of the earliest Christians, who seemed to expect Jesus to return to earth fairly imminently after his resurrection, was softened by the time of the writing of the later epistles of the Pauline school (such as Colossians and Ephesians), what did and does it mean for Christians in the age 'between the times' – now as then – that, as Dunnill suggests, marriage no longer signifies quite as it did before?

In English usage, 'being given in marriage' is not just to do with the 'gifting' of spouses from one family to another. In norms and patterns of marriage, a whole host of other things (gender, sex, sexuality) have also tended to be assumed or (conceptually) 'given' (assumed, known, fixed, taken as read) – the kind of 'givenness' to which someone like Oliver O'Donovan (1982) can appeal as the irreducibility of our circumstances as intended by God (and use as an argument against altering the body via, for example, sex reassignment surgery for transgender people). We might note, for example, that 'being given' in marriage is more commonly used with reference to women, who are sometimes understood as being passed from the care (or ownership) of one male (the father) to another (the husband): most often, though not universally, men give and women are given. The English 'given' has etymological roots in a Germanic term and has connotations of having been allotted or fated in a particular direction. The end of 'being given' in marriage might also be read as meaning the termination of *a priori* givenness related to assumptions about what sex one has to be in order validly to enter into marriage; or about the way that sex in marriage has been taken to communicate something about divine–human patterns of relationship (as for Barth and Balthasar among others). The term *gamizontai*, as in Mt. 22.30, is passive: being given in marriage is something done *to* one or on one's behalf, not something one does for oneself. But in the new order which Christ initiates, humans are no longer passive participants: we are not simply given by others, but have the capacity to mean and signify more expansively – both (individually) in our self-identification and (relationally) in the broader social recognition of the multiplicity of our sexed, gendered and embodied stories.

As Dunnill (2013) emphasizes, biological generation matters very much when it is a case of maintaining a population and preventing one's community from dying out. But once death itself has been reframed, relativized, even conquered, biological generation to stave off the death of a people is no longer crucial in the same way: 'The primary existential fact which underlies the eschatological crisis … is that of mortality. Only for mortal bodies is there need for the constantly vulnerable process of regeneration' (119). This is not meant to be a supersessionist statement rubbishing the significance of cultural and familial commitments, as I will make clear in Chapter 5. Rather, it is a recognition that to generate entails affective care and responsibility that goes far beyond the bare fact of biological reproduction and is not limited by what we might characterize as biology's 'natural' preferences for the preservation of kin and the transmission of familiar genes.

Generativity and Responsibility as Life Stage

Erik Erikson

To some extent, I am drawing here on the accounts of psychologists Erik Erikson and John Kotre. In the work of Erikson, generativity is understood as a life phase which comes about during mature adulthood (see Erikson 1994 [1959]: 103–4).

Chronologically, it is a stage of psychosocial development which happens after the necessary preceding stages of trust, autonomy, initiative, industry, identity and intimacy: for many people, Erikson believed, it would come about in middle age or after. Each stage is contrasted, in Erikson's typology, with a competing aspect against which it tussles: those who do not adequately develop intimate relationships, for example, are likely to experience isolation which precludes their subsequent thriving psychosocial development. For Erikson the 'opposite' of generativity is stagnation: generativity provides meaning, purpose and a sense of integration with a broader community. This is significant given that, in Erikson's model, the generativity stage is followed, towards the end of life, by the integrity stage, whose opposite is despair: a sense of integrity relies on knowing that one has lived meaningfully.

Any typology of the kind set out by Erikson and by Kotre has its shortcomings. It is easy to see the drawbacks to Erikson's system: it is linear and monodirectional in a way that may not be representative of a diversity of life-paths and reinventions of the self; it takes too little account of the reality of adverse circumstances, including the changing realities of physical particularity, in which many individuals find themselves and which may 'interrupt' the process of psychological adjustment; it assumes too much in the way of resilience and non-dependence as being universal goods. Nonetheless, it is possible to extract what is helpful – and generative – for practical use without taking on the entire system wholesale.

Generativity, for Erikson, is about producing and guiding the next generation. In his earlier work, Erikson does seem to link generativity strongly to actual reproduction and the dynamics of parenting, and suggests that mere 'creativity' is a poor substitute. For example, in a 1959 version of an essay originally written in 1950, Erikson (1994 [1959]: 103) says, 'Generativity is primarily the interest in establishing and guiding the next generation, although there are people who, from misfortune or because of special and genuine gifts in other directions, do not apply this drive to offspring but to other forms of altruistic concern and of creativity, which may absorb their kind of creative responsibility' (Erikson 1994 [1959]: 103).

Later, however (perhaps, suggests Bonnie Miller-McLemore (2007: 21), in light of his re-assessments once his own children had grown up), Erikson expands his definition. By 1968, he writes, 'In addition to procreativity, [generativity] includes productivity and creativity; thus it is psychosocial in nature' (Erikson in Schlein 1987: 607). He comes to distinguish between production and care: one can produce a person or thing without care, so procreation in its own right is not necessarily properly generative. Care is 'broadening concern for what has been generated by love, necessity, or accident' (608). True generativity – which often does follow biological parenthood, though not universally – entails generosity, a curbing of self-indulgence and self-interest (Miller-McLemore 2007: 21; Erikson 1994 [1959]: 103). One *comes* to care for what has been generated, and this can include ideas and the products of one's craft as well as other persons. Care may licitly be understood as a virtue needed for living well (Halwani 2003: 71; see also the more technically philosophical discussion of care or concern as characterizing the disclosure of *Dasein*, being-in-the-world, in Heidegger (2008 [1927]: 225ff)); care is often but not always reciprocal, and caring appropriately for others without expectation of reciprocity is precisely one of the mechanisms by which virtuous character may be cultivated. We therefore require caring and generative exemplars, and communities in which care and responsibility are cherished and esteemed.

Bonnie Miller-McLemore

Miller-McLemore (1994) picks this up in her own discussions of generativity, where she insists that an account of generativity which properly disrupts too-close associations between biological sex and particular types of gendered work necessitates, also, close attention to the kinds of work which do not appear obviously instrumental or 'productive', such as the largely unseen work of pregnancy and the often thankless and higgledy-piggledy work of raising young children. Significantly, making time for women's self-actualization via generative work which is not just to do with child-rearing often necessitates 'outsourcing' the actual physical graft of cleaning, changing nappies and so on to another group of 'exploited, silenced women': 'lower class mothers, the baby-sitter, housekeeper, cleaning woman, day-care staff … and so forth' (145). The capacity (mental, physical and emotional) for what looks generative may be eroded by grinding fatigue, so a two-pronged response is necessary: first, changing the conditions which mean some people bear this fatigue disproportionately; and second, recognizing more fully that even work which does not seem to go anywhere or *do* very much is also, often, generative in its way.

Generativity is, then, closely bound up with generosity towards others; but it also, I suggest, means the continual generation of the *self*, via gratification in and identification with one's work (with the provisos Miller-McLemore notes about not thereby devaluing the often frustrating grind of childcare). On Kotre's reading (below), continual generation is profoundly connected to the possibility of hope: in order to properly care for the persons and things already generated, one must believe that they are worth saving, and also affirm the possibility of future generations' own potential generativity. In situations where there seems to be no possibility of a future – where despair outweighs hope – generativity seems futile. At times, securing the future will entail 'the maintenance and the rejuvenation of institutions' by the old in order to attract and ensure the energy of the young (Erikson 1994 [1959]: 167). (I will return to the theme of futurity below in conversation with Lee Edelman and José Esteban Muñoz.)

Miller-McLemore (2007: 41) claims that 'one cannot create without creating someone for whom or something for which one must care and assume responsibility', but I am not sure that this is quite right. After all, I might create a book or a piece of music or a painting which gets sent out into the world to make its own way and have its own afterlife without my involvement. It is not the job of the artist to curate and control every response and reaction to her creation: to attempt to do so would not be 'responsible' (as in H. Richard Niebuhr's terms, which I discuss below); it would, rather, be stultifying, controlling not of the thing itself but of others as they react and respond to it out of their own circumstances. Children, by contrast, do require ongoing care; though even this will change as time goes on. Parents do not stop being parents once their children reach adulthood, but the time nonetheless comes when it is no longer appropriate for parents to assume responsibility for them (and when, indeed, in many cases, it is adult children who must take the caring role and assume legal responsibility for their parents). Still, in some accounts, generativity specifically has a sense of futurity about it: it is 'about care and responsibility … that *move down the generational chain* and connect to a future' (Kotre 1996: xv). For Erikson (1994 [1959]: 103–4), the key is that lack of generativity is 'lack of some faith, some "belief in the species", which would make a child appear to be a welcome trust of the community'. Inadequate development of the psyche beyond the stage of selfishness and self-interest is more than narcissism: it is also a kind of nihilism, since it fails to uphold the possibility of a value or future to communal existence.

John N. Kotre

Generativity also figures in the work of the Roman Catholic psychologist John N. Kotre, who holds that generativity is driven by two desires: to create something that will outlast the self (symbolic immortality), and to be needed. Kotre's (1996) typology outlines distinct but overlapping forms of generativity: biological; parental (which includes the guiding work of grandparents, adoptive parents, mentors and other responsible adults, not just biological parents); technical (in terms of passing on specific skills or expertise); and cultural. Awareness of one's culture – which may involve either an adult appreciation of one's culture of origin, or a discovery of a new culture later in life – is figured as 'nourishment' for the imagination and will and itself leads to 'cultural fertility' (260). Discovery of a new culture therefore provides a 'second chance' at generativity for those for whom parenthood has not been possible or fulfilling (260). Unlike Erikson, however, Kotre considers generativity not as a life stage, but as 'an impulse released at various times' across adulthood which will be followed by 'episodes of fertility' (262). For Kotre, generativity is therefore also not something that can only come about in mature adulthood once one has transitioned through a number of other stages. It is not simply the purview of the established or middle-aged, as Erikson's account hints. In Kotre's case studies of eight men and women, moments of generativity were sometimes prompted by what seemed like crises. And it is not insignificant that in some sense he portrayed his subjects as having *birthed themselves* in a process of creative self-generation (263). The child is parent to the adult (though adulthood should not be understood as an unproblematic *telos* into which childhood disappears), and each of us creates ourselves in dynamic relation to our divine and other causes. We do not arrive as finished articles. But nor can we curate ourselves independently: we exist, always, in relation to God and our fellow-creatures. In both Kotre and Erikson, generativity 'helps us to consider our very nature, as the creature of awareness who knows that an end to this life will come, hence the need to make something out of it: the only choice we have (here in this world, at least) to make a difference to others, and thereby join a community of one's fellow human beings' (Coles 1996: xii).

H. Richard Niebuhr

Kotre's and Erikson's accounts of generativity chime, I suggest, with H. Richard Niebuhr's (1999) more theological concept of responsibility. Indeed, I think they are approximately what Niebuhr is getting at when he portrays 'responsibility' as capacity to *respond*, to be responsive: to God, to other humans and to other stimuli still. But 'responsibility' also, of course, carries a sense of conscientiousness and trustworthiness. To be responsible is to own and to be accountable for one's reactions and activity. One can be responsible for – that is, one can speak to and be answerable for – one's action and its legacy (even if, as we have already noted, actions and creations also have 'afterlives' and are subsequently interpretable otherwise).

Responsibility assumes power. We are answerable for actions about which we had a choice. We can still cause consequences unknowingly, and thereby be blameable for them only to the extent that we caused them to happen: but no one holds a baby *responsible* for the dry-cleaning bill caused by his posseting on his grandmother's best coat, even though the baby was the person whose activity brought about the result, and was therefore its strict cause. In twenty years' time, however, when the same baby, grown up, rolls home after a drunken bender and vomits on grandmother's coat again (poor grandmother! Poor coat! And by now a vintage piece!), we might more reasonably hold that he is responsible for his actions. He has chosen to undertake an activity which has impaired his judgement and had adverse physical results. He is therefore still answerable for the consequence. True 'irresponsibility' is when we refuse to be charged with the effects (for good or ill) of our free choices.

Mature selves, therefore, for Niebuhr, are responsible selves, which know and can own their own voices and reactions. The action of Christ, and the context of salvation history, means that such responsibility is not a condemnation to failure and guilt, but has the potential to be a positive and assured vehicle of conscious, co-creative activity with God. Niebuhr does not mean this to be individualistic or overly triumphalist: rather, he assumes that we are responsible agents living in a community of other responsible agents, and that there is continuity in terms of both persistence of the responsible self, and 'in the community of agents to which response is being made' (65). We are therefore responsible not only for our own reactions and responses, but for the effects that these, in turn, in chain, have on other responsible actors.

Now, Niebuhr is well aware of the restraints and influences to which we are all subject as members of society. Our freedom is limited in the sense that we are responsive to the circumstances in which we find ourselves, which would often not have been of our choosing. Responsibility, however, for Niebuhr, is about making right choices – appropriate choices – in light of actual circumstances. Figuring humans as responsive to shifting circumstances means that pain and suffering need not be figured as overwhelmingly dreadful, irruptive events. They are still real and problematic, but because Niebuhr does not start from a position of assuming that humans ought somehow to be 'above' them or able to float free from them, his theological anthropology is a dynamic one in which the arising of the unexpected is simply an aspect of living as a relational self. Responsible persons have the capacity to revise and reinterpret both the meanings of others' actions upon them and of what this means for their ongoing self in relation to the newly understood world: 'Freedom from the past or newness of understanding and movement toward more fitting response does not come through the rejection of the past but through its reinterpretation. ... The reconstruction of our past can be a large part of our hope for the future' (104). Kotre (1996: 11) comments, '*Creativity* connotes ... that something new is made, while *generativity* connotes that something old is passed on': generativity, then, is the effect of the *integration and transformation of circumstance* (the 'old order') *such as to bring about an altered reality* (the 'new order', informed by the old) moving forward.

I am borrowing from Kotre's account of generativity with its implications of both continuity and discontinuity with previous forms and circumstances. Indeed, I want to suggest that this is precisely what is going on in theological remakings and reconceptions of categories such as marriage, parenting and family. Such remakings are not necessarily losing faith with or denying these institutions' genealogies, but may, rather, conceivably, be recognizing them more fully for what they are as phenomena which human cultures and societies continue – appropriately, and necessarily – to shape. If these are gifts of God, then they are gifts to be used responsively and dialogically. How far can such things be remade before they have gone beyond the point of no return in terms of resemblance to the things God gave in the first place? Part of the answer is that there is no 'in the first place' beyond the real cultures and societies in which norms of constancy, commitment, covenant and so on are worked out. God gives capacities and tendencies, not fixed institutions. Undoubtedly, institutions can function, when they work well, to protect the interests of the vulnerable. Nonetheless, to hold that given institutions have always been a certain way often serves to attempt to make static and fixed what should properly be recognized as dynamic. When Reverend Libby Lane, the Church of England's first woman bishop, was consecrated bishop of Stockport on 26 January 2015, a lone protestor, Reverend Paul Williamson, interrupted the service in York Minster holding that warrant for the event was 'not in the Bible' and that this constituted an 'absolute impediment' to its taking place. Most Reverend John Sentamu, the archbishop of York, presiding at the service, responded that the event was now lawful and reflected the will of the Church of England. The fact that there had not been women bishops in the Church of England until that point – and the fact that the consecration of women as bishops was a departure from the protocols of much of the rest of Christian history – did not in itself make the consecration of women as bishops impossible, illegitimate or illicit. As Stanley Hauerwas (1981: 14) has commented,

> Good societies enable the argument to continue so that the possibilities and limits of the tradition can be exposed. The great danger, however, is that the success of a tradition will stop its growth and in reaction some may deny the necessity of tradition for their lives. The truthfulness of a tradition is tested in its ability to form people who are ready to put the tradition into question.

Unchanging traditions are wont to become tyrannical, suggests Hauerwas; 'in contrast, … substantive traditions are not at odds with reason but are the bearers of rationality and innovation' (26). This is particularly important when the phenomenon or institution already lends itself to accruing traditions positive and negative around it; this is why Frances Clemson (2016: 70), following Mark Jordan, holds that, when it comes to norms of marriage, 'the past *matters more* and matters *more complexly* than is allowed for by some of those who summon "the ghosts of weddings past" for or against reform'. Here, again, is original sin, the sin of apotheosizing origins. Clemson says,

> Arguments by reference to such genealogies often presume either that the constancy of a line of sameness across time – excluding irrelevant distant branches or illegitimate divergences – can be taken as an authoritative pattern for today, or that the identification of a significant lost ancestor, in some way at variance with the main line, legitimates and provides a model for further variation in the present. (70)

Similarly in some respects, Joseph Monti (1995) holds that the church's 'problem' is really about negotiating historical change and modernity, and it is only secondarily that it ties itself in knots about sex and marriage and their putatively unchanging character. The key, therefore, he suggests, is to discuss sex and marriage *alongside* and *in terms of* more thoroughgoing reflections on what it means to be 'constructive communities of moral discourse' (x). Marriage in itself is not an ideal to be apotheosized and cosseted; rather, it points to a broader ideal, namely, all that is sacramental. In fact, Christian overemphasis on sex and marriage becomes a means 'to repress … deeper challenges to our Christian character-identity' (x).

So what could we as members of human societies do to marriage or make of marriage that would erode beyond the pale its capacity to mediate grace to those involved – and, we might add, to others less directly involved? Would a more thoroughgoing dissociation of marriage and procreation really be to the political and theological detriment of both as Milbank claims? At this juncture, I want to engage not with Milbank himself, but with a theologian who has argued from a slightly different angle that a disruption of the marriage–procreation dyad entails an erosion of their theological richness and capacity to signify grace.

Singing a New Song? Robert Song's 'Covenant Partnerships'

One of the most interesting engagements in recent years with the relationship between marriage and generativity – in this case, the subset of generativity that is procreation – is that by Robert Song in his short book *Covenant and Calling: Towards a Theology of Same-Sex Relationships* (2014). Although in this book I am primarily concerned with non-biological generativity, I am choosing to engage in some depth with Song's account, because my responses to it usefully demonstrate some of my misgivings about apotheosizations of procreation elsewhere in the tradition. To begin with, it is important to note that Song's starting point is to explore what, if anything, renders same-sex relationships different enough from heterosexual ones that only the latter can licitly be understood as marriages. In other words, he comes to procreation and generation as concerns secondary to pastoral–ethical imperatives surrounding same-sex relationships, even though, in practice, procreation and generation become important carriers for large parts of his argument.

The greatest strength of the book is that Song has attempted something truly new, which hints at a specific rationale for a specific theological place for same-sex relationships. He wants to set up a *distinctive* account of same-sex relationship; and this may be very attractive to those who have been circumspect about the wisdom of simply writing same-sex couples into marriage as though marriage were already an unproblematic and always life-enhancing institution (which Rees (2011), Edelman (2004) and many others have persuasively argued is not necessarily the case, from both theological and queer-theoretical cultural-critical perspectives). Plenty of critics have noted that marriage has often functioned to reinforce and institutionalize relationships of inequality, where those left without economic independence (which usually means women, and any children of the partnership) are at heightened physical and emotional risk. Why, they have asked, should gay people clamour to be allowed on board this leaky vessel, and patch up something imperfect and unjust? Song's (2014: 27) account might, therefore, be favoured by those who want to emphasize the potential distinction of same-sex relationships from marriages, and the attendant possibility of setting up a new and less compromised form of officially recognized relationships with 'their own integrity'.

The flip side of this is, however, that it still seems to deal in exceptionalism, where heterosexuality and the ability to procreate are the default setting from which other things are deviations. Now, to give Song his due, he explicitly wants to state that marriage is *not* superior to celibacy, nor, conceivably, to the new category he terms 'covenant partnership'. For Song, the significant difference between types of relationships is whether or not they are open to procreation, not the sexes of the partners. Relationships open to procreation may meaningfully be called marriages, since they stand in continuity with a Christian tradition which has always held procreation as an important good of marriage. Relationships not open to procreation – whether between heterosexual or same-sex couples – are not in continuity with marriage in the same way, and would be better classified otherwise, possibly as 'covenant partnerships'. Nonetheless, as I will discuss further below, I fear that, by seeking not to exclude gay people from having relationships which can be meaningfully theologized, Song has not expanded the definition of marriage, but rather narrowed it so that even more people are potentially excluded. For this reason among others, I do not go all the way with Song's arguments.

First, and from the outset, Song – like the Church of England's Faith and Order Commission – wants to say that marriage is a created good (3). By this he means 'created by God' – and the implication is that human beings are therefore not at liberty to jettison or substantially alter it. Of course, this is to assume that there is a continuous 'kernel' of marriage which exists and can be discerned and recognized in marriage in all its various forms across time and culture. Indeed, Song insists that marriage is 'universal' (8). But if marriage is created, it is not created by God alone. God is not the sole creator; creation is not a solely divine act. God has initiated a creation in which God's creatures, notably human creatures, may act as co-creators, and may continue to influence and act upon what is around them. For Barth (1962: 172), creation is God's theatre, the place within and means by which redemption is played out; but God, too, should, as the 'director', be open to surprise, with any limits imposed on the creation those which in turn generate further creativity (see discussion in Gorringe (1991: 72–9)). Creation expresses divine faithfulness – but humans may also act more or less faithfully upon it. Humans' relationship to creation is *transformative*: we till it (Gen. 2.15), curate it, make it into something which we then offer back to God. But, crucially, what we offer back is not precisely the same thing that we were offered, as I discuss further in response to Milbank's 'Can a Gift be Given?' below. God's creative work is not over and done with; God creates eternally, in dynamic relationship with the creative and generative work of the creation. It is imaginable (conceivable, even), therefore, that even if God *had* 'originally' given marriage to be a solely heterosexual institution, God could subsequently create and generate through same-sex marriage just as God's creatures have already done so. The 'original' creation is not the final word. This is part of what it means for the divine will and purpose to be planted in creation: the plant grows up dynamically with its environment, and evolves in dynamic relationship with it. As we have seen, Niebuhr characterizes this as *responsibility*: it is as those who can respond to God's call that we as humans may, in turn, be responsible to and for others. Humans do not receive institutions independently of culture: rather, humans shape and transmit culture, as well as being shaped by it. We all act upon our collective institutions in giving them continued assent, in challenging them, in reshaping them. These are creative acts.

Song does acknowledge, later on, that humans can enter into and be part of the creativity of God. Indeed, he believes that procreation is a significant way, perhaps the most significant way, in which they may do so. In the key thesis of his book, Song (2014) suggests that the major significant difference between a marriage without procreation and a 'covenant partnership' without procreation is the presence or absence of the partners' *openness* to procreation. Marriage is *not morally possible* without an openness to procreation (31). If the spouses are *open to* procreation, then they are married, whether or not it turns out that they are actually able to have biological children. If the spouses are *not open to* procreation (except in very exceptional circumstances, such as a high risk to a woman's health from any pregnancy), then, according to Song, what they have is not properly a marriage, and might be better termed a covenant partnership even if they are heterosexual. The logic here is indebted to Roman Catholic canon law on openness to creation, but Song also again apparently follows Barth, assuming that couples who are fertile but choose not to have biological children are rejecting God's gift to them.

But need this be characterized as a *rejection* of something? Is politely saying 'No, thank you' to something really a rejection to be framed in negative terms, or merely a way of saying 'yes' to another possibility? Where does human freedom come in – or is what we are being presented with here one of those theological double-binds where 'real' freedom means only ever choosing to be fulfilled in the 'right' way (and how confident may we be in the Barthian interpretation of true human possibility in God – which is, after all, still his interpretation [cf. Kärkkäinen 2014: 114])? Furthermore, Song's position seems to make the existence of the marriage contingent on something other than the spouses' gifting themselves to one another, since the assumption is that this self-giving must entail openness to procreation (and is therefore instrumental, directed towards something else). This seems to be at odds with, for example, the position set forth by the Church of England General Synod's Marriage Commission (1979: 33), countering the argument that marriage exists for the sake of (which, we might note, can imply *for the good of* or *to bring about the existence of*) children:

> Marriage is best understood as 'for' husband and wife. It is their relationship with each other which is the basis of marriage. On this is built their relationship with their children. Arguments, therefore, in favour of the life-long nature of the married relationship must be seen to stem from the character of the husband-wife relationship itself, whether or not there are children.

And, furthermore, it is at odds with even an Augustinian account of the relationship between marriage and procreation. Augustine's notion of the sacramentality of marriage shifts between his various treatments of it, but, at least in his 'On Original Sin' (*On the Grace of Christ and of Original Sin*, book 2, chapters 39 and 42 in Schaff (1887)), sacramentality lies in the uniting of the spouses, not in either openness to procreation or in procreation itself. Here procreation, chastity and sacramental union are all portrayed as consequences of marriage, but are clearly distinguished (in other words, it is not procreation that facilitates the sacramental unity). Sacramentality, mediating grace, might therefore be understood as a possible consequence of marriage, rather than being inevitably coincident with it.

Crucially, then, procreation is surely not the only way in which humans may act creatively and as co-creators. Indeed, I take issue with Song's implication that God's creativity is necessarily a *procreative* kind of creativity, so that human procreation can especially echo and participate in it. Song's account owes something to the sort of assumption Hans Urs von Balthasar sets out in the *Theo-Drama III* (Balthasar 1992), in which human fruitfulness is significant because it images God's fruitfulness, but where there is a fairly crude and unproblematic association between divine and human male 'initiative' and human female 'response' which seems to map on to biologist assertions about what goes on in the act of penetrative penile–vaginal sexual intercourse. Why assume that God's creativity is most closely imaged and echoed by human procreativity rather than by all the other many and manifold types of creativity and generativity of which humans are capable? Now, it is possible that Song is saying *not* that procreativity is closer to God's creativity than other kinds of creativity are, but, rather, that procreativity particularly participates in God's creativity simply because it is something God institutes – because it is a *gift* of God. But, in that case, why elevate it above other gifts – especially given Song's insistence that marriage is not better than celibacy, and that (following, I suspect, Barth in *Church Dogmatics* III/4) procreation is no longer a necessity for Christians because procreation has been 'completed' in Christ, but serves as a continuing sign of God's giving character and endorsement of the goodness of the created realm? As Barth (1961: 268) says: '*Post Christum natum* the propagation of the race ... has ceased to be an unconditional command. It happens under God's longsuffering and patience, and is due to His mercy, that in these last days it may still take place'.

I also take issue with one of the main foundations on which Song's argument seems to rest: namely, that, because in Gen. 1.27–28 the pronouncement that humans are made male and female in God's image is immediately followed by the commandment to be fruitful and multiply, there is an inherent link between marriage and procreation. In this Song seems to follow the logic of, for example, the 1930 papal encyclical *Casti Connubii (On Christian Marriage)* (Pius XI 1930). But after all, and at the risk of stating the obvious: sex is clearly not *inherently* or *intrinsically* procreative, or else far more acts of even uncontracepted sex would lead to conception than actually do so. Sex and procreation are not even inextricably bound up within the biblical narratives, or there would be no lamentation over infertility, and less anxiety about infidelity: the biblical writers know full well that sex does not always lead to offspring. I am therefore not persuaded by Song's (2014: 4) claim that 'as presented in Genesis, the procreation and nurture of children is an inseparable and intrinsic good of marriage'. Similarly, later on, Song repeats the idea that the Genesis commandment to be fruitful and multiply is to do with *marriage*. I would counter that it is, in fact, to do with *sex*, and that any reading of it which projects marriage onto it (including that of Jesus as portrayed in the Synoptic gospels) is a later overlay (demonstrating, as I have already stated, that marriage is a cultural and encultured phenomenon from the start). For Song, children are a product of marriage and relationship (48): actually, however, children are a product of *sex*. Sex can, and frequently does, involve and happen in the context of marriage and relationship; but it also frequently does not. Song risks over-spiritualizing what is, in basic terms, a biological process. Unlike Song, I do not necessarily recognize whatever is instituted in Gen. 1.27–28 as unproblematically contiguous with what we now call 'marriage'. It certainly seems to be to do with sexual reproduction, but it is not evidently to do with marriage as a cultural, social and religious overlay on sexual reproduction. Song wants to maintain a close link between marriage and procreation, such that procreation is what makes marriage as an institution distinctive from other kinds of relationship, but I do not think (and do not conclude from the rest of his book) that procreation is all that even he thinks marriage is about.

Song wants to say that procreation has already been fulfilled in Christ – so that, per Barth, it is no longer necessary as a Christian obligation or for the perpetuation of the faith. Song (2014: 19) also notes that it is difficult to make a case for having children on the basis of the New Testament. But he seems to imply *both* that procreation is now redundant and basically theologically insignificant, *and*, simultaneously, that it is theologically significant for those who partake in it because it gestures towards participation in the divine creativity – so much so that procreation's presence or absence can be set up as the determining factor for whether or not a given couple's relationship is legitimately a (created, God-given, 'universal'-type) marriage rather than what Song terms a 'covenant partnership'. If, as Song says, procreation is fulfilled in Christ, then why should we continue to delineate so strongly between procreative relationships and relationships which are not procreative but also share with other relationships the qualities of faithfulness and permanence frequently ascribed in the Christian tradition to marriage?

I am also uncomfortable with Song's implication that procreativity is the main or only significant creativity or fruitfulness of even procreative marriages (28). After all, that a relationship is biologically procreative does not prevent its also being creative and generative in a host of other ways; moreover, a marriage may be biologically procreative yet also emotionally and psychologically stultifying for those concerned. Similarly, while Song attempts to set out a positive constructive theological account of non-procreative relationships by noting that they can free the spouses up for other things such as adoption or missionary work (30), I have some deep reservations about the idea that both spouses' participating meaningfully in public life and mission is inherently unfeasible if they also have biological children. After all, it should not be impossible to build a society where it is a realistic choice to have a meaningful career, mission or ministry *and* raise a family. If this is difficult in practice, it is largely because we have not put adequate infrastructure in place to make it possible. Career, mission and ministry should not be consolation prizes for those who cannot have children, nor placed out of the reach of those who do have children and who want to be generative in these other parts of life too. This assumption is, indeed, part of what underlies Don Browning's (2007: 255) appeals to 'equal-regard marriage', in which 'both husband and wife have, in principle, equal access to the responsibilities and privileges of both the public world of citizenship and employment and the domestic sphere of household maintenance and child care' – even if, in practice, Browning and his team have endorsed a narrower range of manifestations of family life than I am seeking to do here.[2] (For further discussion

---

2. Browning's account of equal-regard marriage has also been criticized on the grounds that it is too contractual and does too little to recognize the sometime good of agape love – that it reduces marriage to being 'a willed association of autonomous persons for reciprocal advantage' (Jackson 2007: 138), rather than a situation of mutual self-sacrifice. Furthermore, while being generally supportive of Browning's conviction that both mothers and fathers should be able to seek paid employment outside the home – ideally for no more than sixty hours a week between them in total so that each may also continue to be directly involved in childcare – Rebekah Miles (2007) suggests that Browning does too little to interrogate why such *paid* activity specifically (rather than volunteering or other non-stipendiary service) seems to correlate with better mental health outcomes for parents, and, in turn, children. Do such theologies, asks Miles, capitulate to models of happiness and worth based on money-making capacity?

on this theme, see Miller-McLemore (1994), Ruether (2000: 206ff) and – for specific reflection on 'equal-regard' marriage – Witte, Green and Wheeler (2007)).

An additional objection to Song's argument might be simply that it seems odd to have what look like two identical relationships (a man and woman, partnered, without children) going by two different names (marriage in one case; covenant partnership in another) depending on what is going on 'underneath' (which we might suspect is, after all, this couple's private business). Song (2014: 29) notes that 'covenant partnerships' would be a vocation in their own right, and that 'not everyone is able to live in a relationship where it was known from the outset that children would not be the fruit of their partners' one-sex union' – though he does not discuss the fact that, for heterosexual couples who have not been sexually active prior to their legal union, or have been using contraception, it is fairly unlikely that this would in fact be 'known from the outset'. Who would be called upon to judge whether any given relationship of this pattern might properly be called a marriage? In what circumstances might such a distinction be made, and what would be its implications?

But another, and, I think, more insurmountable objection, is this: Song seems to me to be assuming that same-sex couples *could not* feel called to procreation. Now, this might seem like an odd objection: the argument might be that, if gay people cannot by definition have biologically procreative relationships with one another, then they cannot by definition be open to procreation. But I do not judge that this is so. First, that argument would imply that sexual orientation is an ontologically inbuilt and unchanging thing, which I do not believe is always the case: we cannot unproblematically say that each and every gay person was 'born that way'.[3] Second,

---

3. The answer to the question of whether there is a biological 'cause' for homosexual orientation remains contested, and I am not attempting to take a position on it here. Some Christians hold that even if prenatal hormonal, genetic or other biological factors do influence later sexual orientation and 'cause' homosexuality, this is a difference which can be ascribed to the results of the Fall and does not render homosexuality morally immaculate. However, other Christians strongly attest that if gay people are born that way – if homosexual orientation is in no meaningful way a 'choice' – then it also cannot be a perverse moral choice, and gay people should not be excluded or pilloried for being gay and following their natural inclinations. This is a very attractive position for pro-equality Christians, but it is still not an unproblematic one. It assumes that anyone who *could* choose to be heterosexual *would* choose to be heterosexual: that heterosexuality is still the 'innocent' default from which anything else is a deviation. It therefore bolsters heterosexuality's supposed naturalness, ubiquity and goodness. Far more challenging to heteronormativity is a position which says something like, 'Sexuality is a complex web of causation, socialization, dissemination, influence, control and helplessness. To figure human beings as having *no* power of agency in their sexuality is to figure them as unable to act upon and live in dynamic tension with their circumstances. Compulsory heterosexuality is not an innocent default, but something which has brought about more than its fair share of death, violence, exclusion and heartache. Why should heterosexuality be set up as something anyone would choose if they could? What's

and more compellingly, some gay couples *yearn* to have their own children and are shattered and heartbroken that they cannot. They *burn* to be procreative. They are absolutely as open to procreation as they could possibly be. If they could have a biological child with their partner, they would do so. They long for a baby with a mixture of their physical features, just as many heterosexual couples do (and some utilize reproductive technologies to get as close as they can). Now, someone might object, 'Well, that just proves that they're disordered in some way – because the yearning they experience is actually a sign that what is natural for them, as for everyone else, is to be drawn to be sexually intimate only with someone they actually *can* procreate with'. However, things are somewhat more complicated than this. The desire to have children is a whole web of desires mixed up together. It might be a desire to see one's genes and one partner's genes combined and sent on in novel and exciting ways. It might be a desire to have a child who will learn the history of one's family: who will be initiated into and cultivated into being a member of one's cultural tribe. There are many, many gay people who want this in and for their children, and who are saddened and frustrated that they cannot have children via the means of plain old penile–vaginal sexual intercourse. However, and crucially: *there are also plenty of heterosexual people who want this and cannot have it via the means of plain old penile–vaginal sexual intercourse either.*

To be fair to Song, he explicitly does not want to draw a bright line between homosexual and heterosexual couples. The difference for him is about procreation. Song (2014: 48) claims, 'Without procreation the reasons for sexual differentiation become moot'. But sexual differentiation is less utilitarian than that. After all, why cannot sexual differentiation be part of the variety and diversity of creation – much of which appears to be entirely non-instrumental, not *for* anything at all other than delight? Delight and desire are present in Song's account, particularly, unsurprisingly, where he engages with Rowan Williams (whose essay 'The Body's Grace' is among the most beautiful and perceptive theological accounts of sexuality in the English language) – but they recede again rather quickly and are not borne along in what reads to me as an extremely functionalist account of sex and sexuality. And if it is functionalist, it is also prescriptive. What I take away from Song is the implication that, if one is gay, one *can* only be called to covenant partnership, and not to marriage. Song (2014: 81) insists that marriages are to do with creation and procreation, and that covenant partnerships are eschatological signs of the age to come where there will be no more marrying and giving in marriage, and no more need to perpetuate the species. He makes a valiant attempt to construct 'covenant partnerships' as something potentially theologically significant and licit in their own right. Nonetheless, his

so good about it? Isn't there power in making a statement of choosing otherwise?' In other words, it maintains a possibility of figuring homosexuality – sometimes, in some forms, for some people – as an active positionality, a thing in its own right; not heterosexuality-with-different-body-parts, not 'but gay people are *just like you!*', but a different kind of thing altogether – without disputing the fact that heterosexuality is *also* constructed, and is *also* an active positionality.

justification is too dualistic for me. Procreative and non-procreative partnerships alike are *both* concretely immanent and concerned with this world, *and* concerned with (and able to participate here and now in bringing into being) the age to come. I do not recognize the need to demarcate the two or set up a typology where each type of relationship is characterized in only one way. Song says that 'it is moot whether couples embarking on marriage knowing that they will not be able to have children are better regarded as entering into marriage or covenant partnership' (85), because, in his account, marriage is not *better* than covenant partnership, but, rather, a different thing. But it is very far from moot to many people *who want to be married* – who want the right to call their relationship marriage and to have it recognized as such, regardless of whether or not they have children (just as many, many childless marriages have been recognized down the centuries by the church – though Song does not believe that the church has had any particularly compelling reason for characterizing them as such).

Song's argument might be particularly exclusive of people who, because of their physical specificities, cannot have biological children with their spouse. In one part of the book, Song insists that *openness* to reproduction is what makes a marriage a marriage (34); elsewhere, however, he implies that covenant partnerships do not become marriages just because children are parented within them, if the children are not the biological product of the union (xi). This latter position seems to me to set up an unacceptable *a priori* distinction between, for example, non-fertile intersex people and others (some intersex people are infertile, but not all). Song says that there is no reason not to refer as marriage to a relationship between those who know, because of their age or previous treatment for medical conditions, that they will be unable to have biological children. In this case, he says, 'They would not be deliberately thwarting creation: it is just that a post-menopausal body or the result of treatment for testicular cancer or similar contingent circumstances have made it factually impossible' (34). So it is not clear to me why those intersex people for whom biological reproduction is *also* 'factually impossible' because of 'contingent circumstances' should be relegated to the category of 'covenant partnership'. There is a pastoral imperative here which Song does not really address. I think this is because of his genuine belief that 'covenant partnership' might come to be considered just as good as marriage but a distinctive thing in its own right; but I strongly suspect that, pastorally, this would not be the case, and that it would be perceived as exclusive (and, as an aside, it would be extremely difficult to justify it in light of equalities law). People who want to be recognized as licitly married, and feel they are being prevented from this on the grounds of something beyond their control (such as their being intersex, or being the same sex as their partner), are unlikely to be mollified by being offered in place of marriage something '*even better*, and especially designed for *you*!' (The speed with which civil partnerships for same-sex couples were followed by full same-sex marriages in England and Wales demonstrates this; while some same-sex couples explicitly did not wish for same-sex marriage, plenty did, and, for them, civil partnership was, at best, a consolation prize which did not prevent further campaigning for full equality.) Song believes that there are 'different calls' – to marriage which produces children; to celibacy; to non-procreative 'covenant partnership' (50) – but seems to be predetermining in advance who *could* be called to what, which seems to me to be theologically dubious as well as pastorally unsatisfactory.

How far, then, is choosing not to procreate also choosing not to generate? How far is it a rejection of a divinely instituted gift?

God's Gift: Hope and Expectation

Procreation may be generative, but generativity is far more than procreation. Modes of relationship which are not (and never could be) procreative are no less generative on that account. For Julian of Norwich (1342–1416) Christian life is inherently generative; indeed, incarnating God in this way is far more a central and inbuilt mode of human love and eroticism than biological reproduction is: 'As we learn to stretch ourselves erotically – that is, to pour ourselves out, in love – toward others, we make more manifest the body of Christ in our own time and space' (Ahlgren 2005: 38). In this sense we birth Christ, but it is also Christ who births us; Julian wrote, 'Our Saviour is our true mother in whom we are endlessly born and out of whom we shall never come' (*Showings*, Long Text, chapter 57; Julian 1978: 292). The reciprocity is key, and means we do not receive from God passively or with no capacity to hone, critique or change what is given.

Marriage and choices about reproduction have already changed: marriage is not, never was, exclusively Christian property, either in the description or in the execution. Need marriages be biologically reproductive in order not to be rejections of what God has given? Crucially, marriage is *human* property, even if it is also a gift of God. I suspect Milbank would argue (much as Barth does) that true freedom is the fulfilment of one's life in God, one's response of 'yes' to God's initiation or God's gift. In other words, freedom is not limitless possibility to signify or receive however one chooses, but rather is the possibility of signifying or receiving as one was designed to signify or receive. Yet there is tension here with Milbank's (1995) own account of gift. For Milbank, gifts are gifts precisely because they are *not* returned exactly like-for-like: to give you back exactly the thing that you gave me would be not an endorsement of the gift,[4] or an appropriate means of exchange-value, but a rejection of it (cf. Bourdieu 1977: 5). Moreover, 'If gifts are

---

4. There may be exceptions to this rule: a pre-empathetic child might, for example, be able to give no kinder or more genuinely generous gift than the one they would most have liked themselves: even if mothers and uncles and nursery school teachers may, in their heart of hearts, be less than thrilled with a decapitated Barbie or a live frog or a handful of mud, it would be churlish of them to show it to the eager young giver who has given the most exciting gift they can imagine. Likewise, someone who had once given the child a lollipop would be impolite to be visibly disappointed at receiving an identical lollipop from them at some soon stage: clearly the expectation that such a lollipop is a good and exciting gift has already been established.

only given in order to render indebted, to ensure a return of honour, and if debt drives the whole system to ensure continued exact compliance with what has been laid down, marked out by the powerful, both dead and living, then there can be, we must judge, no real gift' (Milbank 1995: 129). It would be pleasant if my giving you a gift disposed you to feel warmly towards me (and Milbank holds that, in the gift of God, 'Only gratitude and "good use" are expected in return' (148), since nothing humans could 'give back' to God could possibly 'add' to God, who lacks nothing), but, I suggest, it cannot be contingent on this, not least because I can guarantee no such thing (just as a gift given in good faith to a homeless person or my pre-teen nephew or a dubious friend might well nevertheless provoke anger or sneering or pity rather than gratitude and pleasure). Milbank rejects Jacques Derrida's and Jean-Luc Marion's constructions of gift because, he believes, they are reduced to exchange: receipt of a gift provokes gratitude, a warm-and-fuzzy prize – or reciprocation – in its own right. Its 'giftness' is thereby nullified. It sets up an opposition between giver and recipient, rather than acknowledging their irreducible interrelation and mutuality of existence (though Catherine Keller (2006: 31) holds that Milbank's own outworking of such reciprocity and interrelatedness is not yet 'thick' enough).

Now, in Milbank (1995: 135) this is complicated because humanity not only receives God's gift but *is*, in itself, God's gift; and for him this means that the very stuff of human being must be gratitude. Milbank holds that humans, the gift, do not exist at all prior to the event of the gifting (Keller 2006: 31). Since we exist *as* gift, for Milbank, there are more and less appropriate uses of ourselves, just as there would be more and less appropriate uses of other gifts. And we cannot help but return gratitude to God, by our very existence. For Milbank, in effect, creatureliness can only exist at all because it participates in the univocal being of God. The person's being exists only because it shares in that of the Trinity, and not in its own right. Ultimate freedom only exists in the context of God. Of course, the problem, as ever, is about who gets to decide exactly what is natural, self-evident, God-given and the rest; and what is and is not a legitimate form of life as gratitude. Because Milbank wants to say that activity and receptivity are mutually constituting – I cannot act without receiving, I cannot receive without acting – it seems to me that, in his conception, a gift cannot be deemed to have been given until it has also been received (see Milbank 1998: 95–6). Now this is a little odd: if I tasked Interflora with delivering flowers to you, and the bouquet never arrived, you might well wonder why I had forgotten your birthday, but no fault would lie with me, for I would honourably have discharged my duty to provide you with a gift. Interflora's failure to deliver the flowers is annoying, but does not detract from the sense in which they were a gift (any more than your refusing the delivery would undermine the sense in which they were a gift). Or, to take another example, a child who saves pocket money for several months to send to help refugee families has no less made a sacrificial gift if the money is intercepted nefariously along the way and used for a less worthy purpose. In each case, we might justly chastise Interflora, or the corrupt charity official; but we would not chastise the giver or hold that the sacrifice involved in the gift had been rendered meaningless.

Contra Milbank, and closer to the accounts of Derrida and Marion which he repudiates, I suggest that, for a gift to be a gift, I need not only to be able to reject it out of hand, I also need to be free to do something with it that would horrify the giver. If you, as a cogent adult, gave me wool for my birthday and I gave it back to you for Christmas, that would be strange and a form of rejection of your gift, and of our relationship, even though I had given you something of exactly the same value you gave me (per Bourdieu (1977: 5), 'If it is not to constitute an insult, the counter-gift must be *deferred* and *different*, because the immediate return of an exactly identical object clearly amounts to a refusal'). If you gave me wool and I gave you back a garment I'd knitted from it, however, that would be different: in that case, the value of the gift would lie not so much in the wool, but in the time and skill it took me to transform it into something else. But if you gave me the wool freely, I would also be free to burn it and give you nothing back; or sell it and donate the proceeds to a charity I knew you despised; or keep it in my craft stash and never look at it again. None of these options would necessarily reflect well on me; but I would be free to do any of them, because your gift of the wool (if it really was a gift) incurred in me no debt to you. If you had given me the wool with the expectation (voiced or not) that I *would* knit you a sweater with it, then it would not have been a gift at all, so much as an advancement of resources for a specific purpose.

Now, this does not mean that the giver cannot be disappointed if the gift is used carelessly, wantonly or not as they would have hoped. If we did not give gifts in the hope that the recipient *would* enjoy them, then that would be rather chilling in its indifference (Keller 2006: 20). The difference, for Catherine Keller (here in conversation with Milbank's *Being Reconciled* (2003)), is *hope* versus *expectation*. We may *hope* that our gifts will be appreciated and enjoyed, but we cannot *expect* or *demand* it. Now, if my nephew did indeed callously mock or reject a gift from me that I thought I'd chosen with care, I'd be within my rights (though perhaps a little petty, especially if he were of an age where he was still learning to navigate social niceties) not to bother with him again. But God, who is boundless generosity, cannot make the giving or otherwise of future blessings dependent on our response to an earlier one. And God, I suggest, contrary to the ransom streams in atonement theologies, is not in a hurry to discharge God's debts: therefore as creatures we should also not be over-eager to 'pay off services rendered or gifts received' (Bourdieu 1977: 6). This is not about conceptualizing ourselves as perpetually lacking and in thrall to our obligations, but about recognizing the interdependence between creaturely entities, and in relation to divine entities, that is our reality.

For the process-theology-inflected Keller (2006), the fact that interrelatedness and reciprocity also contribute to the continued becoming of God is significant. And it is this that means there is space for response to God to not exist only along the lines of a more or less appropriate reaction to a singular gift, but more diversely and mutually:

> The 'gift of God' is indeed, as Milbank avows, always already being received. But might this 'always already' – unlike that of Milbank or Derrida – signify that creation is itself absolute gift? The cosmos as explosive, radiant, endlessly

generous, unfolds within its intergeneses infinite reciprocities. It thereby offers infinite opportunities for the gift of the spirit to come, to come differently, asymmetrically, anew. (34)

The cosmos may not be quite so endlessly generous as Keller supposes, but, nonetheless, here is a construction which acknowledges that God is responsive to human (and other creaturely) response to God. This may entail discontinuity with earlier forms; it may mean a rediscovery of forgotten ones; it may mean engaging more wholeheartedly with dynamism (which also brings risk) without assuming that any change is a change for the worse. And there is precedent for this: such dynamism is pneumatological and finds affinity in the work of those whose consciences have prompted them not to take for granted the received wisdom about the mind of God. Indeed, some groups of Christians have testified that marriage is disordered when the institution is rendered overly static: when it cannot stretch to accommodate those whose relationships challenge its limits.

Earlier on I said that, if children, and the possibility of conceiving them, are understood as divine gifts, then they cannot entail any obligation on the part of the putative recipients. Throughout this chapter I have tried to show that, when 'traditional' models of marriage and family are held to be the places in which sanctification and grace may peculiarly – or uniquely – occur, there is a diminishing of other possibilities, a damping-down of the coals of mercy which smoulder elsewhere and in their turn ignite new fires. For as well as responsibility to and for our institutions, and to and for those in our care who may be deemed vulnerable or in need of special protection, we are also responsible to the Creator with whose creativity and capacity for generation our own chimes. In this sense, responsibility really does mean answerability: not because God is going to say, 'How dare you get it so wrong? How dare you change what I gave you?', but because God may ask, 'What did you make with what I gave you? Show me what you've done'. Gifts are given not to be buried in the earth so to preserve them from any possibility of damage, but to be invested in, built with and upon, such that in use they are not fungible but transformable (Mt. 25.14–30). Friends of mine recently bought a house from an elderly woman who had lived there for many years and raised four children there. She was very sad to leave, and my friends promised to take good care of the house. But this did not entail keeping dated features, worn carpets and crumbling plasterwork intact: rather, it meant choosing their own paint colours, remodelling rooms, making the space work for themselves and their own family. When they invited the former owner back to see what they had done, she did not feel the changes were a betrayal of her memories: rather, she delighted in their creativity and vision to make of the space something new.

Conclusion

The heaviest of burdens crushes us, we sink beneath it, it pins us to the ground. But in the love poetry of every age, the woman longs to be weighed down by the man's body. The heaviest of burdens is therefore simultaneously an image of life's most intense fulfilment. The heavier the burden, the closest our lives come to the earth, the more real and truthful they become. (Kundera 1984: 4–5)

That Milan Kundera's account of the attraction of 'weight' in *The Unbearable Lightness of Being* is so gendered is not incidental. The image is not just of sexual intercourse along gendered lines, but of the 'burden' that may result, that of the family conceived in the act. But, as we have begun to see, this is not the only sexual relationship that may occur, nor the only means by which families are created. In some relationships the family may manifest in biological children; in others the children may be adopted; in still others it will exist predominantly in the relationship between the partners themselves. There is something to be said for the 'burden', the responsibility and desire to generate, which many people come to experience. Commitment need not be understood as something to be escaped or transcended, but can become something in and through which humans are fulfilled.

Crucially, and in a way Song does not quite adequately acknowledge, openness to family does not always have to mean openness to children. A family forged in marriage is already a family. To hold that those who choose not to have children are 'thwarting creation' is to delimit how creation (and creativity and generativity) manifests. In her interviews with Christian women who had chosen to be childless, Dawn Llewellyn found that some described their capacity for self-offering, and sense of vocation, as being fulfilled via teaching, research and ordained ministry. Some challenged the assumption that, because they were not mothers, they did not have families (noting that they were still, and already, partners, sisters and daughters). Others saw their responsibility and generativity manifesting in care for existing others, rather than putative new others. Llewellyn's (2016) participants rejected the notion that infertility was the only legitimate reason for a Christian not to have children. Margaret Farley (2006: 278–9) and Cristina Richie (2013: 139) note that in both Roman Catholic and evangelical accounts, while procreation is held to be a duty and a good of marriage, infertile heterosexual couples are let off the hook but same-sex couples, and heterosexual couples who choose to remain childless, are not. Richie (2013: 140) suggests that this is because otherwise procreation is separated more absolutely from marriage, thereby removing at least one theological objection to same-sex marriages.

Where responsibility also means answerability, we are answerable for what we do and do not make of our institutions. Our responsibility extends to how gamely we take on our role as transmitters, disseminators and shapers of the culture we pass on (to our social and cultural mentees as well as our own offspring). This weight may sometimes feel like a burden, but, like other burdens, it is one appropriate to (and even desirable as a marker of having arrived at) a particular stage of life.

Nonetheless, as Nietzsche held, we sometimes fear the power of all that we could be. For this reason, perhaps, we have not always pushed the envelope of our institutions as far as we might have done. We have not always adequately interrogated what is stultifying and life-sapping about them and what might require change on the grounds of justice. We have failed to redefine our institutions in the most generous ways possible rather than reinforcing their boundaries to keep transgressors out. Unlike with the Nietzschian concept of eternal recurrence, though, we are not fated to experience again replays of our past lives: rather, we may progress ourselves and our institutions towards more just incarnations. This means that, once more, we become both parents and children of our institutions, shapers of them as well as shaped by them.

The fear of all we could be is, I suggest, part of the reason for our lack of institutional imagination. It explains our appeals to slippery-slope arguments, to originist accounts of family and marriage, to exclusive rather than expansive definitions. Nonetheless, we might ask how un/familiar an institution has to be before it no longer has any clear continuity with what it has been in the past. In the next chapter I focus on marriage as one example, and, more specifically, the assumption that it may solely be figured as a relationship of two and only two spouses.

Chapter 3

THE CONTENT OF MARRIAGE: TWO AND ONLY TWO?

Introduction

In the last chapter I showed the disruption of the apotheosization of biology that already exists both within the Christian tradition and within other discourses inflected by broader notions of generativity. As we saw, some scholars, notably Robert Song, have lamented the disruption of the association between marriage, biology and parenthood which such accounts may accentuate. In this chapter I examine the extent to which discontinuities between forms of relationship being forged today and marital relationships as understood in the past mean that these already cannot be understood as the same kinds of phenomenon, regardless of whether they are biologically procreative. In particular, I explore the sacramental symbolism of the exclusivity of two partners, and note that there is already good warrant in the Christian tradition for disrupting and relativizing dyads of this kind. I am not necessarily arguing in favour of the recognition of polyamorous relationships as marriages, nor am I claiming that polyamorous arrangements are inevitably preferable to monogamous ones. However, I am noting that these types of relationships share enough features in common with one another that they may conceivably be understood as *both* being able to mediate grace in their different ways, and that attention to the generosity, expansiveness and critical consideration of the detail of ongoing consent and consultation which many polyamorous relationships exhibit may be a significant catalyst for monogamous marriage's own ongoing self-reflexivity and reform.

Christians Do Not Own Marriage

As we saw earlier, in their responses to social changes such as the legal recognition of same-sex marriage, Christian denominations have sometimes appealed to an irreducible kernel of ontological existence which stands apart from human culture and society.

But, whether they like it or not, Christians do not own marriage and cannot define it on behalf of other people. Marriage is not, and never has been, a uniquely Christian institution. It is a *human* institution, instituted and lived out in different ways across different societies. Even where Christians have owned this on the one hand, they have sometimes pulled it back with the other: the 2013 Church of England document *Men and Women in Marriage* holds on the one hand that 'neither the state nor the Church can claim a prior right over marriage, nor does either of them "make" marriages, which is done by God's providence working through the public promises of the couples themselves' (Archbishops' Council 2013: 13), yet at the same time makes claims (such as the one that marriage was instituted by God in creation) which precisely *are* theological ones and *do* seek to define and delineate marriage in a universalizing way on behalf of others. 'God has given this gift [marriage between one man and one woman], and it will remain part of our created human endowment' (16), they claim; yet there is little sense that part of its createdness is precisely the fact that it is created and recreated *by humans*. Indeed, they say, '[Marriage] is not simply a cultural development ... nor simply a political or economic institution. ... It is an expression of the human nature which God has willed for us and which we share' (2). The claim that marriage has somehow existed conceptually before human societies ever practised it is a loaded theological assertion: it says that human marriage is an imitation of a previously existing form.

However, while God can undoubtedly act in and through human institutions, God did not invent marriage. Humans invented marriage, and humans can and do reinvent it too. The Church of England seems to want to claim that marriage existed as an *a priori* concept or *eidos* before human beings ever practised it; but it is perfectly possible to claim, rather, that marriage arises as a response to God's love, and echoes something of the divine propensity for relationality and faithfulness which humans share, without also claiming that marriage had a cosmic significance before the fact.

For even if human creativity reflects divine creativity and springs out of divine creativity, this does not mean that nothing truly new may be done with it. Only God creates ex nihilo, but this does not mean that novelty is impossible for those who create from existing materials. Humans (and other creatures) manipulate and shape their environments; they fit the pieces together in new ways; they conceive (of) things that have not existed before; they take risks, precisely because they do not know for sure how things will turn out. Noam Chomsky and some other linguistics theorists figure this as 'generative grammar': the apparently global ability of young children quickly to discern the rules and norms of their own native language(s) such that they are able, with remarkable consistency, to generate grammatical sentences even from components they have never before encountered being used in these specific ways, and not just as mimicry of what they have explicitly heard. Just as there is something about every child which is truly new and veritably itself despite and alongside its biological and cultural causes, so there can be innovation in human culture and invention even if the tools and materials used are, necessarily, in continuation with what humans have been able to find or synthesize from the resources they have. We really can create new meaning even within the grammar of our language. So, we might say, we are predisposed along certain human lines via our creaturely status – but there is a wealth of opportunity for growth and newness within that. We would never claim that a poet's work is not 'original' just because *all* she has done is to put existing words in a new order. We recognize veritable newness in this activity. In her research on creativity in education, Anna Craft describes its nub as 'possibility thinking' (see Craft 2010), but in some respects this is a misnomer: 'possibility thinking' invites imagination towards implementation of what is *not yet* possible, *as if* it were possible. Behaving already as though the not-yet had come about: what could be more eschatological than that?

If for Plato the form or *eidos* is the most real thing, and does not need to be made manifest in the material world in order to be truly real (and if grasping truth is not the acquisition of truly new knowledge, but *anamnesis*, the recollection of what has been lost in sensory illusion), then for Aristotle the manifestation of a thing is just as significant as the concept and neither can exist without the other (though there is still some prioritization of being over becoming). For Kant, form is nothing but an interpretation of matter, a sense of order in the eye of the beholder. I am suggesting that marriage exists somewhere in between Aristotle and Kant: marriage *may* echo a real pre-existing relationality in God; *may* share in common qualities with divine characteristics of love, fidelity and the rest; but it is what it is as an institution *because we as humans understand it that way* rather than because of anything it was *a priori*. We lay an interpretation over it. We meet it in and through *marriages*; they, not the mythic ontological concept of marriage, are our starting point. Marriage is not, as the Church of England claims, instituted in creation: not if that means at the *moment* of creation, and not if that means that it is somehow written universally onto all human cultures and societies in response to human sex differentiation.

For the Church of England, there is something incontrovertible and immutable about marriage that cannot be eroded or altered: 'The reality of marriage between one man and one woman will not disappear as the result of any legislative change' (Archbishops' Council 2013: 16). We might point to similar essentialism in the Roman Catholic and Orthodox traditions too. In this logic, same-sex marriage is simply not possible; it is not part of the *eidos* of marriage, which requires the partners to be of different sexes. In that case, someone might counter, what is the *harm* in allowing same-sex couples to call their relationships marriages if they want to? After all, by the Church of England's own logic, this could not change the true reality of marriage. But the Church of England holds that calling a same-sex relationship marriage would not only be misleading and cause pastoral distress (whether to same-sex couples who believe themselves married when they are not, or to heterosexual couples who may now feel their heterosexual-only, unchangeable marriage is not so unassailable after all, is not made clear); it would also (for reasons on which they do not elaborate) make 'the disciplines of living in it [i.e. heterosexual marriage] … more difficult to acquire, and the path to fulfilment, in marriage and other relationships, more difficult to find' (16).

For Aristotle, matter is how form manifests, and the arrangement of matter truly becomes the form. Could it be that human sex is only *materially* and not cosmically or eternally significant? In that case, marriage as human institution might be understood as a manifestation of an *eidos* which exists *only in and through* the matter from which it is made. Marriage, then, would exist wherever humans make it, and, if human sex is only materially significant, then the sex of the human participants would have no bearing on whether or not marriage existed between them. Someone might, again, counter that this could not be the case, because the form of marriage is necessarily an idea of something that exists between a man and a woman. But for Aristotle a single form may become manifest in several different ways, through several different kinds of matter. We might want to say that marriage is necessarily made manifest in and through *humans* – we might, that is, want to continue to claim that marriages may only take place between two humans, rather than a human and a tree, or two elephants – but still note that the sexed matter of the individual humans in which the idea manifests may differ (sometimes being a male and a female, sometimes being two females and so on).

Marriage is a *human* institution, a thing created by humans for humans, rather than a thing created by God or a thing that somehow pre-exists human society. This does not mean that marriage cannot provide a valuable image of social interrelation and *perichoresis* such as that which exists between the persons of the Trinity. But the point is that the symbol of marriage is *like* these intratrinitarian relationships of love and mutual exchange: it is not the *same* as them. Marriage exists only because human beings have made it. Human beings can and do remake it too. There have been many societies in the past, and there continue to be many societies now, which hold that marriage is a uniquely male–female possibility. There are also societies which have come to hold that marriage may equally and licitly take place between two persons of the same sex (or, more accurately, which hold that the sex of the persons contracting the marriage is of no relevance to whether or not the marriage is possible).

Opponents to same-sex marriage have sometimes said, 'But we can't say that marriage just is whatever we want it to be! If we allow same-sex marriage, then we might as well allow marriage between polyamorous groups, or parents and children, or people and their pets. That's not our decision to make!' (See Köstenberger and Jones (2012: 35) for a warning about what happens when 'biblical' principles for marriage are replaced by 'civil' ones.) I think this is not so much a slippery slope-type argument (though it may be that, sometimes, for some such objectors) as one which appeals to the inalienability of the *eidos* of marriage in a Platonic sense. In this logic, marriage is what it is because it always was that way in formal essence – or because God created it and intended it to be that way (which comes to roughly the same thing for a Christian Platonist). But if, as I am suggesting, marriage is understood in Aristotelean-cum-Kantian rather than in Platonic formal terms, then we are faced with a different and perhaps harder set of questions. These might include: If marriage no longer necessitates involving a male and a female of its kind, then does it require categorical 'otherness' at all, and if so, on what grounds? What are the licit limits, if any, to our recreation of marriage? What would have to happen to marriage before it had lost all resemblance to what we as human cultures and societies have known as marriage in the past? Would that matter? If it *would* matter, would it matter because a theologically significant symbol had been lost, or because it would be detrimental to human good, or both, or neither?

In this next section, as a thought experiment which shows some of the difficulties of such reframings of the essence of institutions whose content we have often considered self-evident, I turn in more detail to one of these kinds of questions, namely: *why* must there be two and only two people in a marriage, given the deep commitment of most polyamorous people to explicit consent, open lines of communication and proactive ethical attention to the good of all those involved in polyamorous relationship (see Easton and Hardy 2009; Veaux and Rickert 2014)?

Forsaking All Others?

Counting genitals is a rather reductive view of erotic life. It forgets that many erotic activities do not directly involve the genitals. It overlooks the complex relations between erotic roles or selves and genitals or bodies. *All* erotic relationships, except perhaps the briefest and dullest, are polyamorous. They bring together multiple erotic roles, sexual identities, and real or fictive persons. (Jordan 2013: 182)

The imagery of multiplicity in the Eucharistic liturgy, the joining of many bodies in the Christ whose blood is poured out for all of them, means, holds Mark D. Jordan (2013: 167), that 'joining bodies promiscuously is the great Christian Mystery'. Eucharist is eschatological, disturbing here-and-now conceptions of bodies and how they should relate. Similarly, 'Since the eschatological assembly of the church supersedes the biological family, eschatological rethinking of human relations need not begin with the couple' (170).

Yet Christians have not tended to be comfortable considering the possibility of expanding understandings of marriage beyond two and only two spouses. Even if they have sometimes been fairly pragmatic about not insisting that converts to Christianity abandon the commitments entered into via polygamy (like the nineteenth-century bishop John Colenso of Natal, who held that African converts who already had more than one wife should not desert them, but should also not take on any additional wives; or, earlier, Gregory the Great, who advised Augustine of Canterbury that English converts to Christianity who had more than one spouse should be rebuked but not required to end their marriages),[1]

---

1. Gregory wrote to Augustine, 'But, since there are many in the nation of the Angli who while they were yet in unbelief are said to have been associated in such unholy marriages, they should be admonished, when they come to the faith, to abstain from each other, and be made to understand that this is a grievous sin. Let them fear God's tremendous judgment, lest for carnal delight they incur the pains of eternal torment. Yet they should not on this account be deprived of the communion of the Lord's body and blood, lest we should seem to punish them for what they had bound themselves in through ignorance before the laver of baptism. For at this time holy church corrects some things with fervour, tolerates some things with gentleness, connives at and bears some things with consideration, so as often to

more frequently they have restated in the strongest terms the theological and semiological significance of the exclusive *twoness* of spousehood. Indeed, even in 1988 when the Anglican bishops at the Lambeth Conference acknowledged that polygamy remained a live issue in some countries and resolved that polygamous men could be licitly baptized as Christians along with their wives and children as long as the local Anglican community was in support, they also restated, 'This Conference upholds monogamy as God's plan, and as the ideal relationship of love between husband and wife'. In some instances, supporters of same-sex marriage have responded by emphasizing the fact that same-sex couples *also* seek exclusive, two-person covenant marriages just as many heterosexuals do (this assumption underlies, for example, the Episcopal Church in the USA's 2012 liturgical *Resources for the Witnessing and Blessing of a Lifelong Covenant in a Same-Sex Relationship* – Church Pension Fund 2012).

But the fact remains that, within both heterosexual and homosexual lives, there are Christian polyamorists asking serious questions about the recognition of their own relationships, and prompting hard consideration of whether marriage could ever be licitly understood to involve more than two spouses. John Witte Jr (2015: 2) argues that discussions about the extent to which polyamorous relationships – including both more traditional forms of polygamy, and newer forms of polyamory – may be recognized legally are likely to succeed discussions about same-sex relationships as the most pressing concern facing Western family law in the coming decades. In the remainder of this chapter I reconsider some theological and ethical objections to polyamory, and ask to what extent un/familiar theology might stretch in this direction.

In *Indecent Theology* (2000), Marcella Althaus-Reid holds that Christian condemnations of non-monogamy are mostly about upholding the legal and economic import of marriage. Theologies based on exhorting the good of community should be able to recognize and endorse the good of (extended) communities of sexual intimacy too, yet have not done so (142). Yet, she holds, 'intimacy with others has a divine nature' (143), not always but often sexual, and this should not be limited only to one-on-one relationships. If we reject the idea that women, slaves and children are male property, we may also reject the idea that women having sexual relationships with more than one partner is an offence against male property rights (140–1). The notion of polyamory 'challenges a heterosexual monotheistic system from the grassroots of human relationships, the one God, one husband and one phallus system' (141). This picks up on objections from within and beyond the Christian theological tradition that marriage has,

repress what she opposes by bearing and conniving. But all who come to the faith are to be warned not to dare to perpetrate any such thing: and if any should perpetrate it, they must be deprived of the communion of the Lord's body and blood, since, as in those who have done it in ignorance the fault should be to a certain extent tolerated, so it should be severely visited in those who are not afraid to sin in spite of knowledge' (Book XI, Epistle LXIV in Schaff 1898).

in practice, been a carrier and transmitter of inequity and exploitation, and that enforced monogamy has been one facet of this which needs to be challenged on the grounds of justice. If Christians are wary of anything that looks like 'free love', why is that? If Christian modes of love are not to be understood as 'free', why is *that*? On the one hand, we might suggest that 'God's way' of monogamy is the most truly free because it is within these bounds that humans are most truly able to be themselves, to be as God created and intended them to be. (This is the gist of the logic that underlies Barth's *Church Dogmatics*, especially III/4.) On the other, we might ask whether Christians resist the idea of 'free love' because they are more familiar with accounts of love, economics and atonement which are built on a foundation of debt. In this case, we might ask whether a reconsideration of monogamy is likely to help root out some of the rot Althaus-Reid and others have suspected is at the heart of the system.

1 Theological Objections to Polyamory

a The Disruption of Sacramentality

Yet even if we recognize the frequent iniquities of marriage-in-practice, one of the most compelling Christian theological arguments against the consecration of polyamorous relationships as marriages is a sacramental one, the argument that introducing a third or fourth or fifth element interrupts dyadic marriage's capacity to mirror divine–human relationship. Just as God gives Godself fully and unreservedly in the service of creation, mediating grace to it, runs this account, so the spouses are to mediate grace to one another via their own (albeit inevitably less-than-ultimate) self-giving. This self-giving anticipates the eschatological time – the time to come, and the time already coming into being – when there will be no alienation between God and creation. As such, whatever else marriage is, it is a sign of the eschaton, a symbol of the perfectly integrated, non-alienated communion between God and creation. For John Paul II (1981) in *Familiaris Consortio* (The Fellowship of the Family), drawing on Augustine, the exclusivity and indissolubility of marriage-between-two is a potent symbol of 'the absolutely faithful love that God has for man and that the Lord Jesus has for the Church'. If marriages are imperfect, this is unfortunate but ultimately immaterial, since marriages echo and gesture towards something better, and marriage itself has the capacity to do formative and transformative work towards bringing it into being.

This account is indisputably beautiful and lofty, but does it put too great a pressure on marriage? That is Geoffrey Rees' (2011) argument in *The Romance of Innocent Sexuality*, in which he holds that the power of marriage has become so over-stated in some theologies of sexuality that it is endowed with an almost soteriological potency. Augustine objected to polygamy not on natural law grounds, but because it disrupted marriage's capacity to foster 'spiritual goods' and mediate 'mutual fidelity and sacramental stability' (Witte 2015: 98). But to exhort marriage as redemptive and the training ground for redemption and grace, let alone the most potent communication available to us of God's love for the world, is, quite simply, suggests Rees, to assume *too much* about what marriage is and can do, and to elevate it beyond what it can sustain. We might add that it also leaves those who wish to be married but are unmarried in the position of wondering whether they are missing out on not only a form of social recognition but also of a crucial locus for ontological change into the likeness of God. Furthermore, we might hold that to anticipate absolutely no distinction whatsoever between God and creatures in the eschaton does violence to both their natures. There can still be difference without alienation. We might therefore be suspicious of accounts which imply a merging or disappearing into one another of distinct, discrete identities. So while self-giving is a potential good, if there is no limit on it, it risks doing conceptual violence to the integrity of each self.

b *The Disruption of Full Self-giving*
Self-giving similarly underpins John Paul II's (1981) account of family life more broadly:

> The family is the first and fundamental school of social living: as a community of love, it finds in self-giving the law that guides it and makes it grow. The self-giving that inspires the love of husband and wife for each other is the model and norm for the self-giving that must be practiced in the relationships between brothers and sisters and the different generations living together in the family.

Again, this is underpinned by the assumption that (heterosexual) marriage may uniquely provide this foundation; but also, again, it is grounded in the treble assumptions that human males and females are complementary and 'nuptially' directed towards one another; that, in this way, they (uniquely) capture in microcosm the essence of human community; and that complete self-giving may only be to *one* other person (even if, as here, it is purported to be *for the sake of* potentially multiple other persons). In part, the stumbling-block is that 'self-giving' is here a coy euphemism for non-contracepted sex; but if we take John Paul II seriously and ask in what *else* 'complete self-giving' might inhere, the question of how far it is necessarily unique to monogamy remains a live one. After all, conceivably, a casual or anonymous sexual encounter might be understood as having *more* at stake – carrying more risk, giving more away – than one that takes place within the context of a permanent relationship. If we recognize that the image of spouses in marriage as standing for God and humans is already humanly constructed and is built on assumptions about what we know (some) human marriages to be like, perhaps it need not be understood as incontrovertible. It is plainly not unproblematic, given heterosexual marriage's often violent and patriarchal genealogy and legacy. Furthermore, there are plenty of ways in which the Trinitarian imagery of the Christian tradition interrupts the good of dyadic tropes.

Beyond the Catholic context, for Barth, the logic of two-and-only-two is clear; for someone less invested in the orderliness and process of order and procession, or less swayed by the notion that marriage exists in and through divine command, the reasoning may be less obvious even if the conclusion is the same. Per Barth

(1961: 196–7) (who is discussing polygamy rather than polyamory more broadly, though I suspect his logic would be largely the same on the latter),

> In marriage as such ... they are faced only by the duty and task of full life-partnership in which their choice has to vindicate itself. ... They are confronted by this task and duty, and it can be accomplished only by a couple, not by three or four. The two who have chosen each other have to prove themselves in it. There can be no third person alongside them. How can that mutual liberation and freedom in fellowship which is so constitutive of marriage be genuinely attained if at the same time it is also demanded of a second partner and can be to the advantage of this or that third party? And how can there be fellowship in this freedom if the orientation on each other in which alone it can be realised has to be constantly divided between two very different second partners? And how can the order of life-partnership be fulfilled if there are two firsts and two seconds? In every dimension a third party, whether male or female, can only ... disturb and destroy full life-partnership. If marriage as such, under and in virtue of the divine command, is full life-partnership, it is necessarily monogamous.

Barth, suspicious of maximizing any natural theology, cannot say that we recognize order and procession in God because we already know it from intra-human male–female relationships. For Barth, part of the problem would also be that any marriage with more than two spouses would inevitably involve at least two people of the same sex. Barth cannot countenance same-sex relationships, because they also disrupt the sense of unity-in-diversity which Barth believes exist in male–female relationships. Attraction to sameness rather than otherness is narcissistic idolatry. However, Barth objects to homosexuality – and other kinds of homosocial relationships – largely on the grounds of seclusion. Human males and human females are the poorer when they do not share in one another's society (165–6). Arguably, then, a marriage of three or more spouses including *at least two* sexes might be preferable to a dyadic male–male or female–female marriage, since it would acknowledge (what Barth understands as) the incompleteness of single-sex relationship. And as I have commented elsewhere, Barth assumes difference on the grounds of sex (or gender) is self-evident and irreducible, but this is *not* incontrovertibly the case, and similarity and difference may manifest along many lines (Cornwall 2010: 75–89).

It is not insignificant that Barth probably came closer to sustaining a polyamorous relationship than any other key theologian of his era. The exact nature of his relationship with Charlotte 'Lollo' von Kirschbaum, the assistant and companion who lived with Barth and his wife Nelly Barth-Hoffmann, is unclear, but it is evident that Barth found Kirschbaum an intellectually stimulating interlocutor and deeply respected her ideas, on which he drew in his own theological anthropology. Several of their friends and students assumed Barth and Kirschbaum were lovers; they would take holidays together without Barth's wife or children. On at least one occasion, Barth asked Barth-Hoffmann for a divorce, which she refused (Selinger 1998: 7–8); thereafter, the three lived together with

Barth and Barth-Hoffmann's children, and Kirschbaum was eventually buried in the Barth family tomb (10). Whatever the realities of Barth and Kirschbaum's life together with Barth-Hoffmann, there are undoubtedly many faithful Christians, including some eminent theologians, who have maintained relationships with a primary partner (usually a wife) as well as one or more additional lovers (male or female), often over a period of many years. In situations where this is an open secret, and where it is clear that the primary partner is not trapped in the marriage unwillingly (which is questionable in Nelly Barth-Hoffmann's case), one can only assume that the primary partner is also content with the situation for reasons of their own. Polyamory is clearly not something which occurs only beyond the theological community; one of our questions might, then, following Althaus-Reid, be why it has so rarely proven possible to articulate the nature of such relationships as part of these scholars' and priests' publicly avowed lives.[2]

Pair-bonding arises across many animal species. It has proven itself an often effective way to promote stability and security for those involved, including offspring. Nonetheless, it is clear that social pair-bonding and sexual pair-bonding do not always coincide. There are plenty of instances of cultures which have on the surface promoted monogamy (and where certainly legal marriage is only possible between two spouses) but which have actually commonly entailed multiple clandestine sexual relationships. If polyamory brings to the surface what had been hidden, and foregrounds consent, disclosure and accountability between all concerned, it may prove a more ethically satisfactory system.

With this in mind, it is perhaps especially significant that there is another part to Barth's public objection to polygamy, similar to John Paul II's: that full life-partnership, full commitment, can *only* be given to one other, not to more than one. We might characterize this as an ontological objection: per this logic, a marriage of three or more persons just *cannot* be a marriage, ontologically *is not* a marriage, simply because a marriage by definition involves exclusive commitment one-on-one. Of course, this has patently not always been the way that marriage has been organized: the Hebrew Bible is replete with polygamous arrangements, and the question of whether polygamy is compatible with Christianity is still live in parts of the African churches. Men of the Greco-Roman era were quite comfortable with the notion that different partners fulfilled different roles: boys for sexual pleasure, male peers for intellectual stimulation and wives for reproduction; there was no

2. Althaus-Reid (2000: 49) writes of Barth's 'hypocrisy' in 'writing on the values of the traditional family while he obviously could not suffer the occasionally idiotic nature of married life'. The point is expanded in her comments on Paul Tillich: 'What is to be condemned and regretted is not that Tillich was a sadomasochist, but the fact that he did not find "the courage to be" out of the closet of his sexuality; a sadomasochist theologian, for instance, reflecting on an issue of importance in his life as in the life of others. Our difficulty with Tillich is his lack of integrity and not necessarily his developed taste for bondage practices, which were probably shared by many other academic colleagues, fellow priests and everyday fellow Christians' (88).

expectation that a wife need provide all these. The Bible (notably, for example, the book of Hosea) utilizes imagery of God as a jealous husband; but this seems to be based on the assumption that jealousy is a legitimate and understandable quality in a man protective of his property (and the problem in Hosea is, in any case, probably not non-monogamy, but cultic transgression). Ronald E. Long (2005) believes that jealousy is almost inevitable in human sexual relationships because of the fear of being left out. He concludes, therefore, that 'a polyamorous heaven may be the theoretical, the eschatological, ideal, but in human affairs, the sexually intimate couple remains the practical ideal most transparent to the heavenly one' (45). Yet this is to assume that the way human beings have arranged their relationships in the past delimits how they may arrange them in the future. The question is to what extent a putatively polyamorous eschatological future (in which, per Mk. 12.25 and Mt. 22.30, human marriage will not be organized as it has been organized in this realm) could be anticipated and implemented in the present.

c　The Disruption of the Imagery of Complementary Pairs
Another form of the ontological objection says that the imagery of pairs, of twoness, arises again and again across the biblical literature, and that to expand marriage to more than two partners therefore undermines the ways in which marriage echoes other pairings built into the very structures of creation. In this account, just as God creates the heavens and the earth and separates the waters from the land, just as night contrasts with day and each has its own illumination ('the greater light to rule the day, and the lesser light to rule the night' – Gen. 1.16), so God creates humans as a pair. For some interpreters, it is significant that this pair is the male and female of its kind; for others, it is simply the twoness itself that matters, since this represents diversity and otherness. The two-becoming-one of marriage echoes the uniting of other dyads: Christ and the church; humanity and divinity in Christ; humanity and divinity, again, in the reconciliation by God in Christ of all things to Godself (Col. 1.20; 2 Cor. 5.19).

However, we would do well to note that there is also plenty of imagery in the Bible, and in the Christian tradition more broadly, which is *disruptive* of dyads. The tradition points not just to either-ors, but to both-ands; to instances where oppositions (both social and ontological) are relativized (per Gal. 3.26–28), and where difference between two groups does not equal animosity. In instances where there seems to be dyadic reciprocity (as in the instructions to wives and husbands, fathers and children, or slaves and masters), the implication is that this is possible precisely because there is a mediating third party, God. And as the narrative develops it is clear that the rhetoric of the early Christians is that God is the God not only of Israel (as a jealous husband), but a God of multiple nations and peoples, who has love enough to go around.

Indeed, proponents of polyamory have countered that to say one can only fully love and be committed to one other person makes no sense if one accepts that it is possible for parents to love more than one child equally; in fact, that it is possible for love to grow and expand to include as many children as necessary. Dossie Easton and Janet Hardy (2009: 56–62), for example, hold that many traditional relationships are built on 'starvation economics' while polyamory seeks to promote and celebrate abundance. Surely jealousy is not a desirable quality in human relationships? A spouse may well wish to be their partner's one and only, but just so do plenty of firstborn children resent the arrival of younger siblings and wish to keep their parents to themselves. Granted, a relationship between parents and children is not mutual in quite the same way as that between spouses: a father may have five or six children, but each child has only one father. On the other hand, plenty of children do count several adults as their parents and draw no hierarchies between, for example, fathers and stepfathers. Similarly, children brought up predominantly in the care of a grandmother, aunt or nanny may consider her as much their mother as their actual mother is. For Easton and Hardy, monogamy is no guarantee that jealousy will not exist, so better is to do the work of working out what is at its root: 'The challenge comes in learning to establish within yourself a strong foundation of internal security that is not dependent on sexual exclusivity or ownership of your partner' (115).

As we have seen, those who appeal to the existence of pairs across the structures of creation do not always hold that such pairs within human relationships need necessarily be heterosexual. Nonetheless, the imagery of two-and-only two may also be held to map more specifically onto the sexual difference of the spouses, as in the arguments of some detractors of same-sex two-spousal marriage. Echoing the emphasis on human sex as having a 'nuptial meaning' also found in John Paul II's *Theology of the Body* (2006, based on his 1979–84 lectures), Pope Francis (2015a) holds,

> It is not man alone who is the image of God or woman alone who is the image of God, but man and woman as a couple who are the image of God. The difference between man and woman is not meant to stand in opposition, or to subordinate, but is for the sake of communion and generation, always in the image and likeness of God. … God entrusted the earth to the alliance between man and woman: its failure deprives the earth of warmth and darkens the sky of hope.

This is also clearly influenced by the Augustinian principle of fidelity between the (two) spouses.

But if we expect to find completion in relationships of marriage, we may – as Rees (2011) hints – risk making marriage an idol and imbuing it with almost soteriological significance which it cannot carry. Veaux and Rickert (2014: 9) observe, 'Polyamory can feel threatening because it upsets our fairy-tale assumption that the right partner will keep us safe from change.' Spouses, whether two or more, cannot be everything to one another. Jordan (2013: 171) notes that there is a certain romance attached to the idea of one perfect partner who holds together all our desired qualities – even in communities where exclusive two-partner relationships are relatively rare, as among some portions of the gay male community. But this is, precisely, a fantasy: *no-one* can be our one and only, providing all we need in terms of human interaction and community. Samuel

Wells (2006: 96) describes marriage like this: 'Marriage is the great proclamation of abundance. All is focused on a single other – but the truth is that, far from being not enough, that one person is more than enough. … One other person is always more than enough, when you believe that that person will listen to you until you run out of things to say.'

This is attractive in some respects, but I do not think it is the only possible picture. And I wonder whether it is slightly in tension with the expansive vision of marriage as being for the whole community: Wells does *say* that marriage is about discerning what is good for 'the service of others' as well as the spouses' mutual flourishing; but, even so, the picture of marriage he *shows* – as one person being enough, more than enough, for the other – could quickly shade into co-dependence, isolation from other relationships and insularity. It might also negate the possibility of change, and of seasons where spouses are alternately more and less closely involved in one another's lives. Jordan (2013: 183) holds, 'Change is built into an erotic relationship and the persons who constitute it': perhaps we should not understand monogamous relationships as inherently any less shifting or uncertain than polyamorous ones.

d The Disruption of Fidelity

That said, even if one is not inclined to have all one's emotional or sexual needs met by one single other person, there might still be an argument for saying that one's self-giving to a single given person can be greater if one is able to channel all one's energies into them rather than splitting time and labour between several recipients. In certain models of polyamory, notably those where there is a primary partner and then subsidiary 'secondaries' and 'tertiaries', the non-primary partner usually has neither the responsibilities nor the rights of full life together (Easton and Hardy 2009: 163). Where a non-primary partner is figured as being there only for the fun times, this might be understood as incomplete and shallow. Theodore W. Jennings (2013) suspects that, despite the many possible strengths of open relationships, what they are less likely to do well is to recognize the fullness of long-term life together *beyond* the sexual. 'It is all too easy', he remarks, 'to use openness as a way of avoiding the work of building trust and trustworthiness over the long term' (195). Where the 'more' of open or polyamorous relationships occurs mainly along sexual lines, the importance of sex at the expense of care, responsibility, structures of affect and quotidian day-to-day life may be overemphasized. Such arguments in favour of entire self-giving have long underlain Christian objections to divorce and to sex outside marriage (notably in documents such as *Familiaris Consortio* – John Paul II 1981). John Paul II (1981) holds,

> The total physical self-giving would be a lie if it were not the sign and fruit of a total personal self-giving, in which the whole person, including the temporal dimension, is present: if the person were to withhold something or reserve the possibility of deciding otherwise in the future, by this very fact he or she would not be giving totally. … The only 'place' in which this self-giving in its whole truth

is made possible is marriage, the covenant of conjugal love freely and consciously chosen, whereby man and woman accept the intimate community of life and love willed by God Himself which only in this light manifests its true meaning. The institution of marriage is not an undue interference by society or authority, nor the extrinsic imposition of a form. Rather it is an interior requirement of the covenant of conjugal love which is publicly affirmed as unique and exclusive.

If self-giving is a good, there may be fears that, the more people are involved in a relationship, the more they will be likely to shirk and not pull their weight, emotional or otherwise. The need to take into account a range of people's needs and preferences may make the relationship such hard work as to be unsustainable. John Paul II insists that ultimate self-giving means sharing *everything* about one another's 'life-project', not just sex or parenting. However, this exhortation is rooted in his assumption that there is a natural male–female complementarity such that a two-and-only-two heterosexual marriage relationship is already synecdoche for the human community in toto. We might counter that, if complementarity is removed from the equation, the sex of the partners is already irrelevant. The question for our purposes is whether the number of partners is irrelevant too, and whether a polyamorous relationship – or rather, the persons in it – may similarly be deemed an appropriate target for continual outpouring of the self.

The principle of fidelity, significant as one of the three goods of marriage Augustine repeatedly emphasizes – the others being procreation and sacramentality – is sometimes appealed to as the quality which particularly echoes Christ's loyalty to the church (see Mohler 1991: 75). However, given the aspect of Christianity often deemed (not unproblematically) generous and expansive – the extension of the covenant beyond Israel to a church which is diverse and contains many members – this does not in itself make the case for why such fidelity must be understood as exclusively dyadic. Could Christ not be faithful to multiple 'brides'? Fidelity, for Augustine, includes the commitment of the spouses to one another's spiritual well-being and to do for the other what they require to prevent them from falling into sin. Again, however, it is not self-evident why this may only be a two-way commitment. In Ron Haflidson's (2016: 65) translation of the *Literal Commentary on Genesis* 9.7.12, Augustine insists, 'What fidelity means is that neither partner should sleep with another person outside the marriage bed' – but this is open to a whole host of interpretation should one choose to be imaginative. Could there be a case for holy threesomes (or more) within the 'marriage bed' – in which case the principle might be that there is a distinction between involving a third person in a marriage (or in the sexual activity between married spouses) if that third person is unmarried, and between involving a third person who is themselves married (since this would involve removing them from their own 'marriage bed')? This case is harder to make from, for example, James Hammond Taylor's (1982: 78) translation of the same passage: '*Fidelity* means that there must be no relations with any person outside the marriage bond'. Nonetheless, some creative exegesis might still lead us to ask the question of whether the marriage bond itself – rather than simply the 'relations' or sexual activity – could conceivably be expanded to encompass more than two without sacrificing the good of fidelity per se. This is especially the case given that – as Haflidson (2016: 64) notes – it is clear from *On the Good of Marriage* that Augustine conceptualizes fidelity as being more about mental than physical faithfulness (discussing *On the Good of Marriage* 4.4). If fidelity is about attitude of mind, it is not necessarily absurd to conceive of a form of fidelity which is not inherently dyadic even if it remains exclusive of others beyond the (multi-partner) arrangement. By this logic, as I have hinted, it might be more possible to justify polyamorous marriages (where three or more partners commit to one another) than 'open marriages' (where the committed partners also have relationships with one or more people outside the marriage).

The question of fidelity is, indeed, paramount, and far from alien in discussions within the poly community. People in polyamorous relationships are precisely invested in *relationships*, not just in sex, which they could presumably access via other means; as Christian Klesse (2007: 112) remarks, 'As a love- and intimacy-related set of discourses, polyamory can be presented as superior to other forms of non-monogamy that more strongly emphasise the pursuit of sexual pleasure'. Indeed, for this reason, polyamory which assumes stability of relationship, albeit between more than two partners, may be understood as too limiting by people who advocate for 'freer' or more open or anonymous sex that is more radically disconnected from ongoing relationship (111). The ascetic argument against polyamory says that 'too much' sex is profligate and undisciplined; of course, some early Gnostic-influenced Christians were not persuaded that any sex at all was licit, even in marriage, let alone sex with multiple partners (Jordan 2013: 160), and sexually ascetic streams have recurred ever since. However, as we have seen, polyamory does not necessarily entail more frequent or 'excessive' sex (however that is to be defined). Furthermore, Jordan holds that Christian exhortations of sexual asceticism may be a distraction from more beneficial ascetic practices such as resisting the lure of advertising, and notes, 'The urgent Christian discipline for sex might be to engage it generously and attentively rather than greedily and abstractly' (178) – in other words, asceticism in these terms may not equal a restriction of sexual partners to one, but may, rather, govern one's behaviour *with* and *towards* one's partners.

e   Disruptions of Procreative Intimacy
As well as the argument from asceticism, Jordan (2013) suggests that there are three main theological objections to polyamory: from procreation, from adultery and from intimacy. Thomist-influenced Natural Law–type accounts insist that all sex must be open to procreation. People in polyamorous groupings may well not be fluid-bonded with all their partners; nonetheless, they frequently are with their primary partners, and Jordan notes that polyamorous relationships which include heterosexual males and females might well be open to procreation, and, indeed, that a partnership of one male and several females might lead to *more* rather than *less* procreation (177). Indeed, as Witte (2015: 91) notes, Augustine could hold that polygamy was entirely natural and proper from a procreative angle. The objection that polyamory threatens procreation is therefore not insurmountable.

A sub-objection might be that children of polyamorous marriages could not be the child of more than two of the spouses, interrupting the association between sex, spousehood and parenthood. It is not currently possible in most jurisdictions for a child to have more than two legal parents, let alone biological ones. But same-sex couples who have children in creative ways – such as lesbian couples who conceive using sperm donated by male friends – have already had to navigate the difficulties that arise when moral and emotional responsibilities cannot be recognized legally. Discussions in recent years on so-called 'three-parent embryos' (those where mitochondrial DNA in the mother's ovum is replaced by DNA from another woman's ovum) betray concerns about the links between genetic heritage and the notion of parenthood. But the point is precisely that such difficulties already arise, and would not therefore be unique to polyamorous marriages. As I argue elsewhere in this book, the association between spousehood and parenthood already is non-absolute, and apotheosizing it is theologically unsustainable.

The argument from adultery, says Jordan (2013: 177), holds little water given that the Hebrew Bible recognizes that it is possible to have multiple simultaneous licit (i.e. non-adulterous) partnerships, as with men who have more than one wife, or a wife plus concubine(s). In other words, adultery is not coterminous with just *any* relationship involving sex outside a two-person marriage. Finally, the objection from intimacy holds that it is simply not possible to maintain intimate relationships with multiple partners – but Jordan points out that there is likely to be enormous variation on this (178), and that those who do not have the disposition for polyamory themselves should not assume it will be impossible for others.

2 Ethical Objections to Polyamory

a Children's Stability

The arguments noted thus far are all, in various respects, theological. There might, however, also be Christian *ethical* objections to polyamorous marriages. These are likely to centre, in particular, on concern for those who may be found vulnerable in the relationship, including children. If children are not sure who their parents are, or cannot trust that there will be stable adult figures in their lives, this is likely to be detrimental to their emotional and mental health (and, possibly, their economic well-being). Should children be exposed to intimate life with adults who are not their parents? Part of the everyday run of life for many families might include young children showering or bathing with their parents, seeing them naked and sharing beds with them. There might be an argument that for children to see adults who are not their parents in such situations is potentially damaging or dangerous. But, again, as important as these concerns are, there is nothing about them that is unique to polyamory. A traditional two-spouse marriage may also break up (even if statistically more partners mean more possible break-ups); a succession of monogamous relationships between the child's parent and various others could be just as disruptive to the child as a succession of different poly partners who come and go. Unmarried parents who have sexual partners already have to make decisions on an individual basis about whether, when and how it is appropriate for their partners and children to share in intimate everyday life. Some step-parents are very comfortable about their young stepchildren kissing and hugging them and seeing them naked or in bed; others are not. This is less a moral issue than a cultural and dispositional one.

b Power and Objectification

Additionally, however, polyamory might raise ethical questions about the accrual and concentration of power. Jordan (2013: 173) notes that polyamory has too often failed to trouble the dynamic in which older males have much of the control and privilege, so that 'polyamory just by itself does not make for revolutionary equality'. Laura Betzig (1995: 183) argues that monogamous societies are more likely to be democratic and polygynous ones are more likely to be despotic, and remarks on the many hundreds and thousands of women to whom powerful men have gained sexual access. Witte (2015: 20–2) notes that objections on the grounds that polygamy (in particular) violates the natural rights of women and children have been the most consistently invoked by proponents of monogamy in the Western religious and legal traditions for almost 2,000 years: polygamy sets up rivalry for scarce economic and emotional resources between competing wives and children; it alienates younger and less powerful men who may be unable to marry; it diminishes children's right to be supported to adulthood by both their parents (454–5). This certainly looks like an argument for being circumspect about the accrual of more and more sexual capital by fewer and fewer men – but is not necessarily thereby a compelling argument against polyamory in its more egalitarian forms.

The ethical objection about polyamory as promoting the objectification of others may seem more unique, but if, as Elizabeth Stuart (2003: 37) holds, such objectification is a function of patriarchy, we might similarly find it in monogamous partnerships. Detractors may assume that people in polyamorous relationships are at heightened risk of exposure to sexually transmitted infections – but proponents counter that polyamorous communities are deeply invested in consent and open communication, and that, where multi-partner relationships need not be secret, there is also less incentive to have clandestine unprotected sex with unknown partners, or to avoid disclosing the possibility of exposure to infections (Emens 2009: 278).

c Social Stability

Another ethical objection might be characterized as the social one. In this account, everyone knows what the 'rules' of marriage are when they enter into it. By contrast, poly relationships have to be navigated anew and perhaps no two arrangements will be exactly the same. This might be understood as threatening the stability of society, since it may be unclear whether or not someone is 'off limits' to an external party. Boundaries give freedom. When everyone is aware of the rules, it is easier to be free within them. People need not live in fear of being punished or resented for something if everyone is happy to own that that particular activity is already sanctioned. Marriage, we might say, provides boundaries of this kind.

In contrast, polyamorous relationships seem to require constant negotiation and checking-in, to ensure that everyone is comfortable with what is happening, and to reassess a relationship whose dynamics and boundaries might have changed since the last encounter. This kind of constant active work might end up being the opposite of life-enhancing. Polyamorous relationships in which everyone involved is not doing the necessary hard work of negotiation and consent-seeking might, quite simply, become contexts in which bad behaviour is easier to get away with. On the other hand, many monogamous relationships have undoubtedly fallen into lazy and stultifying patterns, and could benefit from some stirring up and restating of expectations every now and again. Easton and Hardy (2009: 30) suggest that a fuller awareness of relational negotiation (which requires articulacy, self-reflexivity and emotional resilience), and less complacency, makes for greater respect precisely since nothing can be taken for granted and everyone is held continuously accountable for their part.

Constancy is often invoked as a good in affective relationships, yet, as we have seen, constancy means faithfulness through change, not a denial that change occurs. Could there be any value in a sanctioned, recognized suspension of monogamy for those who are married, which would allow them to come back together afterwards with no remorse and no hard feelings to hunker down, renewed, for the next chunk of shared life, more sure than ever that they were making a conscious decision to continue being committed to this family? Or would this prove too costly, particularly for the others – especially children – on whom the relationship impacts? The purpose of the period called rumspringa (literally 'running around') among Amish youth is precisely to allow them to sample modern life beyond the community before they make a better-informed decision about whether to submit voluntarily and joyfully to its disciplines in their own right (Stevick 2014). While a large percentage of those who go through rumspringa do choose to return to the Amish community, a number prefer to stay in the wider world, and never go back, some losing all contact with family and old friends as a result. Marital fallow years would, similarly, undoubtedly lead to some casualties. There would be hard pragmatic questions about who took care of the children many couples have, and even harder ones about what would happen if the returning spouses brought more than they had bargained for (new ambitions, pregnancies, sexually transmitted infections) back to their life together. But the principle of jubilee might be invoked in marriage in other ways, by building in conscious time for the reassessment of dynamics and patterns of work, sex and parenting which have become stultifying.

Edgard Danielsen-Morales (2015) insists that polyamory must not be set up as superior to monogamous relationships. Rather, each should be understood as a legitimate way of loving others. Proponents of polyamory are not usually evangelistic about it in the sense that they believe everyone else should also be polyamorous. They are usually happy to hold monogamy as a legitimate and positive possibility, not one which should be derided as puritanical, square or narrow-minded. Margaret Robinson (2009: 3) notes that an ideal might be a theology which recognized *both* that monogamy need not be predicated on female subordination and male ownership, *and* that polyamory need not be 'modelled on a capitalist premise of accumulation and consumption'. We might hold that, for those who remain convinced that monogamy is the best or only legitimate way, it is better to exhort monogamy on the basis of good reasons (a conviction that this is the mode of relationship which genuinely allows the most flourishing for those involved) rather than of bad ones (jealousy, fear, guilt, shame).

However, that is not to say that polyamory does not still trouble the symbolism of two-spouse marriage as celebrated and explored across much Christian history and in some of the world's great literature. Marriage has long been understood as a relationship which is, at its best, mutual and reciprocal. There may be some polyamorous forms more troubling to this ideal than others. A poly triangle in which all three partners were in mutual and equal relationship to one another would be less problematic from this angle, perhaps, than an 'N' with four partners in which each individual was in a full partnership with only one or two of the others. Mutuality assumes shared, egalitarian power-structures; it assumes consent, and a continued commitment to the well-being of the other. But it also implies reciprocity: A can trust that as much as they do *for* B will also be done for them *by* B – not in a cynical process of horse-trading or score-keeping, nor, even, in a like-for-like manner, but in a process by which selfishness is increasingly eliminated as each prefers and privileges the needs of the other. Is this kind of reciprocity possible in a triadic or otherwise multi-partnered relationship?

The Content of Marriage

Questions about the content of marriage, and what changes push it beyond being legitimately defined as marriage at all, are hard, but they are important ones, because they require us to get to the heart of what we believe marriage is. And if we know what we believe marriage is, then perhaps it will become clearer whether marriage is really something endangered, whose boundaries need to be shored up, or whether its centre shifts but in a way which still bears witness to what it has been (and allows for what it may yet become).

Marriage is a location (not the sole or necessary location) in which humans learn vulnerability and patience with one another. They promise to give one another time: both mutual attention, and the space to experiment and grow and not know at the beginning how the story will end or even whether the main characters will still be recognizable by then. It involves making promises, and prompts humans to become their better selves, as well as providing a place in which they feel safe enough to act poorly on occasion knowing that there is space to do so and to receive forgiveness. Love in marriage is not always unconditional: where it is, it may tend towards being abused, and become a cover for mutually destructive dynamics. Marriage is a host of small and great and ancient words: love, comfort, honour, protection, faithfulness. It is a pledge to make these words reality against the odds.

Marriage is an agreement, once made, to which the parties go on agreeing by mutual consent. Where there is no longer consent, then the legal aspect of the arrangement may continue, but the spirit of it is over. This does not mean that every time the spouses anger or argue, the marriage is finished: rather, the consent they give each other includes consent to vent these things and to know that the existence of the anger or the disagreement has not in itself marred the promise. The promise is about *even if* and *even when*: *even if* you are poor and sick and less than your best self, our mutual agreement towards love, comfort, honour, protection and faithfulness still persists. *Even when* I fail you and you fail me, the first question we must ask is whether things can be mended. Seamus Heaney (1966: 50) writes in 'Scaffolding' of a couple between whom 'old bridges' seem to be crumbling, but who can nonetheless be confident that the 'wall' they have built together is stable and will not fall. There are, of course, important questions about what types or modes or extremes of behaviour push the agreement past breaking point, particularly given the propensity of some Christian pastors to counsel that abused spouses must remain in their marriages to witness love and forgiveness to their abusers even when their own and their children's lives are endangered – a tendency which has caused and exacerbated gross and inexcusable exploitation. The instinct to fix can become a toxic one.

Faithfulness is one of the important keys to understanding what marriage really is, theologically, and how, in and through it, we may understand more of what we are as creatures in relation to God as well as to each other. But faithfulness is not just about the avoidance of adultery or emotional deceit. Faithfulness testifies to some kind of persistence of identity: it says that I can trust that there is a continuity between the person you were yesterday and the person you will be tomorrow, even if you change your politics or gender expression or religion, because the person you will be tomorrow has as part of their identity a history of promise-making. It says I can trust that when you make a promise you intend to keep it and will endeavour to do so. What faithfulness does not mean, however, is impassibility or ever-unchangingness. Faithfulness means *keeping faith*: keeping faith with a changing spouse; keeping faith with the changing dynamics of lives and relationships. Faith implies trust, not knowing ahead of time that everything is locked in. It will likely include pain and distress, as when a spouse whose partner experiences dementia, memory loss or severe changes in personality as a result of illness or trauma feels that they no longer really know the person to whom they are covenanted. This frustration is summed up well in the Irish poet Micheal O'Siadhail's (2015) poems about the last two years of the life of his wife, Brid, who was suffering from Parkinson's disease. Marriage is, then, an ongoing process, and needs continual assent and reassent. It used to be the case that marriage meant an assumption of consent to sexual activity thereafter. There was no such offence as rape of one's spouse, since rape is sex without consent, and in marriage consent was already a done deal. Now we recognize in many jurisdictions that consent can be withdrawn even after it has been given; that spouses continue to have rights as individuals. Adrian Thatcher (2002: 235) would remind us that, far from being things with a concrete beginning, marriages have fuzzy beginnings, and a public ceremony will – if it takes place at all – almost always happen somewhere along the road down which the spouses have already journeyed some way together. Marriages may well have fuzzy endings too: the moment of legal divorce is clearly rarely, if ever, exactly coincident with the moment of the relationship's death. Marriages which have been legally dissolved may nonetheless exert an emotional pull for many years thereafter.

Beyond this, I am not sure it is helpful to set up a normative account of what marriage is or should be like. It happens in some contexts, and it is very appealing: 'Here is what healthy marriage is like; here is what constitutes it; all happy marriages are alike.' Well, such accounts might tell a partial truth. And I could tell you what my own happy marriage is like, and the ways in which I think it might chime with a broader set of goods that I would like to be widely available; and it might ring true with you, or it might not. In point of fact, there is no way to tell you all the things I think I am getting right, through a mixture of good judgement, good fortune and pig-headedness, without sounding supercilious. Marriage is diverse and multiplicitous. It looks like lots of different things. It is not the case that all happy marriages are alike. And things which someone might want to say are good can all too easily turn bad in another context.

This is one reason why the appeal to nature in many theologies of marriage is so slippery. After all, nature is also not something static or unchanging. It is often cyclical, but almost never constant. There are patterns of non-identical repetition from season to season, habitat to habitat, epoch to epoch, but the uncomfortable common truth underlying all of it is entropy and decay. To be natural is to be in a state of flux. Aquinas and his acolytes might respond that nature is in flux because nature is already damaged, and that constancy is a higher good to which we should aspire and to which state we may one day be elevated; but for me that will not do, because it seems to have too little to do with the ways in which bodies as we now know them live and work and interact. If no change took place, then there could be none of the delight attached to seeing a moon-faced baby become a melon-bellied toddler before transforming into a skinny, leggy child. There could be none of the shy, tentative excitement (admittedly, along with frequently tortuous bafflement, self-doubt and self-loathing) of adjusting to a body going through the mysterious revolutions of puberty. There could be no witnessing of time-lapse personality becoming ever-more visibly inscribed in the lines of a face; there could be no endorsement of the goodness of bodies that are old and crumpled and no longer fertile if they ever were. The fickleness and wastefulness of nature is something we rail against and fight with all our might; yet death and decay are there in the rotting leaf-mould, the drying and dropping of seeds, the tiny deathly sacrifices of intestinal bacteria in the interests of keeping their host animals alive a while longer and all the other invisible processes underpinning life as we have known it (the same life as this into which God became incarnate). I wonder whether this is what Dunnill (2013: 128) is getting at when he says,

> Paul is celebrating in baptism something more than a 'sign' of the new age. For him, resurrection is the actual transformation of the mortal body of Jesus, the

reversal of the deathward trend established by Adam: not merely the resuscitation of a dead body but a change in his mode of being human which begins with death and moves outward into life.

In nature, despite all its deaths, we continue to affirm that there is something new coming into being. If nature is decay, it is also a recalcitrant tenacity for life. And so it is in and through a series of deaths and disjunctions that we move forward.

What's so good about forward motion? That sounds like a question that the anti-futurist queer theorist Lee Edelman might ask, as we will see in subsequent chapters. Why not stop subsuming our nows to our tomorrows? Why not endorse the goodness of right where we are? Well, there is a lot to recommend endorsing the sacrality of each moment; but justice demands that we recognize that here and now is not all there is. And it is for this reason that generativity of institutions, communities and new modes of work continues to matter. Edelman is suspicious of the rhetorical uses of mythic children; there might, however, be ways in which 'children' are all those whom social hegemonies have tended to deem expendable and who are therefore exactly those for whom Christians are called to care (Dunnill 2013: 131) – not as a justification for jettisoning the ugly, the difficult, the queer and those who refuse to fit in, but as a recognition that these precisely *are* God's 'children'.

Conclusion

Attention to the generosity, expansiveness and critical consideration of the detail of ongoing consent and consultation which many polyamorous relationships exhibit may be a significant catalyst for monogamous marriage's own ongoing self-reflexivity and reform. Ethically reflective polyamory seems to offer distinctive endorsements of phenomena such as communality, consent, honesty and a lack of jealousy perhaps more effectively and incisively than many justifications for monogamous marriage have succeeded in doing (and this where monogamous marriage has been self-critical enough to allow for such consideration in the first place). Monogamy no more has a monopoly on ethical behaviour than Christianity does on marriage. And proponents of polyamory and open relationship are keen to remind their detractors that there is plenty about monogamy that has been violent, oppressive and harmful.

Of course, such critique also occurs within the Christian tradition – at least when the tradition is operating at its least defensive and most self-analytical. Rachel Muers (2015: 160–1) notes that Quakers have held that certain norms of marriage are disordered, such that seventeenth-century versions of Quaker marriage can be understood not as a rejection of marriage all told, or even a rejection of the idea that sexual relationships need ordering, but rather as 'a specific attempt at the *right ordering* of marriage – seeking to follow the guidance of God in setting marriage into order, within the wider context of God's transforming and reconciling work'. The implication in her following sections that a similar reading might be made of the Quaker discernment of the need to recognize and affirm same-sex marriages in our own time is clear. As she notes, theological (and other) endorsements of same-sex marriage are often met with gloomy charges which 'seem to be based on the false assumption that any break with a given order is a fall into disorder' (171).

Marriage has changed. Augustine argued that polygamy had been appropriate in the era of the Hebrew Bible's patriarchs, and that one of the problems with it in his own day was precisely that it was no longer customary – it was, in some sense, no longer fitting to the culture. The implication is that it is appropriate for theological goods to be reframed and reinterpreted alongside and in light of the social mores of the day. (See Augustine's *On the Good of Marriage* 17.)[3] Witte's (2015: 98) gloss of the Church Fathers' objections to polygamy, and explanations for why God could allow polygamy in the Hebrew Bible era but not later, suggests four kinds of justifications of God's apparent change of heart: on *historical* grounds, as in Tertullian who suggested that in times past polygamy had been temporarily necessary to increase the population more rapidly in a way that it no longer was; on (similar) *prudential* grounds, as in Jerome who suggested that necessity might mean that God's command sometimes overrode natural law; on *developmental* grounds, as in John Chrysostom who held that what had been virtuous in less mature societies was no longer virtuous in more advanced ones; and on *structural* grounds (as in Augustine's appeal to marriage having both procreative goods – which polygamy could bring about – and sacramental goods – which it could not). Only after the Council of Trent in 1563 did polygamy come to be consistently condemned as 'a heretical violation of the exclusive and enduring marital sacrament' (Witte 2015: 450); according to Witte, it was *after* this, not before, that appeals to monogamy on the grounds that polygamy disrupted natural law and justice really came to the fore. The change in the culture and the change in the theology were mutually influential.

Just as some supporters of same-sex marriage have held that it is only in making a sacramental, exclusive institution open to same-sex couples that goods such as permanence, stability and faithfulness may be nurtured in their relationships, so some supporters of the broader acceptance (including legal recognition) of polyamory argue that this is the best means to bring it into the open and ensure that it does not act as a channel for injustice or exist merely in a shadowy world beyond state or mainstream religious accountability (7). But, conversely, just as some commentators hold that the expansion of marriage to same-sex couples

---

3. 'For there is not now necessity of begetting children, as there then was, when, even when wives bare children, it was allowed, in order to a more numerous posterity, to marry other wives in addition, which now is certainly not lawful. For *the difference that separates times causes the due season to have so great force unto the justice and doing or not doing any thing*, that now a man does better, if he marry not even one wife, unless he be unable to contain. But then they married even several without any blame, even those who could much more easily contain, were it not that *piety at that time had another demand upon them*' (as translated in Schaff 1887a; my emphasis).

rings the death knell for same-sex relationships' capacity to be subversive and to stand against some of the violences and injustices that the institution of marriage has perpetuated, so some pro-polyamorists believe that polyamory's potential lies precisely in the fact that it so often flies under the radar of state control. It seems to me, however, that, while it is far from a perfect one, legal recognition of un/familiar relationship configurations brings with it a level of responsibility from both sides which is likely to be a useful means to uphold the well-being of those impacted by such relationships who may be deemed vulnerable – including children, and people who for various reasons are entirely economically dependent on other members of the household. Similarly, a mechanism for providing religious acknowledgement of relationships beyond 'traditional' marriage is likely to increase their visibility and encourage the development of and accountability for such relationships in the context of a spiritual community. This already takes place in small ways, as when (increasingly) marriage services include prayers of thanksgiving for the children that the couple already has together, or prayers of unity for the existing children that each spouse brings to the marriage from previous relationships. How daring might Christian churches be in publicly giving thanks for what is good in unconventional families of other kinds?

If Adrian Thatcher (1999: 142ff; 2007: 134–41, 152ff) and Don Browning (2007) are correct that what makes for good marriages is what best promotes the flourishing of children (and, we might add, other vulnerable persons), the key question at stake is how far polygamous family configurations may do so. Thatcher (2015: 603) insists that Christian *support* of those in a range of familial structures need not equal proactive *advocacy* of all such structures, and fears that diminishing support for some – what we might call more 'traditional' – models of family might itself erode these models' capacity to promote flourishing for those in them. But if so, we might counter, does this not imply that what is really important is *not* the familial institution itself, but the goods promoted in and through it – which are highly unlikely to be found in *this* iteration of the institution alone? For, as Thatcher himself continues, 'The churches will do well to recognize that the values it [*sic*] associates with marriage – fidelity, commitment, unconditionality, fruitfulness, hospitality, and so on – are often found in families where formal marriage vows have never been made. Such recognition … does not "lessen" the value of marriage but "expands" it' (603–4).

One problem, of course, is that some of those who advocate polyamorous arrangements do so in tandem with actively refusing *any* possible continuity between their own relationships and marriages (deemed expressive, exploitative, demeaning and likely to foment jealousy and – ironically – secrecy and infidelity). But this does not mean that such rejections cannot *also* be motivated by a desire to promote the good of 'innocents'. (Another problem is that Browning makes certain assumptions about kin altruism and its promotion by marriage that I reject: for Browning, parents are more invested in their biological offspring than in others, which is part of why biological offspring raised in wedlock do better. I will show in the next chapter, on adoption, why I believe such appeals to kin altruism do not tell the whole story.)

Furthermore, whether or not we are persuaded by Browning's and Thatcher's convictions that monogamous marriages are what make for the best outcomes for children and should be privileged over other forms for that reason if no other, the fact is that *neither theorist's argument rests on claims that marriages which are good for children are all that marriages have ever been.* In short, they appeal *precisely* to revised, what might in some respects be termed un/familiar, modes of understanding which place something other than the apotheosization of a particular form of marriage-for-marriage's-sake at the centre. Thatcher (1999), for example, shows that children are *not* in fact central to biblical accounts of marriage, and that latter-day appeals to the centrality of procreation sometimes function as means to legitimize sexual activity. He notes, 'A doctrine of marriage which begins with children can be consistent with biblical models for marriage, but it cannot honestly be said to be based on them' (133). So here we have a picture of marriage which is open about the fact that it has necessarily been refigured, reshaped and remodelled in the service of upholding what is claimed as a related but distinct good. If theological appeals to marriage are now sought, says Thatcher, they must be grounded in pragmatic evidence for how and why marriage 'works' to promote flourishing in the present day, rather than in outmoded assumptions about gender hierarchy and body–soul dualism (142).

In short, God's responsiveness to the creation, and that of the creation to God, conceivably engenders dynamism. There is warrant for recognition of this dynamism from early on in the Christian tradition. In this chapter I have tried to show that neither the continuities nor the discontinuities between historical and emerging forms of marriage and family are absolute, and that claims to any absolute or unchanging quality of these are likely to be disingenuous. This means that there is space for newness, for things to be other than they have been before, and other than they were destined to be in 'givenness' from the beginning of time. This is the underpinning for the next chapter, in which I explore, via Grace Jantzen and Hannah Arendt, the potential for the uses of the concept of natality in formulating and interpreting our un/familiar theologies and asking what it means to relate to un/familiar institutions.

Chapter 4

NATALITY: REPRODUCTION AND THE POSSIBILITY OF NEW BEGINNINGS

Introduction: History/herstory

In May 2015, after months of eager anticipation by royalist members of the public in Britain and beyond, it was announced by Kensington Palace that the Duke and Duchess of Cambridge had had their second child, a baby girl. This baby, named two days later as Charlotte Elizabeth Diana, Princess Charlotte of Cambridge, became fourth in line to the British throne after her grandfather Charles, the Prince of Wales; her father William, the Duke of Cambridge; and her older brother, Prince George of Cambridge, himself not quite two years old at the time. Bookmakers had been taking bets on the new baby's sex and names ever since the pregnancy was first announced; keen royal-watchers had camped outside the royal residences in London for several weeks before the child was born, hoping to be among the first to hear the news. Within days of her birth, Princess Charlotte had become the recipient of gifts from around the world: some from governments and national authorities, some from individuals and community groups within and beyond the Commonwealth countries and others from local well-wishers. In some respects, Charlotte had been known and expected from long before she was born, with a version of her destiny already mapped out for her (as well as, of course, a traceable and attestable family tree stretching back centuries).

In the same week, in Scotland, a funeral took place for a six-week-old baby boy who had been found dead, abandoned on a path in Edinburgh, two years beforehand. He had no name; the police and local authorities had been unable to trace his mother or other family. Their only clue was the white Primark blanket in which the little boy had been wrapped. But this anonymous child's short life and death did not pass unmarked: in response to an advertisement in a local newspaper, over two hundred people attended the funeral. The *Guardian* reported:

> Wellwishers had gathered from across Edinburgh and eastern Scotland. There were bikers from the Royal British Legion Scotland, a representative of Leith's Sikh community, several of the city's politicians from rival parties putting the election campaign aside, and mothers who themselves had lost children. ... A captain in the 154th (Scottish) transport regiment based in Glasgow, Macnab

said many others in the 700-strong branch were saying prayers, in Orkney, Stornoway in the Western Isles, Stranraer on the Irish Sea and Berwick-upon-Tweed. … The minister from nearby Tranent parish church, Erica Wishart, told mourners: 'Everyone gathered here today is grieving. We represent everyone in this community and beyond who feels deep sadness that this tiny baby is never going to have his chance to grow up and live his life. [We] are here to mourn a life that could have been.' (Carrell 2015)

This child's story and history were unknown, yet those who came to mourn him insisted that his brief life mattered. They claimed him as a member of their community and wove him a biography where no known biography had existed before.

Story and the transmission of culture are significant to each of our coming into being as persons. Princess Charlotte was born to a life where she already had a story resonant with expectation and history. The unnamed Scottish baby's history and genealogy were unknown. The dizzying newness and discontinuity from the old self and old life which comes with an entry into the world for the child, and into parenthood for those who care for the child, is summed up well by A. S. Byatt (1995) in her novel *Still Life* – which also contains the most visceral and unrelentingly truthful literary account of childbirth I know. Of the new mother Stephanie, sister of protagonist Frederica, Byatt writes:

> There was her body, quiet, used, resting: there was her mind, free, clear, shining: there was the boy and his eyes, seeing what? And ecstasy. Things would hurt when this light dimmed. The boy would change. But now in the sun she recognised him, and recognised that she did not know, and had never seen him, and loved him, in the bright new air with a simplicity she had never expected to know. 'You,' she said to him, skin for the first time on skin in the outside air, which was warm and shining, 'you'. (114)

Stephanie's child is at once entirely familiar and entirely mysterious – and so, it becomes clear, is the new mode of life in which Stephanie finds herself. In this chapter, then, I reflect on the tropes of life and newness and the significance of potential and possibility for formulating un/familiar accounts of familiar institutions, drawing, first, on the work of Grace M. Jantzen.

Born of a Woman: Natality in the Work of Grace Jantzen

At the time of her early death, Jantzen had planned an extensive six-volume opus on the theme of death and the displacement of beauty. The first volume, the only one which appeared in her lifetime, focused on necrophilia and violence as the *habitus* of the West, which Jantzen traced back to dissociation from and disavowal of materiality and the feminine in Greco-Roman texts. Two further volumes appeared posthumously, compiled from Jantzen's draft chapters and notes by Jeremy Carrette and Morny Joy. These addressed the outworkings of death and necrophilia in the Christian tradition, and the potential of the Quaker tradition for recovering accounts of natality and beauty. The final three volumes were never completed.

Jantzen (2009) returns again and again (both in this *Death and the Displacement of Beauty* series, and in her earlier works such as *Becoming Divine*) to the concept that, just as all humans die and are therefore marked by death, so all humans have in common that they were born and are therefore 'natals' with the capacity to create. She says, 'Natality is linked to the fact that we are born; but it is not reducible to birth any more than the category of mortality is reducible to death. Natality, rather, is the potential for newness and for hope, the creative possibilities of beginning again that are introduced into the world by the fact that we are all natals' (8).

The Christian philosophical and theological tradition, she argues, has tended to focus on death, sin and the human need to be saved from ourselves, rather than on the wellspring of human creativity and generativity which echoes that found in God. However, she suggests, 'It is not violence and the victimage mechanism but creativity, desire springing from fullness rather than premised upon a lack, which is the root of hominization and the foundation of culture; and that its paradigm is the newness of natality. ... Without creativity ... newness cannot emerge' (34).

Christian and other disparagement of natality has come about in part because this discourse is always already gendered: she finds significance in the fact that we are natals because we have been birthed, and birthed by women. Western males have wanted to escape mortality: this has often meant escaping (associations with) femaleness, the womb-tomb. Suppressing this anxiety leads to the acting-out of violence and death-making activity. 'Necrophilia' – a preoccupation with death and dyingness – is, therefore, simultaneously a phobia and a desire (Jantzen 2010: 186). Mara Willard (2013: 230) suggests that Jantzen's imagery of birth is too unproblematically life-affirming, 'obscuring more complicated analysis of maternality' – yet the emphasis on flourishing and affirming interdependence is unsurprising given that Jantzen is actively seeking to reclaim the concept of birth from associations of alienation and violence.

Indeed, Jantzen critiques psychoanalytic theory for setting up a relationship of violence between pregnant women and the fruits of their wombs. Psychoanalysis figures birth as expulsion from the womb, which sets up patterns of alienation. Jantzen (2009) suggests that this is not quite right: women late in pregnancy *do* want their babies out (often quite emphatically, when they are huge and uncomfortable and full of mysterious octopus limbs, with a foetal skull continuously pressing on a bladder whose capacity is already seriously restricted; or when prolonging the pregnancy would mean heightened risks to the woman's or baby's health), but this is usually because they want them to be *born* and interact with them, not so they may be rid of them altogether. The child itself, from the time it is born, responds to the world not (or not only) as a dangerous and inhospitable place from which it wishes to retreat back into the womb, but as a place full of stimuli, so that the child is 'grasping for new experiences, desiring life and responding to all its wonder. Desire, surely, is here premised on possibility and the active grasp of the newness and creative impulse inherent in natality' (198).

Jantzen holds that although only God can create ex nihilo, human creativity is more than simply mimesis. There is a possibility for novelty and innovation: we are not condemned just to do and do and do again what we or others have done before. Humans can create veritable newness – even if, inevitably, they do so out of existing materials (200). I want to build on this idea further here. Even when one has a child biologically one is not simply reproducing oneself. One is 'replacing' oneself as a unit of population, but one is not replicating oneself as an individual. One can create only out of the materials one has – genes, gametes and nutrition, sometimes with help from reproductive technologies – but the person created will always be more than the sum of their biology. Even from before birth, humans begin to respond to their environments. For this reason, what one transmits in one's culture and values is as significant as what one transmits biologically. Moreover, any transmission of culture always, in some sense, involves a making of new connections: the recipient does not receive passively, but actively weighs and tests the new knowledge against their existing body of knowledge to work out if and how it 'fits'. The fact that parents and other carers are often baffled by the questions that children pose them reminds us that children are quite capable of making connections they have not explicitly been 'taught' to make.

Starting with birth and life rather than the inescapability of death could, holds Jantzen (2010: 181), alter the entire imaginary and consciousness of the Western self:

> A moral imaginary of natality would necessarily be very different from a moral imaginary of death. Natals require care and protection to flourish. They rely on interdependence; and unless they are welcomed into the world, they will not survive. A moral imaginary that proceeds in terms of atomistic individuality simply could not get off the ground if we were thinking in terms of natality. Moreover, it is precisely the fact of natality that makes for possibility: natality is the condition of new life entering the world. It is therefore the condition of hope, and of future.

Futurity is not an unproblematic good for queer-inflected scholars: the work of Lee Edelman and those who have followed him makes that clear. Yet it is also clear that, for Jantzen, the thrust of the Western philosophical tradition has been lacking in hope: it has been hopeless, and it is because of this hopelessness that it has understood and reinscribed death as the most significant thing all living creatures will share. But as we see with the insistence by the unnamed Scottish baby's community that his death not be the only known fact of his life and existence, there is also a shared human imperative to make and understand one another's lived and living stories.

Ruptures and Disjunctions: Natality and Witness

Jantzen, of course, borrows from and expands on Hannah Arendt's notion of natality. Arendt (1958: 8) writes,

> The miracle that saves the world, the realm of human affairs, from its normal, 'natural' ruin is ultimately the fact of natality, in which the faculty of action is ontologically rooted. It is, in other words, the birth of new men and the new beginning, the action they are capable of by virtue of being born. Only the full experience of this capacity can bestow upon human affairs faith and hope, those two essential characteristics of human existence. ... It is this faith in and hope for the world that perhaps found its most glorious and most succinct expression in the few words with which the Gospels announced their 'glad tidings': 'A child has been born unto us.'

For Arendt, the shared fact of having been *born* is, then, the thing in which human freedom is grounded. Arendt's concept of natality is about humans' capacity to act freely. Arendt takes from Augustine's (1984, book XII, chapter 21) *City of God* her key for the natalist project: that the first human was created to provide a beginning to the souls destined for union with God. In consequence, being a new beginning, and the capacity to make new beginnings, is a characteristically (and universally) human quality. Arendt (1958) finds in Augustine an account which insists on human beings' dual origins, both from their human genitors and from the divine. This reminds humans – or should remind humans – of their inescapable interconnectedness. Humans' 'bornness' is also a reminder of our multiplicity: we are individual yet interconnected persons, not an amorphous and faceless singularity (7). This should not, however, lead to individualism: we exist in the world with others. Mara Willard (2013: 231–2) notes that, in commentators such as Hanna Pitkin, Wendy Brown, Mary O'Brien and Adrienne Rich, Arendt's account is represented as unhelpfully hiving off the 'private' business of birthing and maternality from the political activity of the public sphere, rendering leaky, needy embodiment a messy and embarrassing distraction from political action; but I read Arendt more as Jantzen does, as insisting on the centrality of universal bornness as prerequisite for recognizing the contingency of all who shape and participate in the public imaginary.

Namsoon Kang takes a different line on natality, focusing on Jesus's birth (in the Christian tradition, to a virgin) as disruptive of the normal run of things in a slightly different way from that of Yvonne Sherwood and John Dunnill:

> His birth has no previous memory, history, tie, cause, or origin, but itself alone constitutes the very credential for who he is. ... In order to understand Jesus' Virgin birth in Matthew, one must deconstruct the very genealogy of Matthew. In the process of deconstruction, of radical discontinuity with the very tradition, one can reencounter, reinterpret, reconceptualise, recontextualize, and reconstruct the meaning of the tradition as if one is inventing a new tradition

out of nothingness – a *nonhistory of absolute beginnings*. (Kang 2013: 107; original emphasis)

Rather than focusing on the subversion *within* the genealogy, Kang majors on the departure from it. Here, born-ness is interruptive, which makes sense, given that birth itself is frequently violent and always bloody. Kang's account is deeply political, grounded in a postcolonial concern to disrupt hegemony and empire. Kang is right that the tradition of the virgin birth relativizes genealogy and makes exclusive tribalism unjustifiable; nonetheless, precisely *because* the Christian tradition holds that Christ was born not ex nihilo, but *ex Maria virginae*, Mary's own concrete humanity is a tie to human materiality more broadly. Kang picks up on Arendt's belief that birth itself is a continual pointer to hope and new generativity even when things seem hopeless (Kang 2013: 110). This means holding custom, history and the status quo lightly, or the memory of them will strangle our capacity for newness (112). Others, of course, have noted that Jesus's birth of a virgin is disruptive of the old order in more ways than just the political one: the doctrine of conception and birth with no human male element is also a departure from the established norms of biological reproduction. For Tina Beattie (2002: 125), the disruption of biology here is also a significant disruption of phallocentric ideology and power: 'Mary's virginal conception might signify an event outside the domain of the phallus, in a way that is not circumscribed within the values and laws of patriarchy'. (For further discussions of theological and hermeneutical traditions surrounding the virgin birth, see Lüdemann (1998); Borg and Crossan (2007); Crisp (2008); Lincoln (2013).)

Rosalyn Diprose and Ewa Płonowska Ziarek (2013) emphasize the more-than-individualistic nature of natality. They note that all births involve witnesses who, to some extent, experience the process of birth more fully than the one who is actually born. The child born certainly cannot witness its own birth: at a bare minimum, the labouring woman is present to witness. In contexts where the labouring woman is unconscious, medics or others are likely present. Consequently, 'To be a beginner is to be witnessed and welcomed as such and this is to be in relation to otherness' (111). This chimes with Margarete Durst's (2003: 778) account:

> Birth ... is the tangible sign of how the relationship of alterity marks the entire length of our life, because the fact of being born causes alterity to emerge both in the form of conditioning and in the form of difference, that is, from the dependence to which our coming into the world is subject, and from the caesura that each new human being introduces into the continuity of others' history.

For Diprose and Ziarek, this otherness, this alterity comes primarily from the mother (in their account, the principal witness to birth), and secondarily from the broader community. As such, 'The beginning announced by natality is already the event of human plurality insofar as its meaning and happening is *disclosed to others* before it happens to me' (111). In Diprose and Ziarek as in Jantzen and in Arendt herself, 'this orientation presents the mother as a necessary (if only ever implicit and abstract) agent in the realization of human appearance' (Willard 2013: 235).

Women are not always conscious witnesses to their own children's births: in the early and mid-twentieth centuries, many women gave birth in a state of 'twilight sleep', induced by opiate drugs, such that they did not feel or recall any pain from the delivery. Even epidurals and lesser painkilling drugs can leave women feeling detached from their own bodies and as though they were not quite 'there'. Labour pain itself can be so overpowering that there is no time to reflect on the rest of the experience. Many women have given birth, vaginally or by Caesarean section, while in natural or artificially induced states of coma. Still, women's bodies themselves testify in their own ways even if the women have no conscious memories. Foetal cells may remain with women for decades after they have given birth (Bianchi et al. 1996; Pritchard and Bianchi 2012). Changed breast shape, feet that may never shrink back to their pre-pregnancy size, crêpey bellies, distressed pelvic floors, stretch marks and so on all send a message that someone else – or an entity which has since *become* someone else – was once there.

But, crucially, in Jantzen's account as in Arendt's, women, and especially women as mothers, are not the sole witnesses. The pause, the caesura, happens to other others too. Fathers and other birth partners are, notably, often able to help new mothers piece together what happened during their labours, having quite possibly been more aware of conversations between midwives and obstetricians than the women (influenced by medication and fatigue) were themselves. As Margaret Kamitsuka notes, Jantzen does not intend to romanticize motherhood itself. Rather, Jantzen 'argues for natality as a semiotic reality of divine-human integration, which presents natality's unambiguous goodness at the cost of obscuring the material and discursive conditions that constitute us as subjects' (Kamitsuka 2007: 86–7). So, in Kamitsuka's account, Jantzen has not quite succeeded in remembering materiality: how and to whom we are born, suspects Kamitsuka, is less important to Jantzen than the fact we simply *are* born and are therefore, ontologically, natals. This is why Willard's critique, which suggests that Arendt and Jantzen in their different ways both instrumentalize women-as-mothers and repeat the idea that women are uniquely 'reproducers' of (implicitly male) productive citizens, only 'sticks' if birth is read as solely literal. It is true that if Arendt and Jantzen are interpreted as reducing women to a maternality constructed in the service of the *polis* then this fatally compromises women's agency (Willard 2013: 236) – but I read in them a less narrow account of birth. For Willard, Arendt's account displaces the concreteness of women, rendering them merely mother-ciphers, tools used in the service of political life (240, 243) – yet if birthing is always *both* concrete and symbolic, *both* animal and conceptual, I suggest that what we have here is, rather, a conception of natality which recognizes the simultaneous irreducibility and inadequacy of human life without sociality. It is an irreducible fact that humans are human already at the moment of their birth, without having made any contribution whatsoever to public life or discourse; but it is also true that humans, almost universally, make their marks on one another immediately, socializing one another into webs of intercourse which are always already politically inflected.

The fact of the existence of mothers is irreducible, then, but, contra Willard, I hold that neither Arendt nor Jantzen is hung up on mothers' biology. While there are rare occasions, as with the Scottish baby, when a child is 'adopted' by a whole community, and more common occasions, as with Princess Charlotte and other royal or 'celebrity' babies, when the child is treated as semi-public property, frequently it is specificity of connection we value more than 'publicness'.

The woman who has given birth will always be the one whose body remembers and bears testimony to the birth. This will be the case even if the woman does not *consciously* remember; even if she in fact *suppresses* the memory; even if she gives up the child immediately after birth; even if she was comatose at the time. But the others who encounter the child – fathers, siblings, grandparents, adoptive parents, midwives, nurses, doctors, friends – continue to be able to testify to the fact that *this child was born*. This might seem like a truism, and such a workaday fact as to be insignificant: *of course* we were all born. It goes without saying. Yet the point Jantzen wants to make is that it does *not* go without saying: that, in fact, we always and constantly forget this obvious and unforgettable fact about all human beings. Each birth is miraculous, and each person is born a miracle, with the miraculous power to remake and recreate (both, eventually, through their own actions, in most cases; and via the changes they provoke in others, in all cases). But we focus too frequently on condemnation to death.

It has sometimes been suggested that, prior to the advent of modern medicine when infant mortality was much higher, parents were less attached to their babies as individuals (Ariès 1973: 37). Some have argued that the practice of giving several children in the same family the same given name testifies to a sense of interchangeability among them: that if a child died early on, it did not really matter, since another would probably come along a year or so later. Lawrence Stone (1977: 57), for example, claims,

> Nothing better illustrates the resigned acceptance of the expendability of children than the medieval practice of giving the same name to two living siblings in the expectation that only one would survive. The sixteenth-, seventeenth- and eighteenth-century practice of giving a new-born child the same name as one who had recently died indicates a lack of sense that the child was a unique being, with its own name.

But this, I think, is to misinterpret what those parents who lost child after child and yet still kept using the same names were doing. Actually, this practice is a highly anticipative, propitious act: it testifies to a hope against hope that, despite what has happened in the past, *this* John or *this* Elizabeth or *this* Mary will be the one to survive to adulthood and to pass on the name. When Stone characterizes an eighteenth-century woman, Mrs Thrale, who could not bear to look at her ill premature baby, as having taken an 'instant dislike' to the child, he misses the element of pre-grieving attached to care for an infant whose survival is unlikely. Mrs Thrale was not, I think, being cold or heartless towards her gravely sick daughter Susanna Arabella, but rather attempting to prophylactically insulate herself from her anticipated pain. Such a defensive, survivalist strategy may also underlie Mrs Thrale's words on her next daughter, Penelope, who died at ten days old: 'One cannot grieve after her much, and I have just now other things to think of' (in Stone 1977: 57). Stone gives too little credit to the human propensity for trying to talk oneself into believing something is true. Mrs Thrale is a woman doing anything necessary to convince herself that her world has not ended.

While children do not remember their actual births, and may never remember meeting those who birthed them, what all human beings must never forget is the fact that they were born – for in Arendt, says Miguel Vatter, 'in remembering the origin, man is oriented towards "loving" God's love (for man), as manifest in Creation, and not simply oriented towards "love of God" (where God is a possible object of desire)' (Vatter 2006: 140). That we all had an origin means that we should all be aware of our contingency, our non-aloneness. But it should also guard us against considering any other person dispensable or interchangeable. For Arendt, 'Natality … stands in the way … of finalizing the human species. … Natality only brings forth singulars, radically diverse individuals, but no species "man"' (153). We are simultaneously new beginnings and new beginners: agents of action 'defined by beginnings with the potential to be miraculous because of their unexpectedness and utter dissimilarity from what has come before' (Biss 2012: 764). It matters that I am I and you are you. Someone else would not have done in my or your place instead. It is when we fail to acknowledge another's uniqueness and irreplaceability that injustices are done.

Jantzen takes from Arendt the necessity of the biological fact of born-ness (though neither woman reifies or apotheosizes biological birth). In Vatter's (2006: 138) reading, this is key for Arendt because it reconnects politics to freedom. Each person is born in and as *possibility*, so no one should live with their possibility unreasonably curtailed. Any form of captivity which limits freedom must exist for a spectacularly good reason.

Born to a New World: The Generativity of Death

But while Jantzen's use of natality as a trope clearly has much to recommend it, there are also respects in which it requires further interrogation. For example, she does too little to deal with the ways in which natals, even if they are to be interpreted out of the shadow of original sin, still do live in a world clouded and occluded by sin's effects. The mainstream tradition has perhaps been less guilty of an exclusive focus on guilt and judgement than Jantzen supposes: the essays in Bunge (2001) acknowledge astutely that even those theologians most often associated with notions of depravity and sin from birth were also often themselves loving fathers of young children, or pastors of congregations or communities including infants and children, or also emphasized the capacity for blessing of and through such young people: they were aware that children were blessed as much as they were damned, and that their construction as morally significant and responsible meant acknowledging their potential as spiritual beings, not just their need to be lifted from the mire. (See, in particular, Traina (2001) on Aquinas; Guroian (2001) on John Chrysostom; Strohl (2001) on Luther; and Brekus (2001) on Jonathan Edwards for acknowledgement of the complexities of 'classic' theological accounts of original and structural sin and their implications for Christian constructions of childhood.) Jantzen has to deal with the reality of sin even if her suspicion is that it has frequently been over-accentuated.

Frances Ward's criticism of Jantzen is twofold: first, that Jantzen portrays natality as the one and only legitimate kind of ethical response there is; and second, that Jantzen's reading of the Christian tradition is too weighted to the deathly. On Ward's (2009: 62) reading, Jantzen's accusation that Christianity sanitizes and domesticates enormous and powerful forces such as maternity in order to control them does a disservice to the breadth and complexity within the tradition – which also includes outworkings that are, says Ward, 'stirring and passionate and full of desire, and more complex in terms of gender than I think Jantzen would recognize'. Jantzen, suspects Ward, in her attempt to reject the dualism she sees in the Christian tradition, actually ends up throwing out the possibility of transcendence altogether (67) – which might be a problem when it comes to acknowledging the specificities of real and troubling bodies. As theologians of disability, chronic pain and terminal illness have reminded us, sometimes hope for transcendence of the body is just about the only hope there is (Scully 1998).

Another criticism of Jantzen might be to say that she is simply *too negative* about death. It is true that death is presented, often, in literature and theology and art, as indignity and interruption, a dying of the light against which to rage. Death frequently does impinge this way: while I was writing this book, my dear friend died aged thirty-five. A speaker at his funeral noted that it felt as though a tear had been ripped in the fabric of our lives. He was broken in a car crash and burned by fire: his death made me hope more urgently than I usually do for a resurrection body restored and remade in continuity with its earthly self. But irruption and violent inbreaking are not all that death is. Death is also repose, relief, a fitting rest at the end of a life lived well. When death is early, violent or unjust we most fight and deplore it, but hardly anyone considers a beloved grandparent's peaceful death in sleep at ninety an injustice. Adults sometimes explain death to children as something that happens when a body gets worn out or stops working properly; many young children have difficulty understanding that a dead pet or relative is not coming back again. In the Western philosophical tradition, the permanence of death is a hard lesson we all have to learn.

Even so, death has its own generativity. I have a group of non-theist friends who were worried about how to explain death to their young children. They felt disingenuous telling them a pretty story about heaven when none of them believed it themselves, but it felt too bleak simply to say that death was the end of existence. Some found a scientific narrative of the reuse of matter a powerful tale: 'Maybe you were once part of a star', they told their children, 'and we know you are a person now for a time, but when you die the energy in your body will go elsewhere: to nourish trees or animals, to end up in water and rocks and the air that other creatures breathe'.[1] Others focused on memory, and the concept that we live on in the minds of those who knew and loved us and the legacy of the things we have done and created. That by itself would have been unsatisfactory for my friend, whose exhorted narrative and ground of hope was an explicitly Christian one, and who would have wanted at least to emphasize a persistence of identity as held and known in God; but it is still the case that, in the weeks following his death, lapsed friendships were revived, damaged relationships restored and priorities reassessed by those who loved him and had realized anew that life was precious and short and that human beings were vulnerable in their animality.

Death is generative because the atoms in our bodies will be converted into other things. But death can also free up room at the top. If we did not die, soon there would be no space for new people to be born onto our crowded globe. Death can end an abusive relationship, or curtail a tyrant's reign. And if some of the most influential thinkers and writers of the Christian tradition seem to have had a preoccupation with death, we would do well to remember that death was a much more present threat and daily reality for most of them and for their spouses, children and associates than it is for most of us today (Ward 2009: 65). It is not particularly original to observe that Christianity has a long tradition of figuring death as a gateway to new life. Bodies and worlds are to be rebirthed.

A critique of Jantzen could also be made from another angle: namely, that she renders birth the bright line which characterizes all natals. But as the work of Carol Sanger (2012) and others makes clear, this line is not as sharp as it might be. Stillborn babies and late-term miscarried foetuses[2] are born, but not until after they have already died. There was never a time at which they existed as legally independent beings; there was never a time at which they lived without being sustained by their mothers' bodies. Accounts of personhood around pregnancy, miscarriage and birth are notoriously slippery: debate about how, where and when a foetus's personhood begins is the well-worn stuff of countless ethics classes. Does this mean that they are born, but are not full natals? Perhaps; however, we might

---

1. Similar themes are evident in the American performer Aaron Freeman's 2005 commentary for National Public Radio (NPR)'s *All Things Considered*, entitled 'Planning Ahead Can Make a Difference in the End'. Freeman converted from Roman Catholicism to Judaism as an adult. He suggests that 'the person you want to speak at your funeral' is not a priest or a rabbi but a physicist, who can comfort your grieving loved ones with the assurance that 'according to the law of the conservation of energy, not a bit of you is gone; you're just less orderly'.

2. In the United Kingdom, a stillbirth is defined as having occurred when a foetus of twenty-four weeks' gestation or more dies before or during birth. Deaths of foetuses before twenty-four weeks are classed as miscarriages. Given how relatively infrequent miscarriage as late as twenty-four weeks is, and given that foetuses born under twenty-two weeks are known to have survived beyond infancy, there may be an argument for revising the point at pregnancy after which a miscarriage officially becomes a stillbirth and it is possible to acquire birth and death certificates to mark these proto-lives.

note, these born–unborn creatures still, and absolutely, mark a caesura in their families' and communities' lives. That is the point: their families and communities were *already* their families and communities even before these children were born to them. Death does not divide them ontologically from the rest of us as creatures, for we other creatures, too, will die. This is where death may be understood as democratizing: a commonality, not an indignity.

Finally, Tina Beattie criticizes Jantzen for being insufficiently historically grounded, or nuanced, in her characterization of the anti-natality of the Western theological and philosophical tradition. For one thing, Beattie holds that Roman Catholic theologies after Heidegger are already much closer to Luce Irigaray's (1993) 'sensible transcendental' (wherein the divine and embodied are held and understood as mutually interdependent) than Jantzen would give credence to: they do not, she holds, disparage the incarnational (even if, per Beattie, many Protestant theologies do have this tendency). For another, Beattie (2006: 225–6) suggests that Jantzen does too little to make her project truly *theological*, which, suggests Beattie, means that it will be harder for Jantzen's ideas to be implemented in communities of *religious* practice.

All this said, Jantzen incisively identifies the propensity in some mainstream theologies to a preoccupation with deathliness to the exclusion of life. And her account is a reminder that those of us working in and with the Christian tradition continue to birth it as it births us, just as we are both children and parents of the social and cultural institutions into which we are born and initiated and which we continue to shape, disseminate and pass down.

Reproducing Natality: Ever-old and Ever-new?

Theological traditions have also been invested in (re)productivity and generativity for other reasons. Mike Higton and Rachel Muers (2012: 162) note that this is sometimes because of implicit or explicit theologizations of biological and relational realities, such that male–female and parent–child pairs have been made synecdoche for relational human imaging of God: 'The production/reproduction of human beings, linked in [Gen. 1 and 3] to the image of God, already acquires a significance beyond the biological; the texts and the tradition set up a nexus within which images and concepts of human production and reproduction acquire great symbolic force'.

As they note, the Genesis creation accounts have been read with two slightly different emphases: in the first, male and female together image God regardless of their reproductive potential or actuality. The second 'locates the image of God … in the capacity and summons to *be fruitful and multiply*, to produce and reproduce the human image that is also the image of God' – per Gen. 5.3 (162; original emphasis). Wielded by masculinist interpreters, however, these different textual emphases have too often been used to claim merely that women's role is to be *both* wife *and* mother, rather than moving beyond these and only these characterizations. We might see this kind of reading even in theologians who would be amazed to be described in masculinist terms, like Aidan Nichols (2007: 145), who says, 'It has been suggested that one major reason why there are relatively few women artists (virtually no women dramatists, for instance) is that for women the vocation to continue creation is primarily expressed in motherhood in such a way that artistic creativity pales into relative insignificance by comparison.[3]

Nichols does not identify his specific interlocutors here, but we might suggest that, whoever they are, they have failed to engage with literature on women who specifically choose *not* to have children and to create in other ways, or on women who feel pulled apart by the conflicting calls of artistry and parenthood (see Power 2012: 1–7; Liss 2009; Rosenberg 1995); have ignored the structural reasons why there may appear to be relatively few recognized woman artists (Do women artists get less coverage? Is their art not considered as 'good' or legitimate as that of male artists? Do social constructions of what it means to be a 'good mother', and a lack of financial remuneration accorded to the work of parenting, make professional artistry more likely to be a luxury of childless people?); and have risked universalizing from some women's experience and projecting this onto women in general. Feminist interpretation, suggest Higton and Muers (2012: 163–4), needs to find another way:

> 'Products' themselves – not only persons, but also group identities and the narratives that shape them, religious and political systems and the artefacts that define them – carry with them traces of their differentiated and conflicted origins. In theological terms, this means seeing the image of God, even within the self – and certainly within the community that claims to image God – as appearing in and through the encounter with given and non-assimilable differences over time. Being made 'male and female' in the image of God is, on this reading, being made for a project of responsible encounter with, living with, and production of, different human being. This project is still one of production and reproduction, because the human future emerges from it; but the human future thus produced and reproduced is not simply the perpetuation of what is already given.

As they note, this remains open to a bodily specificity without reinscribing essentialism: there really are real and distinct male bodies and female bodies, but this does not mean that there are *only* male bodies and female bodies, nor that male and female together can stand as an unproblematic cipher for everything-there-is (in either social or theological terms) – as I have commented elsewhere (Cornwall 2010). Additionally, this means that the phenomenon of reproductivity is not limited to biological procreation. The trope of reproductivity and generativity within the tradition is about much more than biological reproductivity itself. Rather, there is potential here for a diversification of and multiplicity of accounts of embodiment, gender and the transmission of thought and culture.

Higton and Muers (2012: 163–4) emphasize the importance of non-assimilable differences over time. This is unapologetically futurist: they are with Jürgen

---

3. I am grateful to Alana Vincent for drawing this passage to my attention.

Moltmann, José Esteban Muñoz and Lauren Berlant (whom I discuss in more depth below), not with Lee Edelman. In what ways does this kind of account chime with other aspects of Christian constructive theology? For one thing, it is profoundly Eucharistic – a version of Eucharist which retains the concept of otherness, or re-making and re-newing, of repetitions with critical difference (as in patterns of thought across Deleuze, Kierkegaard, Catherine Pickstock, Elizabeth Stuart and beyond). For another, it makes the future something shapeable, open to us as we are open to it, not a fait accompli. It is here that David Matzko McCarthy's (2007) account of human generativity is particularly helpful, because it holds together two aspects: biological bodily generativity, and the relational and cultural generativity of the social body. He argues that sex as figured in Western culture today is about expressing the self via desire. Existing as it does within a capitalist logic, this self and its desires cannot be satisfied by sex: rather, sex itself must continue to reproduce desire, to keep us wanting ever more (88). This has implications for the way sex is figured theologically too: nature is invoked as a justification for sexual desire, and we pay too little heed to (and, sometimes, explicitly deny) the ways in which nature and desire are influenced by and constructed through social, economic and political norms (88–9).

Building on McCarthy, there might be a case for an anti-capitalist model of sexuality and reproduction that rejects the trope of constantly hungry desire. If sexuality is to be reframed along the lines he hints at, then, I suggest, it will need to be understood as non-utilitarian (and therefore not, primarily, directed towards procreation), and in tension rather than accord with the capitalist logics of unlimited growth. Augustine longed for a time when sex would take place only in order to reproduce, and when there would be no lust involved – when erections could be willed into being without the complication of libido. I am not talking about a tamping-down of desire of this kind, but, rather, of an expansion and multiplication of our modes of desire. A more satisfactory theology of reproduction, then, would figure it as not primarily about the end result. It is not about whether babies are or are not produced, but about in what ways relationships (with putative offspring, yes, but with others too) are brought about. In other words, this is about the process of relationship-building as much as about the end result. Sex can be natal and new (and new-making, regenerative, re-newing) even when it is not for procreation.

Where sex must always be a means to an end, it loses its capacity to figure in its own right. This is when desire is commodified and instrumentalized: when it is directed only towards making babies, or used exploitatively for the good only of the self and not the other. Rowan Williams (2002) has persuasively shown that same-sex relationships are an important reminder of the non-utilitarian nature of sex: sex is not all about making babies. Insisting that sex must always be open to the possibility of procreation is problematically utilitarian. Now, why is saying that sex is for building relationship any less utilitarian than saying it is for building children? Well, I suggest that it is about process rather than *telos*. Sex is recreation, recreation; any given sexual encounter marks not the end of a relationship, but the potential for its new beginning (be it with a new-found partner or one's spouse of sixty years). This new beginning says that what the relationship may have been in the past is not all it can ever be in the future; it holds tenaciously to the possibility of forgiveness, mutual vulnerability and beginning again. But there is a tension here: many sexual encounters do come with a history, such that the newness is tempered by appeals to a shared life experience.

This is why, for McCarthy (2007), the Christian model of marriage and family presents a good alternative to the desire-capitalism-individualism matrix. Having sex within the marital–familial context, he holds, means that the terms do not have to be negotiated anew every time (as they might have to be in a polyamorous arrangement): the contractual nature of the relationship is lessened. The commitment of marriage is an alternative to 'the dominant reproduction of desire' (89). I think marriage *is* still a contract, even if it is also a covenant and a sacramental mediation of grace: McCarthy's account of the non-necessity of renegotiation, attractive though it is in many ways, might be taken as warrant for a once-and-for-all assent to sexual activity in marriage. As we have seen, on the contrary, having married someone does not mean having consented to engage in sexual intimacy with them whenever and however they desire: changes to the law in most jurisdictions to acknowledge and outlaw marital rape reflect our distaste at the idea of a spouse's being their partner's sexual property. McCarthy might counter that a spouse who rapes or forces unwanted sex on their partner is evidently already in breach of the spirit of the contract. Nonetheless, it is, I think, significant that marriage be figured as, in part, a contract that can be terminated (and whose continued consent and observation does not mean that the spouses have given up all other rights) – though it is understandable that McCarthy himself does not argue along these lines given his location in the Catholic tradition.

But key is that, as McCarthy wants to say, importantly, in the context of family and household and everyday life, sex is, very often, not the most generative thing. All the other things going on *around* and *between* and, often, *instead of* sex are also where the work of sustaining and maintaining and reproducing the community occurs. He points to the non-generativity of sex in the context of the household (which he understands as any group of people living together, sharing resources and co-operating). Households are primarily about *social* reproduction, relationships and networks of support: an intimacy of *being with* others in continuity with more explicitly sexual relationships. Sexual reproduction *may* also take place, resulting in the births of children – but this is secondary. Households exist not just for those within them but also for those outside, who benefit indirectly from the increased stability and interconnection they afford. 'Passion in the household … is only modestly regenerative. … It is free to be nothing at all' (94). It makes sexual practices 'fecund' even when they are non-procreative. McCarthy figures this as spontaneity; I suggest it is also anti-utilitarianism. Jonathan Herring (2014; see also Herring 2013) has made a similar point: namely, that sex is less significant than relationships of care in maintaining and sustaining ourselves and others. If the government ruled that no-one could have sex for a week, says Herring, it might be frustrating for some people, but we would likely all survive; by contrast, if the government ruled that no-one could *take care of* anyone else for a week, things would surely fall apart.

'Okay', someone might respond, 'so we don't necessarily need sex to sustain our relationships – at least not in the short term. But we *do still need sex*, or where are all the new people to come from?' Well, there are at least two possible responses: first, yes, sex *is* useful and necessary for procreation, but it also generates quite other things (among them sometimes love; sometimes reconciliation; sometimes a much-needed release; sometimes plain old bodily pleasure). Why should its procreative function be apotheosized? (I return to this point below.) Second, even if no-one had sex again for quite some time, there would still be plenty of people around in need of care. Generative responsibility is, after all, not only responsibility for infants, but also for older children, for elderly parents, for asylum seekers, for people with intellectual disabilities, for bereaved people, for victims and perpetrators of crime, for all of us. Here is where the ever-new and the always-already meet. When we continue our species we do so not merely for the sake of continuing the species, but because, in Christian terms, we believe we are inclined towards God, and our reproductivity is part of our endorsement of hope. For Stanley Hauerwas (1981: 27), for example, this is one way we are reminded to make better communities: in his analysis of community and story via engagement with Richard Adams's novel *Watership Down* (Adams 1973), he says,

> Rabbits survive by their dogged refusal to let the dangers of life stop them from carrying on – which is nowhere more centrally embodied than in their insistence on having and rearing children. For it is only through their children that the tradition can be carried on. To fail to have children would be tantamount to rejecting the tradition and would symbolize a loss of confidence in their ability to live out that tradition.

We hope because our future is in doubt; we hope because hope will 'keep us faithful to the struggle' (13). So, it seems to me, if as humans we will not build a better future for the sake of strangers, we may yet do it for our own children; in and through this community-building, we may come to recognize our own children as strangers in their alterity, and recognize, as a next step, that other strangers are not really strangers at all but others to whom we are already intimately tied.

The Population Crisis

Is there something rather fatalistic and defeatist about all this? Is not carrying on as normal less a testimony of incorrigible hope than a wilfully oblivious fiddling while Rome burns – particularly given the environmental crisis facing our planet and the undeniable additional pressures placed on resources and the ecosystem by increasing numbers of ever-more consumptive human beings? 'God is working his purpose out as year succeeds to year', says the hymn;[4] but the rapid

---

4. 'God Is Working His Purpose Out' (Arthur William Ainger 1894).

acceleration in polar ice melting may mean that the waters soon cover not only the sea but enormous tracts of land too.[5] Human beings and other land-dwellers may feel circumspect about how far this reflects the 'glory of God' – yet quotidian *behavioural* denial of the environmental crisis is commonplace even among those persuaded by the science, whose motto might be Rom. 7.15 ('I do not understand my own actions. For I do not do what I want, but I do the very thing I hate'.). As Hauerwas (1981: 18) himself notes, socialization often means 'training in self-deception as we conspire with one another to keep death at bay'. Rabbits' lives, as Adams and Hauerwas remind us, tend to be short and violent ones; human life is sometimes brief and bloody too; but, in each case, it is inhabitation of a common story that is more significant than direct biological connection. Rabbits, who have short generations and a vulnerable future, understand that procreation is necessary to ensure survival. Human beings, whose cultural influence is a little longer in the scheme of things, know that transmission of one's history is a communal affair and the responsibility of all who are steeped in it. The human population need not pass eight or ten billion[6] in order to stand as a sign of affirmation that we hope for a future beyond our own lifespan: human generativity exists in different things, and can mean ensuring communities in which growth takes place via improved nutrition, education, healthcare and access to cultural fulfilment for a smaller number of total people, rather than increasing numbers of people wholesale.

The population crisis is just one reason, but a sobering one, why overemphasis on the relationships between sex and procreation on theological grounds is potentially damaging. What made sense in contexts of low population and slow growth, frequently decimated or worse by war, famine, plague and contagion, makes less sense where life expectancies are increasing and preventable diseases are gradually being brought under control. Where procreation is characterized

---

5. A fictional account of how a remnant of humanity will adapt to being sea-dwellers – not without massive loss of life along the way – is found in Stephen Baxter's 2008 novel *Flood*. In 2052, a small band of survivors gather on rafts and flotsam to see the last piece of dry land on earth, the top of Mount Everest, submerged. The children present, well used by now to seeing small pieces of land claimed by the sea, are bemused by why the adults find this one so exceptional.

6. The United Nations Department of Economic and Social Affairs estimates that the eight billion mark will be reached sometime around 2023, nine billion around 2040 and ten billion around 2062. The same data estimates that the *percentage* increase of the population year on year will gradually decrease, to less than 1 per cent by 2099; the actual population change is also projected to decrease gradually, with growth of over eighty thousand people in 2015 but less than thirty-four thousand by 2062. However, the hugely increased overall population by then, coupled with longer life expectancies, means that the overall world population is not projected to fall during the time these figures cover (up to 2100). These figures are based on a 'medium fertility' projection: if each woman had an extra half child on average above these estimates, population would reach ten billion in the 2040s and would surpass sixteen billion by 2100. See United Nations (2013: 1–2).

as a necessary potential outcome of fully self-giving (and thereby theologically licit) sex, sex not directed to this purpose is devalued in a way not justifiable given current population concerns. This also has important psychological implications, given the guilt experienced by some Christians when they do deliberately prevent conception, and the assimilation of the assumption that good sex is potentially procreative sex to the extent that some Christians express enjoying sex only when they know it *is* fertile. We also know that some of the solutions to the problem of overpopulation proposed in the past (such as helping developing countries grow their economies to help financially support their also-growing populations, or opening borders to allow the free movement of trade and labour) now appear dubious on other grounds (like the increase in carbon-heavy technologies which have accompanied the rapid industrial growth of economies such as India and China, and the failure of free markets to create prosperity for all). In the 1950s the US Roman Catholic theologian Anthony Zimmerman (1959: 20) could oppose the use of the 'rhythm' method of birth control on the grounds that

> the Church's answer to an economic problem is to urge an enlargement of the economy, not to encourage a diminution of human beings. Just as a sensible mother will not think of starving her son to prevent him from outgrowing his trousers; she will feed him well, and proudly fit him with larger trousers when he is ready for them.

We should now know better than we did then that growth seems to have limits, defined by the patterns of consumption beyond which our planet simply cannot support us. There may not be enough fabric in the world to clothe the still-growing behemoth-child. After Pope Pius XII, Zimmerman insists that the family is the founding unit of society and that individual couples should not avoid having children for the sake of the wider social common good (24); he takes it as read that having children is a couple's right, and that to prevent this on the grounds of avoiding overpopulation would be a sin against nature and against the couple's right to direct their own family life according to God's will rather than that of the state. Pope Francis's (2015b: para 50) papal encyclical *Laudato Si'* (*Praise Be to You*), despite its generally progressive and pro-environmental outlook and awareness of problems caused by environmental destruction and water shortages, repeats the Pontifical Council for Justice and Peace's claim that 'demographic growth is fully compatible with an integral and shared development' (Pontifical Council 2004, para 483; Francis 2015b: para 50). Francis argues that the problems are caused not by overpopulation as such, but by consumerism leading to an overconsumption of resources. Of course, any recognition that the actual number of the world's human inhabitants was inherently problematic would seem to legitimate birth control, something Francis has not yet publicly entertained. But even Augustine recognized that the mandate to procreate which God had given in former times did not exist in the same way in his own era on the grounds of 'the mysterious difference of times' (*On the Good of Marriage*, 15; see Clark 1997: 56).

Natality and Personalism

So natality and generativity aim to say that sex is not just for procreation, and that there may be a case for majoring on this further given overpopulation. Should we, then, focus rather on sex's capacity to communicate personhood and the kernel of the self? Not necessarily. McCarthy (2007) incisively identifies the shortcomings of one version of the Roman Catholic personalist account of sexual relationship. He notes that, in scholars such as Dietrich von Hildebrand, Andrew Greeley and Mary Greeley Durkin, a great deal is pinned onto sexual subjectivity, rendering it as 'a total unity, integrating physical and psychological aspects of the person' (90) which is so potent yet also so vulnerable that only marriage can sustain it. Sex and desire are 'celebrated as a natural (pre-social) drive to communion that transforms an otherwise isolated self' (90). He notes, too, that great significance is placed by some Roman Catholic personalists in human sex as male and female, since humans' sexuate status is taken to communicate something profound about humanity as such.[7] The positions he describes are the ones taken by those theologians who want to free sex from its instrumentalist direction towards procreation; but, he fears, in over-spiritualizing the capacity for marriage itself, rather than marriage-leading-to-procreation, to signify 'the sacrament of human community as such' (92), they pin too much on this one, necessarily heterosexual, mode of intersubjectivity. McCarthy is right that this kind of model places too much store in maleness and femaleness, to the extent that they become simply 'types'. Rather, I suggest, difference and relationality can be understood as inherent human needs without making them rest in binary sex as a trope. Binary sex is a mechanism for one kind of reproduction, but it is far from the whole human story.

This is why, as Karen Kilby and Tina Beattie among others have shown, Balthasar's theology of human sex in the *Theo-Drama III* is so inadequate. Balthasar (1992: 286) figures woman as 'the fruit-bearing principle in the creaturely realm', whose vocation is 'to receive man's fruitfulness into her own fruitfulness'. Beattie (2002: 93) points out that Balthasar's over-association between human male generativity and divine generativity goes against the counter-cultural nature of the Virgin Birth and its interruption of patriarchal modes of production and transmission. Kilby argues that Balthasar does not really do a 'nuptial' theology, as he claims, but a sexual one, and specifically one based on 'the' act of sexual intercourse (with much emphasis on male ejaculation and female receptivity). Balthasar's imagery is not just gendered but sexual – but it is sexual in a noticeably stereotypical way, such that 'even when seeds and wombs and male outpourings do not specifically appear … it is often still clear that the underlying logic has a good

---

7. There are, to be sure, also other kinds of 'personalist' accounts within Roman Catholic theologies which are less prone to apotheosizing marriage, heterosexuality, procreativity and the family, but which have frequently been shut down or ignored in magisterial pronouncements; they include work by Louis Janssens, Kevin T. Kelly, Josef Fuchs, Bernhard Häring and Joseph Selling (see also discussions in Stewart (2010) and Bonny (2015)).

deal to do with sexual intercourse' (Kilby 2012: 137–8). Even if Balthasar does not necessarily make assumptions about the theological import of *procreation* specifically (Nichols 2000: 110), he does make particular assumptions about male and female roles in and contributions to sexual intercourse, then reads his theology off them. Kilby (2012: 130) says, 'While Balthasar appears to insist on and make much of sexual difference, it is not a *real* sexual difference that he envisages, but one which begins from man and then casts woman as whatever is needed to complement and fulfil him'. Specifically, woman's 'difference' is situated in her physiology, 'one that is an integral part of her unalterable essential structure, matching the inner, pneumatic vitality infused into her' (Balthasar 1992: 355). Quite apart from reading uncomfortably in light of subsequent disruptions of gender supervening on sex, and seeming to repeat essentialist tropes of women as receptive because of one aspect of her reproductive anatomy, Balthasar's account leaves no space for models of human sex which are more than binary ones. Furthermore, it undermines Balthasar's own argument, leaving too little space for the existence of real intratrinitarian difference between the persons of the Godhead. Balthasar (1998: 87) wants to say that the generativity within God is mutual and dynamic; he believes that drawing a parallel with sexual difference accentuates his point, but actually his argument that difference (by which he means binary difference) in creation reflects *two* poles of giving and receiving, initiating and responding, misses the point. Actually, difference in creation is always more than binary, always more than either-or, always more than this-not-that, because it echoes the Trinitarian difference which is always at least tri-directional and therefore cannot be self-absorbed. Indeed, binarizing differentiation and unity themselves (as Balthasar seems to in p. 95) risks making for a static dyad.

Beattie notes the same kinds of problems in Aquinas's *Summa Contra Gentiles* (*SCG*) and *Summa Theologiae*, and points to instances (as in *ST* II-II, 26, 10, and *SCG* IV, 11, 19) where father-males are figured as 'active principle' uniquely bringing conception and generation, and where (as in *ST* II-II, 26, 10) the body explicitly receives its form 'through the formative power that is in the semen of the father'. On the *SCG* passage, remarks Beattie (2013: 348),

> Here, Thomas argues that 'the fleshy generation of animals is perfected by an active power and by a passive power; and it is from the active power that one is named "father", and from the passive power that one is named "mother"' (*SCG* IV, 11, 19). This makes clear that sexual difference is quantitative, not qualitative. The female is not a genuine other but the 'other of the same' (to refer to Irigaray), the negative against which the man represents himself as positive, the passive against which the man represents himself as active, the lack against which man represents himself as perfection. The naming of a woman as mother and a man as father derives not from any fundamental difference between the two nor from any human relationship of love, commitment, and fidelity to one another and the child they bear. It derives only from their biological functions as active and passive in the act of conception and gestation, which in turn derives from the copulative ontology of the pagan cosmos.

As a result of these kinds of accounts, holds Beattie, biological insemination is made synecdoche for 'a whole system of divinely commanded duties and loyalties', making ejaculation 'the cornerstone of the social order' (116).

The same kinds of problems arise in Pope John Paul II's *Theology of the Body* (delivered during the 1980s and published collectively in 2006), and in the apostolic letter *Mulieris Dignitatem* (*On the Dignity of Women*) (John Paul II 1988). John Paul II makes therein the same kinds of assertions about the male and female body communicating something about masculine and feminine ontology. For him, the sexed body expresses the true person in soul and spirit (see 2006: 14:1 and 45:2). 'Womanness' is always and inherently 'motherness': to be a woman is to have a mother's body, a body that can make space for a child even as it 'makes space' for a male partner during sexual intercourse (John Paul II 1988: section 4). Being woman is, precisely, being receptive to insemination, whether human or divine (section 5). But this rests in a too-biologist account of theological anthropology, where observations about male and female interactions during sexual encounter are moralized and made prescriptive and normative in both behavioural and ontological terms. Here women have vaginas and uteruses because it is *the very nature of women* to accommodate others (whether male partners or growing foetuses). Assessments of anatomy are both grounded in and re-ground moral claims about the underlying personhood of males and females – such that to be a person *is* to be male or female. As much as anything else, as I have shown elsewhere, this elides and writes out of existence the full personhood of those who are neither male nor female in biological terms (Cornwall 2010).

Furthermore, I think the same kind of problem arises in John Milbank even though, ironically, it is exactly what he is trying to avoid. When Milbank insists that males and females (or, rather, men and woman) are not just interchangeable types, but that each brings distinctive qualities to the table, he means to respect specificity and difference. But by setting out *how* they differ – male aptitudes including 'physicality, objectivity, transcendence and the need to be in charge', while females tend to be 'actively receptive, embracing and interpersonal' (Milbank 2012); or, elsewhere, claiming that in general 'men are more nomadic, direct, abstractive and forceful, [and] women are more settled, subtle, particularising and beautiful' (Milbank 2003: 207) – Milbank risks perpetuating the idea that males and females differ only along certain lines, and that the most important human differences are those between the (two and only two) genders. Moreover, despite his important acknowledgement that men's and women's different giftings *are* tendencies rather than universals, he does not speculate on how gendered 'aptitudes' are socially reinforced from an early age (so while he knows it is problematic when girls are given only pink things and encouraged to present themselves exclusively as 'pretty' and 'sexy' from an early age, he does not explore the ways in which other qualities are also overtly and subtly encouraged in one gender rather than another from birth).

Now, it is not wrong to give sex, sexuality and bodily specificity a high place in theology. But a problem in all these accounts – in Balthasar, Aquinas and John

Paul II – is, as Beattie notes, the way that their binarization repeats and reinforces systems of lack. This would not necessarily trouble any of them: indeed, for Balthasar, giving-out becomes a mode of kenotic dispossession which is itself generative. In this logic, it makes sense that giving-up and giving-over does not constitute a troubling lack, because, for Balthasar, when God the Father acts kenotically, it is only to make space for the Son and the Spirit. There is, we might say, always more God available to rush in and fill the hole. For Balthasar, God's nature is to give-out and give-over, and it is herein that God's generativity lies. But I am not persuaded that generativity always entails ceding of the self. Generativity, I want to argue, need not diminish, but can augment. Indeed, Balthasar says as much himself. However, this does not stop Balthasar (1992) figuring God's kenotic activity as almost violent in potential. Suffering, sacrifice and death are built into the Godhead from time immemorial (226). Now, what goes on between divine Persons in the privacy of their *perichoresis* is their own business; but when this violence, predicated on lack and risk, is made imperative for the rest of us, we might have something to say about it. What works less successfully, then, is when Balthasarian divine self-expropriation becomes a model for required human behaviour: first, because it is often patterned along stereotypically gendered lines; and second, because it fails to give space for human otherness to be truly other, to not conform to the divinely ordained pattern.

Indeed, another problem is when all human difference is reduced down to sex difference along these binary lines. This does not do justice to the multiplicity and range within human sexes as well as between them; it does not take account of intersex or other factors which complicate the solely binary picture; and it elides the sense in which human beings, while always being rooted and grounded in embodiment, are also not slaves to it. Furthermore, as Rachel Muers (2007a) notes, some attempts to map human sex difference onto divine–human and divine–divine (as in Trinitarian) relationships, such as those in Barth and Balthasar, apotheosize sex and fail to recognize its alterity; she comments of Balthasar's reading,

> The 'ordering' of the sexes on earth that provided an analogy for innertrinitarian relations or the ordering of Christ and the church is in turn valorized or reinforced on the basis of its heavenly analogates. Clearly this acts against any critical interrogation of our assumptions concerning sexual difference. Predetermined understandings of 'masculinity' and 'femininity' are mapped onto the immanent Trinity, and back onto earth, without being affected by the *maior dissimilitudo* supposedly present in every instance of analogy between the divine and the human. (201–2)

The Barthian–Balthasarian account is clearly inflected towards Aristotelianism, but in Plato, too – comments Janet Martin Soskice, via Plutarch – generativity involves the conceptual and material principles together with the masculine as organizing and transcendent. Theologies coloured by neo-Platonism find it difficult to hold that generativity lies anywhere but in maleness (Soskice 2007: 109–10).

So, to summarize the foregoing section:

1. The theological privileging of fertile, potentially procreative sex, which made good sense when communities were small and the human species was at risk of being wiped out, no longer makes sense in a context of a worldwide population explosion.
2. Concomitantly, the continued theological sanctioning or privileging of only one type of sexual activity – that is, fertile penetrative sex between a male and a female – no longer makes sense on the grounds of point 1.
3. An overemphasis on the necessity of binary sex as a precondition for the type of sexual activity described in point 2 is also less justifiable on the grounds of point 1.

I am suggesting that a broader account of generativity which focuses on non-biological reproduction is one way to respond not only to the population explosion itself – necessary as such a response is – but to the pro-natalist theologies which may, consciously or otherwise, exacerbate it. Concomitantly, such non-biological accounts of generativity will also help Christian theologies to move beyond sexual essentialism.

So is there any hope for Catholic theologies of the kind I am discussing? Rachel Muers (2007a: 204) believes that Balthasar's anthropology can be reclaimed along anti-essentialist and even queer lines because he figures the receptive 'feminine' principle as something open and necessary across the community, not just in women. I am less persuaded than she is that this is enough to rehabilitate him (especially given that the model is still a closed binary which explicitly leaves no space for variant sex and gender; and given the hierarchy inevitably bound up in the Balthasarian characterization of woman as *belonging* to man and *oriented* to man (Moss and Gardner 1998: 385)), but I take the point. And, in fact, I want to suggest that elements of John Paul II's writings might also be reclaimed along these lines. Although, as I have noted, the essentialism of his claims is deeply problematic, what he does do effectively is to give space for generativity to be more than about the production of biological children. It is patronizing to say that all women are 'really' mothers because this is what their bodies 'dispose' them for (and may be deeply hurtful, too, especially to women who yearn desperately to have biological children but whose bodies seem to conspire against them despite their supposed inbuilt ontological 'readiness'). However, by figuring (as Augustine also does) the creative, generative nature of virginity, John Paul II (2008: section 18) can say that 'mothers' are not just those who have biological children. I would want to expand his argument and say that fertility is also not just about femininity or the female, but is a capacity open to all human beings. Kinship is 'fictive' for John Paul II to the extent that Christian love should not be limited to one's own children, but expanded to others 'not as outsiders but as members of the one family of God's children' (41). Even if he seems here to consider biological nuclear families a solid centre from which to move outward, rather than something to be relativized altogether, it is clear that he does not apotheosize nuclear structures or flesh-and-blood relationships.

Conclusion

In Jantzen's characterization, the Western philosophical and Christian theological tradition has focused too exclusively on death. But her own account, grounded in natality, finds areas of accord with mainstream theologians too, including Karl Barth. William Werpehowski (2001: 393) glosses, 'Barth repeats the theme that, whether we be "young," "mature" or "old," we are to respond to God's requirements for us "as if we were just setting out." ... He is just as resolute about our being also and especially "beginners" in our response to grace. The mature adult ... must not fail to venture still as a "child at play," a "student," or an "explorer"' (cf. Barth 1961: 613). As new beginners we create newness in and through our interactions with the creation – which is, itself, ever-new in its generation by an eternally creative God who also continues to be made anew in and through the creation. Yet natality and generativity are deeply, profoundly, paradoxically non-instrumental. Per Barth, children must be understood as for themselves, for joy, not for anything else. Each of us was, is, a natal child: we, too, are *for* joy and delight. A non-instrumentalist account of natality and generativity says: you were born to be yourself. You were not born to prove anything to or for another. Is this individualistic? Does it lionize the jettisoning of old loyalties, as I will discuss in the next chapter? Not, I suggest, if it means that we are understood as children of a common God *who cannot be limited to any human story about God*. We exist out of the overflow of divine delight.

So if we want to hold to this non-instrumentalism, it is true, per Milbank, that children should not be treated as commodities (though I am aware of the modern Western bias of this position, in myself as well as in others, as I will note in Chapter 5). Why, then, do people want to have children, if not to prove something to or for or about themselves? What is going on is more subtle and less self-serving than that. Many who yearn to have children yearn to have them because children signal to them a particular life stage which they have found difficult or impossible to explore or access by other means. As in Erikson and Kotre, children are (usually) part of the life stage in which maturity is beginning or bedding in – or only just beginning to be recognized by observers. Per H. Richard Niebuhr, I suggest, care for children is an aspect of the responsible self: one who responds to God and to other persons. In maturity we *want* to be responsible. We want a legacy: not a sinister or self-aggrandizing one, but an affirmation of a continuing hope and belief in new starters (and, concomitantly, a continuing real possibility of new beginnings for each of us): just as seventeenth-century people named in hope and belief that *this* Elizabeth might survive to adulthood, so parents hope today that *this* new baby might be the one who, against all the odds, helps to show how humans can be other than horrifyingly destructive to one another. For, Christians assert, a child already *has* been born whose mission was to make evident that humans can be other than horrifyingly destructive to one another (but who, like every other human, suffered at the hands of some of the undeniable horror).

The imperative for natality, for recognizing the newness and discreteness of each child even alongside their frequent recognizable continuity with their biological and/or social heritage, is part of the reason why even in a world replete with reproductive technologies of various kinds, we tend to be circumspect about actual cloning. Cloning of the self seems to deny the possibility of the creation of 'offspring' who are unlike as well as like us. Even if, as seems likely, environment, nurture and culture mean that a cloned child would grow up with important differences from its parent – as we see already with sets of identical twins differences in whose diets, lifestyles and other environmental contexts frequently lead to divergences in their appearances – clone-children seem (on what I want to argue is quite a visceral level) to elide the possibility of veritable newness. It is the possibility of newness in each child to which I turn in more depth in the next chapter, on adoption. I will hold that as children of our institutions, each of us is made and shaped by them as children of our culture who are both born and adopted. And I will argue that we are, likewise, parents, guardians and custodians of what is passed on.

Chapter 5

Adopting Our Own: Worldless Newcomers or Children of a Common God?

Introduction

The close conceptual link between marriage, sex and procreation in the Christian tradition is a familiar and much-discussed one. Examinations of how necessary, inherent or irreducible this association is have underlain and continue to underlie discussions of topics such as the licitness of contraception for heterosexual married couples, and the extent to which non-biologically procreative relationships, including same-sex relationships, may properly be understood as marriages. But there is, of course, also long warrant in the tradition for recognizing diversity in the ways in which people become one another's parents and children.

For Samuel Wells (2007), the primary purpose of marriage is not the endorsement of the relationship of the spouses themselves, but the protection of vulnerable people – and most obviously, though not exclusively, young children. This protection is the primary purpose, he argues, because the family home is to be a *safe* place – a place where catechesis occurs and character is formed. While the quality of relationship between the spouses may ebb and flow, 'children do not come and go. Once they are born, they are generally there for a long time' (67). Wells is well aware that the Christian tradition has blown hot and cold on marriage and is ambivalent about nuclear families; nonetheless, he implies, faithfulness, care and hospitality are key tenets of the Christian life and of transformed social relationship (68), whatever else marriage and family as institutions may end up looking like.

While it is not clear in Wells's brief discussion why *marriage* should be understood (uniquely or most effectively?) as conferring the necessary 'safety' for vulnerable dependants, he does incisively identify the fact that *protection* of children is not identical to *birthing* children. Joining the absent dots, Wells seems to imply that the characteristic of the protection of the vulnerable may extend not only to children born of the union, but to others (including, perhaps, existing children whom one of other of the spouses brings with them to the marriage; or other children, beyond their own biological circles, to whom they may better provide support and stability than if their relationship did not exist; or elderly parents). In this chapter, I focus on another situation, that where children enter families via adoption. The theological tradition has variously been better and worse at recognizing the diversity of forms of family and community which marriage may be said to uphold. But in at least some recent accounts, there has been an overemphasis on the theological significance of the *biological* parent–child relationship specifically, such that other types and patterns of parenting and care are diminished. But it is through practices of attention and initiation into particular narratives that children become socialized into their families, even when they are being raised by their biological parents; as Janet Martin Soskice (2007: 30) holds, 'The child is introduced to a world of symbols, stories, goals, and practices. By such means, parents … help babies to become "selves"' – though we should note at the outset that some families have proven better at such socialization than others have. Jantzen's (1998: 153) account of natality remains important here, for, as she comments, 'To act for love of the world is to act in such a way as to try to ensure that newcomers will not be worldless, that their uniqueness is valued, so that they need not lose themselves in "the masses."'

In this chapter, then, I will therefore examine the concept of social initiation, particularly through this lens of adoption, and ask what light accounts of adoption shed on constructions of generativity as more than biological, and how far any child may truly be understood as a new beginner, a natal unto itself. I will focus not on the historical use of the adoption metaphor for initiation and assimilation into the family of God either generally across the Christian tradition or more specifically within Calvinism or Reformed Christianity; nor, except fleetingly, on pastoral theologies of adoption or those designed predominantly to counsel existing or putative adoptive families. The former have been addressed thoroughly and effectively in Trumper (2001)[1] and the latter in Stevenson-Moessner (2003) and Nydam (1992). Helpful examinations of the image of adoption, as used by Paul, are found in Peppard (2011) and Scott (1992). I will also not touch, except in passing, on discussions of constructions of adoption as a means to avoid alternatives often assumed to be less desirable, such as abortion and (especially in some Roman Catholic contexts) the uses of reproductive technologies for assisting conception. Rather, what I will do here is to show that the (often assumed) primacy of the biological parent–child relationship might legitimately be disrupted on other theological grounds, and that endorsing animality need not mean apotheosizing biological generativity. I will explore the sense in which adoption is a more focused version of the initiation into community which all persons undergo, as summarized in the words of an adoptive parent to their child:

> I hope over the years you'll keep both of these truths in mind: that you owe much to others, and that we give you credit for what you've achieved. And really,

---

1. Calvin's reclamation of the Pauline trope of adoption for discussion of Christians' inheritance of the Kingdom was itself a departure from understandings of adoption in his own context. In Calvin's France, adoption had largely disappeared, and certainly did not accord adoptive children equal rights with natural ones. See for example Boyle (1998: 232).

you know, even though your case is special because you were adopted, both of these lessons are true for all of us. We're all indebted from the start. (Meilaender 2005: xxv)

Any comments I make here about the initiation of children into families and wider society is made in the full awareness of the narrow specificity of my own context. Resistance to the commodification of children, or exploitation of their utility as producers or economic contributors, may appear ethically uncontroversial and theologically sound in the twenty-first-century West; but the logic may not work so well in other contexts, especially those where survival is more of a close-run thing.[2] This is just one among many good reasons for being circumspect

2. David F. Lancy (2015) argues in his book *The Anthropology of Childhood* that the 'neontocracy' of many modern Western societies is anomalous when compared with the majority of cultures across the world and across known human history. Many societies – 'gerontocracies' – have valued, and continue to value, elders and ancestors more than they value younger people. Individuals may not be accorded full personhood until several years into life. In some gerontocratic contexts, children are pragmatically figured as commodities whose value and labour are to be used for the good of the family, kinship group or society as a whole. There is less sense than in neontocracies that children are to be protected, sheltered from work or considered non-economically productive. In gerontocracies, infants' and young children's worth and well-being may be (what seems callously) ranked well behind that of their parents and elders, but this is a cost-benefit analysis: it is in the social (and genetic) interest of families to ensure that the healthiest and most viable members survive, and that care for children does not take up resources disproportionate to what the parent, family or group can afford: 'Being a "calculating" mother is not synonymous with wickedness; on the contrary, it is adaptive behaviour' (Lancy 2015: 33). By contrast, in neontocracies, says Lancy, '[Children's] value to us is measured no longer in terms of an economic payoff or even genetic fitness but in terms of complementing our own values – as book lovers, ardent travellers, athletes, or devotees of a particular sect' (14). Lancy describes anthropological work on various societies in which decisions about whether to name or fully acknowledge a child as a person have been postponed until it is clear that the child is worth nurturing beyond infancy. Some societies – such as the Punan Bah of Sarawak, Malaysia and the Wari people of Brazil – have likened young children to 'unripe fruit' which must be allowed to develop further before they may be fully acknowledged as members of the group (41). Such tactics of 'delayed personhood' may, he suggests, be a pragmatic response in contexts where infant mortality is high; in some cultures, such as that of the nomadic Fulani people dispersed across Western and Central Africa, they may be a pre-emptive attempt to ward off evil (for if the mother treats a child as too obviously precious or valuable, this may attract malicious attentions – so appearing to regard them casually is actually a tacit protection strategy) (39). Furthermore, such strategies may be understood as endorsing rather than eliding the child's agency: in some cultures, it is considered that infants are suspended between the spiritual and material realms and have 'not yet committed to being human' (41). In many contexts, the death and mourning rites for babies and young children are

about making systematizing theological pronouncements. Some theological anthropologies may seek universal truths about human life and personhood, but theological anthropologists themselves cannot escape their own cultural purview.

Similitude and Difference

The (biological) parent–child relationship is sometimes invoked as so irreducible that it is made the ground for opposition to marriages where biological reproduction by the spouses is not possible because they are of the same sex. John Milbank's (2012) account of same-sex marriage seems, intentionally or not, to disparage adoption and adoptive families. Milbank believes that it is problematic to disrupt the assumed connection between marriage, sexual activity and parenthood: all other things being equal, he argues, we expect (and, he claims, empirical research and 'common sense' show – but see research led by Simon Crouch (2014) at the University of Melbourne for a counter-position) that children do best when brought up by their two biological parents. Milbank wants to say that the technologization of childbirth – which he paints as contiguous with its commodification, its distancing from the 'ordinary' pattern of sexual activity in marriage – is problematic, and that, since same-sex couples inevitably need to use interventions of some kind in order to have children, same-sex marriage and parenting repeat the same kinds of problems of other technologizations (which we might assume to be, though he does not spell this out, the figuring of children as status symbols or resources rather than as persons). It would be a loss, argues Milbank, if society were allowed to become modelled as being fundamentally about state and financial control of reproduction, rather than about locality and extended kinship groups.

In another piece, Milbank (2013) also argues that if the link between marriage and procreation is broken, state intervention will expand to the extent that one's children are only legally considered one's children if the state allows one formally to adopt them (Woodhead 2014: 32–3). Families will become more to do with political will and access to the relevant technologies than about unmediated biology. He says,

> There is a natural link between the sexual act and the bringing to birth of children. This is what binds our nature and culture together in the most fundamental way. If you sunder this link you reduce us to bare animality on the one hand, and to mere rational control which will be handed over to the state on the other hand. (Milbank 2013; Woodhead 2014: 33)

different from those used for older children and adults, or are omitted altogether. Lancy and some other anthropologists take this as further evidence that they are not yet considered full persons (52), though I wonder whether there is also a hint at the concept of young children's moral immaculacy: someone who does not yet seem old enough to sin may also not seem old enough to need to be shriven.

Milbank wants to say that biological relationship trumps state power unless the state has extremely good reason to intervene (such as removing children from their parents to be cared for by foster carers because they have been neglected or abused). He is motivated by his awareness that states have sometimes encroached egregiously upon their citizens' rights, and that so-called universal standards of human rights are only meaningful so long as states and governments recognize and accede to them. But I wonder whether Milbank's argument comes too much from a parental perspective, and not enough from that of a putative child. Children's fundamental needs are for physical and emotional care. The question of whether this is provided by someone to whom the child is biologically related is secondary, as long as the caregiver's commitment to and love for the child are equally strong in either case. It is clear that while there are evidently more and less successful attachments, and more and less successful examples of parental care, these do not map in any unproblematic way onto biological versus non-biological relationships. If there are adoptive parents and step-parents whose attachments to their children have proven less absolute and less selfless than those of many biological parents, there are also plenty of biological parents whose commitment and attachment have broken down and whose children have been parented more effectively by others. (I discuss the question of 'kin altruism' in more detail below; the theme has also been drawn upon extensively elsewhere, most notably in the work of Don Browning and his research team at the University of Chicago. For a critical but broadly supportive overview of this work, see Thatcher (2007). Thatcher is more persuaded than I am that Browning's appeal to kin altruism can avoid unjustifiably apotheosizing biological families, because Thatcher – with Browning – is more persuaded than I am that it is because of the specificities of the biological relationship that many children who live with two biological parents seem to fare better than those who do not.)

I will not attempt to engage in any depth with theological accounts of new reproductive technologies; thoughtful discussions of this kind have been undertaken elsewhere, as in Peters (1996), Waters (2001), Cahill (2005b) and Banner (2014). But I will note here that Milbank does not acknowledge the fact that not all same-sex couples who have children have them via technological means. Same-sex families often are, indeed, broader kinship groups in their own right, intergenerational and expansive 'villages' of care in microcosm. Some parents in same-sex relationships, for example, bring with them biological children from previous relationships (who may or may not also continue to be parented by their other biological parent). Some lesbian and gay people come to their own arrangements with friends, involving nothing more technological than a turkey baster. In any case, it is not obvious that technologization does always entail commodification. Certainly this has been the argument about reproductive technologies like IVF made by scholars such as Oliver O'Donovan. Christopher Craig Brittain (2014: 151) glosses this kind of account: 'Accepting the use of procreative technology reduces procreation to "instrumental means chosen by the will". ... It turns procreation into a "product" of human choice, rather than recognising it as an intrinsic good beyond the control of individual self-interest. In this way, the technology mimes the cultural values of industrial capitalism.' (See also O'Donovan 1984: 39)

But why can children conceived via these means not be understood as *both* begotten (of God) *and* made (of human ingenuity)? Milbank and others sympathetic to his position are being rather utopian if they think that 'natural' reproduction – that which takes place between a male and a female via sexual activity with no technological intervention, possibly within marriage – is not also already interwoven with the functions of the state. Many people in today's Britain, for example, put off having children, or have fewer children than they would have liked, because parental leave and pay, and the cost of childcare and housing, make it financially unviable to have more. State mechanisms such as tax credits, child benefit, free or subsidized contraception, and the provision and quality of state nurseries and schooling also influence couples' decisions about family size and timing – except, perhaps, for those who are so well-off that they would not struggle financially however many children they had. In other words, I am suggesting that what Milbank calls 'market and state tyrannies' do not exist in *contrast* to but rather *alongside* 'natural' norms of reproduction.

Now, Milbank is well aware that relationships can break down, and can be violent or abusive, so that children may be better off being brought up by a lone parent than in an abusive relationship. He knows that children tend to do better being brought up in families than they do in care, so that adoption by same-sex parents might be a lesser evil than upbringing in the state care system. But Milbank's argument against same-sex marriage also has another effect. It over-prioritizes biological reproduction as grounding for family life. For Milbank (2012), gay people are not *really* parents; rather, they are merely 'allowed' (by the state) to perform a 'child-rearing function'. Same-sex couples' function as 'child-rearers' is not a good argument for calling their relationships marriages, he says, for they are complicit in commodifying birth, and their relationships cannot represent the opposite-sex complementarity which (he believes) is also inherent and necessary for marriage.

But how persuasive is Milbank's account? How far is it the case that society loses out when the biological nature of the parent–child relationship is disrupted? And what other theological and other resources might we draw upon in constructing un/familiar theologies of adoption and parenting?

Social Birth and Shared Fate

Is a merely social bond inevitably inferior to a biological one? Work by Browning and his team (e.g. Browning et al. 1997) suggests that non-biological relationships may be statistically less likely to confer good outcomes for children – but this depends on a wide range of other correlates, and accounts by some adopted people suggest that this is not necessarily the case. At a time when Scotland and Finland were the only countries in the world to allow adopted people over seventeen to access information about their birth families, John Triseliotis (1973) interviewed those who had written to or visited Register House in Edinburgh in the early 1970s to get such information.[3] Despite his finding that the majority of people who sought out their birth parents at the time did so because of dissatisfaction with their adoptive families, or frustration at how little information they had been given (55), which had tended to set up further problems for adopted children and parents, several of Triseliotis's interviewees held that they were not accessing the information through any sense of lack, and that their adoptive families were not inferior to or in any sense less 'real' than birth families:

> My real mother and father, as far as I am concerned, were my adoptive parents. … Parenthood is something which is biological but I think at the same time, more than anything else it's psychological. (Anonymous male adoptee, quoted in Triseliotis 1973: 53)
>
> Our relationships were and still are wonderful. … If you learn to get on with people they don't have to be of your own flesh. … It is how you feel that matters and not who you are. (Anonymous female adoptee talking about her adoptive extended family, quoted in Triseliotis 1973: 72)
>
> To me my adoptive parents are my mum and dad and I love them dearly. We had a very good relationship which was built over a long period – it was a real thing and not artificial. I think it is wrong for anyone to suggest that adoptive relationships can never be as real as natural ones. Well, some people think there is nothing like a blood-tie: I think, from my own experience, that it's a lot of nonsense. My adoption was made successful because of the love of my parents. If a child knows that it is loved, that is all that matters. That is the most important bond. All the way through I had a sense of belonging to them. I think a personal relationship is more important than the biological one, I really do. Let's face it, a biological relationship is sometimes purely accidental – it's a matter of what happened one night, so to speak. But a personal relationship is something which is built up over the years and because of this it is a lasting one. (Anonymous male adoptee, quoted in Triseliotis 1973: 73)

Now, we might hold that, psychologically, there is a lot at stake in insisting that one has not been disadvantaged by having been adopted; similarly, there might be good pragmatic reasons for endorsing the goodness and reality of one's relationship with one's adoptive parents. But we might likewise hold that there is much at stake in bolstering up the primacy of biological relationship, particularly if, as for Milbank, there is an additional political or anti-statist imperative in the mix.

3. The Scottish Adoption Act 1930 had made provision for adopted people aged over seventeen to access such information (Triseliotis 1973: 1). Although adoption legislation for England and Wales had been passed in 1926, it was not possible until the Children Act 1975 for adopted people over eighteen to access the names of their birth parents except, in exceptional circumstances, with a court order.

In 1964, the sociologist H. David Kirk offered what he termed the 'shared fate' theory of adoptive relationships. He proposed that adoptive parents tended to operate according to one of two modes: 'rejection-of-difference', wherein they claimed that there was no difference between their own family and a biological family, and 'acceptance-of-difference', wherein there was an explicit acknowledgement of the peculiarities and particularities of families made via adoption. Kirk (1985: 9) held that 'rejection-of-difference' was often psychologically damaging to parents and children alike, and would 'tend to disturb [the parents'] relationship with the adopted child, since it probably inhibited their capacity for empathy with the special problems that only the adoptee experiences'.

In his later book *Adoptive Kinship* (1985), Kirk argued that although the kinship between adoptive children and parents was, on some level, fictive, this was not actually unique to adoptive families:

> Many of the positions we are called on to fill require of us, in the beginning at least, some sort of fiction. We may have thought about parenthood long before we became parents, yet on the day we ourselves entered into that new position for the first time, we had to make believe that we knew how to enact it properly. The majority of people know something of what parenthood is about. ... Yet on the day we ourselves become either father or mother it has a novel quality, so we invent the fiction that we know what it is like and can act it out in confidence. This kind of fiction is both necessary and allowed, for it enables people to learn the ropes of some newly acquired position in social life. (13)

The *social* nature of the contract is significant: what makes someone a parent is *acting and being recognized as a parent*; the biological relationship or otherwise is secondary. When people want to know who a new baby resembles, said Kirk, they really want to know how well the new baby will be able to become 'one of them'. And, of course, this has just as much to do with how well the family and friends socialize and include the baby as it is to do with anything about the baby itself (14).

In her discussion of the legal challenges raised by grieving parents' requests for birth certificates for their stillborn infants, Carol Sanger (2012: 283) notes, 'Social birth – the identification and incorporation of a child into its family during pregnancy – commonly precedes biological birth'. For women who have known they were pregnant by the time they go into labour – which is not universally true[4] – there has been a period of time during which the foetus has begun to be initiated into the broader narrative of their (and possibly a larger family's) lives. Sanger suggests that this tendency to see the foetus as a real-yet-unborn person has been heightened by the use of high-quality ultrasounds. Many people now know

---

4. Between 2009 and 2011, for example, the US cable TV channel TLC ran a series called *I Didn't Know I Was Pregnant*, profiling women who had attributed their pregnancy symptoms to other conditions, or had had few or no symptoms of pregnancy at all. In some cases, women had previously been told by doctors that they were unable to conceive, and so had not considered pregnancy a possibility.

an infant's sex and face, and have chosen and announced a name before the baby is actually born. Many foetuses have already had nurseries created for them and filled with things that are 'theirs', even before they have become a legal individual and concomitantly a licit owner of property. Newborn children are already, legally, members of their biological families (except in very specific circumstances such as surrogacy arrangements where birth parents have ceded all legal parental rights prior to birth; see Snyder and Byrn 2005). In some cases, embryos (such as those leftover from IVF attempts) are now being adopted, such that they 'belong' to their adoptive parents even before they are viable foetuses: Snowflakes, a US-based charity, seeks to match 'spare' embryos with adoptive families to prevent their being destroyed or kept frozen indefinitely (Mayoue 2005).[5] Sanger suggests that neonates are also already *social* members of their families.

Sanger's account may seem to re-establish the priority of the biological, but what I predominantly take from it is the reminder that relationships of care and affect in some sense exceed and bring into question chronological bounds. Being 'known' and welcomed does not necessarily have as a prerequisite that one has independent agency or self-awareness – and, in this way, norms of subjecthood are challenged. (The flip side of this argument is, of course, the insistence that foetuses should be afforded protection and moral considerability before they are born, a conviction which has sometimes led, in extreme pro-life discourses, to a privileging of foetal rights over those of born humans, including – most notably – pregnant women and their already-born children. However, I do not hold that this position is an inevitable corollary of the acknowledgement that social recognition is sometimes deemed to have predated birth.) As Michael Banner (2014: 74–5) notes, such recognition may also be specifically theological: he notes that the Anglican liturgy of the Thanksgiving of Women After Childbirth – sometimes still termed the 'churching' of women by those of elder generations – might often have functioned historically not only as a means of giving thanks for safe delivery and the women's survival, but as the only way possible of publicly acknowledging the existence of children who were stillborn or died neonatally prior to baptism and may not have had a funeral.

Natals and Their Worlds

The impossibility of remaining divorced from social relations is summed up by A. S. Byatt's (1995: 119) Stephanie, in conversation with her husband about the naming of their new son:

'We can call him William. If your Dad chooses to be pleased, that's all to
    the good, really.'
'I wanted him *separate*,' she insisted.

---

5. I am grateful to Cherryl Hunt for drawing the work of Snowflakes to my attention.

[The baby] lay there on the bedcover, separate, seeing their faces perhaps,
    or a haze of light perhaps, or even trailing clouds of glory.
'We could call him William Edward. After my Dad as well.'
'He must have a name of his own.'
Daniel thought. 'What about Bartholemew? That's unusual.'
'That's for your church [St Bartholemew].'
'William's for Wordsworth.'
'He's getting tied into a community and he's only been here a few hours.'
'That's human.'

This social existence is, surely, what Grace Jantzen is getting at when she writes of not allowing newcomers to remain worldless: both adopted and born children are newcomers to their families of care, and all must be initiated into their culture and history. No child understands the story of its own family of care straight away, even if there are particular dynamics and propensities and tropes that will, subsequently, be absorbed by osmosis rather than needing to be consciously taught. This initiation, then, needs to happen for biological families just as for adoptive ones. In a sense, we are all adopted into our own families. In saying this I do not mean to diminish the real specificities and struggles in attachment, trust and development faced by adoptive children and their families – to deny their difference – but rather to emphasize that biological bonds do not magically, in and of themselves, communicate a shared narrative unproblematically or absolutely. As Virginia Burrus argues after Judith Butler, identity is constituted and reconstituted in acknowledgement by others; it is never complete, and never independent of its existence in community, given that, per Butler (2005: 42), 'the identity we say we are cannot possibly capture us and marks immediately an excess and opacity that falls outside the categories of identity'. Particularity is what characterizes us, but also what makes us vulnerable (Burrus 2007: 151–2).

   Studies of people brought up in groups of other same-age children but with limited contact with their biological families – as in Israeli *kibbutzim* between the 1920s and the 1970s – show that such children tend not to form romantic or sexual relationships with their community age-mates as adults: some researchers suggest that the anti-incest instinct across societies is strong enough to make it genetically 'safer' to consider *any* person with whom one has been brought up in close proximity as one's full 'sibling' (Smith 2007). This is the so-called 'Westermarck effect' (after Edvard Westermarck, the anthropologist who first outlined the theory that those who live closely together during early childhood tend not to experience mutual sexual attraction later). Here shared heritage seems to trump biology: there are many tales of biological siblings or other close relations separated at birth who, unbeknownst to each other, meet again years later and experience a special connection, some even falling in love (Greenberg and Littlewood 1995). Theories of assortative mating suggest that choice of reproductive partner is, in genetic terms, often a case of finding a sweet spot between genes that are different enough from one's own to prevent problems caused by inbreeding, without being so different that the individual is considered dangerous or an enemy: studies show that many people rate potential partners as more attractive and, in some cases, more trustworthy when they look more like they themselves, perhaps because similar appearance implies similar cultural background (Alvarez and Jaffe 2004; DeBruine 2002). There is something about our animality and biological connectedness that we cannot, perhaps, entirely explain.

Yet Kirk (1985: 15) held that there will always be part of any new baby that is just, irreducibly, itself, and not simply a composite of its social group. No family can know its new member absolutely straight away: we can delight in recognizing flashes of someone's nose or eyebrows or hair colour in a new infant,[6] and this might be understood as a positive affirmation of our own concrete animality; but plenty of familiar mannerisms and facial expressions later pop up in adopted children too.

Nonetheless, Kirk continued to maintain that rejection-of-difference was likely to be damaging to the long-term well-being of adopted children and their parents. He said that when parents of adoptees recognized adopted children's difference, they could more readily empathize with the questions and doubts children may have about their identity, and that the process of honest engagement with such questions even when the parents were discomfited by them itself enhanced trust and bonding between parents and adoptees (157–8). By acknowledging the difference between adoptive and birth families, said Kirk, adoptive parents could be upfront with themselves, their children and their wider community from the start about their families' specificity. This meant opening themselves and their children up to possible vulnerability: themselves, since there would be no way to avoid telling their children that they were adopted and risk their children's rejection or resentment; and their children, since this opened them up to the risk of feeling different or of being bullied or treated unfavourably. At a time when the majority of adopted children were adopted because they were 'illegitimate', born outside marriage, something which still carried a huge stigma (Seglow, Pringle and Wedge 1972: 166), publicly admitting that children were adopted meant that their friends, teachers and others were more likely to know that they had been born in undesirable circumstances: out of wedlock, and possibly to 'under-educated' or 'criminal' parents. Rejection-of-difference parents could avoid themselves and their children being publicly marked as different.

---

6. When a friend of mine had a baby via an emergency Caesarean section and, subsequently, sent me a photo of her hour-old daughter, I immediately felt that I recognized the mixture of bemusement and indignation on the baby's face as one I had seen many, many times on my friend's own face over the years. It is possible, however, that I was projecting this feeling of foreknowledge onto facial expressions stemming from quite other causes. Sometimes the desire to spot familial similitudes is taken to outlandish extremes; describing my mother, then a one-year-old baby girl, my grandmother had written under the 'family resemblances' section of her baby book, 'Her hands were an exact replica of her grandfather's'.

However, rejection-of-difference also set up a tension or distance between adoptive parents and children, since the parents had to keep the fact of adoption secret from their children (and, possibly, other relations and friends). Children who found out later in life, or from a source other than their parents, that they were adopted were more likely to feel betrayed, more likely to seek out their birth parents and more likely to attribute any problems or shortcomings they had to their adoptive families (Triseliotis 1973: 57). Rejection-of-difference meant a further distancing between adoptive parents and children. By contrast, acceptance-of-difference parents made themselves and their children equally and simultaneously vulnerable – this was, in Kirk's term, their 'shared fate' – but, in so doing, enhanced the bond between them.

What might rejection-of-difference versus acceptance-of-difference mean in theological terms? Jeanne Stevenson-Moessner (2003: 113–14) holds that God Godself gathers a 'family' of adoptive children along the lines of an acceptance-of-difference model where distinctions such as circumcised versus uncircumcised, alien versus non-alien, stranger versus non-stranger are not erased but also do not affect each group's capacity to be reconciled to God in Christ. Another important key might be the association of the acceptance-of-difference trope with contextual theologies, which particularly emphasize the significance of location and locatedness. In this typology, rejection-of-difference would represent those types or modes of theologizing which diminish or underemphasize the significance of location, which may, in fact, tend to appeal too unproblematically to universality as a theological good (or which never feel the need to name their own concreteness, because the wider applicability of their mode of theology is simply assumed). Models of theology which understand themselves as systematic – indeed, also as systematizing – have had and may continue to have a hard time in a world suspicious of metanarratives all told. Of course, 'unworldliness' is not in itself a reason to reject or move away from particular modes of doing theology. Nonetheless, some kinds of systematic theology are precisely that: a rejection of difference; a rejection of otherness; a rejection of the possibility of 'outsides' (i.e. the existence of anything outside the scope of the system – which might, symbolically, also mean outside the scope of reconciliation into the life of God).

Someone might counter, immediately, that such systematization is profoundly levelling and democratizing. There are not some more in need of salvation and reconciliation than others: all, whatever their situation, are affected by sin and alienation. We are all in it together. There is much to recommend this account. And yet rejecting the possibility of 'outsides' has long been bound up with a temptation to speak everyone else's stories on their behalf, telling them what they *really* mean by virtue of their situation inside of, outside of or otherwise-oriented-with-respect-to a Christian schema.

But when we try to make our questions and answers fit the system we are constructing, rather than insisting that any system must be fit for the real phenomena that arise in all their awkwardness and recalcitrance, systematic theology alienates us from ourselves and our quotidian worlds. Apparent coherence at the expense of engagement with life in all its messiness will not do. Life does not always yield to the categories and premises into which we would like to fold it. No more does God. So are there any metanarratives that we can reclaim, or have such overarching tales simply had their day? What new kinds of goods might we appeal to?

Natality and generativity have potential here because in them is an already existing tension between givenness and possibility, which might be understood as the potential for transformation into an important coexistence of two things: first, an emphasis on the truly universal commonality of birth (i.e. the fact we were all born); but second, a refusal to erase context or specificity of situation. In this way, it can affirm that family relationships formed via adoption are really, truly real, but without cancelling out the significance of relationships of biology (which speak into animality and recognition). This matters because it relatives the biological – and calls into question the over-theologization of its significance in familial relationships – while refusing to jettison materiality and location as goods. I will return to flesh out this point in more detail a little later. First, though, let us consider another kind of Christian rejection of adoption.

Bad Blood: Christian Rejections of Adoption

Some Christian accounts of adoption have focused on the difference of adoptive relationships, not from the point of view of the Kirk 'shared fate' model, but because of beliefs about possible curse or generational sin attached to the adopted child. Such associations of curse have not been uncommon: many adoptees, particularly during the era when most were born to unmarried women, have experienced being accused of having 'bad blood' and therefore believe 'that the "badness" of their parents might be transmitted to them and through them to their children' (Triseliotis 1973: 48) via a tainted heredity. In a Christian context, however, this has been more explicitly associated with sin. For example, Bill Gothard, formerly of ATI (Advanced Training Institute) and its parent group IBLP (Institute in Basic Life Principles), the US-based right-wing conservative evangelical educational organization,[7] appealed to texts such as Ex. 20.5, Num. 14.18 and Heb. 7.9–10 in his seminars and teaching materials on adoption, claiming that the 'sins of the fathers' are passed down to their children to the third and fourth generations.[8] This, he claimed, means that children adopted into a family bring with them generational sin from their birth families, which may 'poison' their adoptive parents and siblings and prevent the children themselves from flourishing. This sin could manifest as particular illnesses or diseases. While it is true that some adoptees have health

7. In 2014, Gothard was suspended and subsequently resigned from IBLP, following accusations that he had sexually harassed a number of female interns and had failed to report child sexual abuse that had been made known to him (Bailey 2014).

8. For a compelling study of how this dogma has been applied to the more specific category of children born outside wedlock, whether or not they subsequently went on to be adopted, see John Witte (2009), *The Sins of the Fathers: The Law and Theology of Illegitimacy*.

difficulties as adults because they know little or nothing about their birth parents' medical histories and their own propensities for heritable conditions, Gothard seems to be thinking less of genetic illness and more of propensity to specific sins or moral weaknesses. Adoptive children, holds Gothard, may have been 'cursed' and need to have 'demons' cast out of them. Gothard (1982: 1–2) says,

> Adopted children are affected by the sins of their natural parents, and these sins are usually very severe. … If the child is too young to understand, pray for the child. Confess your sins and acknowledge the sins of the natural parents. Ask God to rebuke Satan and free the child from any unbelief or rebellion from the lives of the parents.

Adopted children should be taught to thank God for having taken away their birth parents, and to see this as part of God's plan (10–11). Adopted children should not be considered by adults in the same way as biological children would be: adoptive parents should 'look at your adopted children as really belonging to their natural parents and only entrusted to you by the Lord' (19). Children should be taught not to be overly invested in their adoptive families: 'Encourage adopted children to focus more on their Heavenly Father than their earthly father. God must be their security, not earthly relationships' (21).

There are a multitude of ways in which Gothard's account is problematic – not least, as John Witte (2009: 5) notes, because in the biblical texts the former cites, there is no distinction drawn between adoptive and natural families or legitimate and illegitimate children; *any* family might find the legacy of its forefathers and foremothers played out in the lives of its children across generations. Indeed, in the biblical accounts, adoption may precisely be figured as an efficacious remedy for the failings of the ancestors (6).[9] Gothard's position is extreme and unusual within US evangelicalism. The history of attitudes towards adoption within this stream of the Christian tradition has, overall, been far more positive, constructing adoption as a work of Christlike love which seeks to accord adopted children the same moral and legal rights as biological children (Presser 2005: 219–26). There has, nonetheless, coexisted alongside this second stream a minority voice closer to Gothard's, one coloured by a Calvinist-inflected suspicion of interference with 'natural' determinism (226–7). However, determinism works both ways: Kathryn Joyce (2013b: 76) notes that, in some contemporary accounts of adoption from conservative evangelical pro-adoption ministries in the United States, there is a fatalistic flavour, with adopted children figured as having been intended by God to belong to their adoptive families, rather than their birth families, from before the world was created. Far from being a positive account of belonging and the

---

9. Like Browning, Witte (2009: 8) is propelled by the assumption that children born out of wedlock even today are condemned to poverty, abuse and higher rates of delinquency. Like Browning, however, I suggest he does too little to interrogate how far social prejudice against non-traditional families itself exacerbates negative outcomes for these children.

endorsement of non-kinship families, Joyce believes that this rhetoric underpins some Christian adoption agencies' construction of children as 'orphans' before they have even been born (76), undermining birth mothers' claims on and emotional bonds to the children, and leading to psychological pressure being placed on pregnant single women to give up their infants for adoption.[10] For Lisa Sowle Cahill (2005a: 165), writing on Catholic social theologies of adoption, love transcends biological kinship, and the reciprocity of connections in adoptive parent–child relationships are just as real as those in biological ones. But her language of 'assimilation' of the adopted child into the biological family is not unproblematic, especially given the tensions around initiation into the culture of origin which continue to exist particularly in the context of interracial adoptions (with, for example, some non-white adoptees adopted into white families feeling that their adoptive families have insufficiently prepared them for the racism they often face outside the home, by inadequately connecting them to their birth cultures) (Patton-Imani 2005). Elly Teman's (2010: 110ff) ethnographic study of surrogacy in present-day Israel draws attention to practices of 'kin claiming' and 'maternal claiming' by intended mothers even while the surrogates were still pregnant, disrupting norms of 'naturalness' and affective ties since they often claimed that becoming parents via a surrogate precisely was itself a natural act and a means to create a natural family (more natural, they deemed, than adoption).[11] This kind of determinism chimes with some kinds of Christian colonialism.

10. This kind of situation is not necessarily unique to the United States. In other cultural contexts, adoption is also made a means to regulate young (usually single) women's bodies: in South Korea, for example, says Hosu Kim (2015: 61), the long practice of international adoption (mostly to the United States) of the children of single women functions as a form of social cleansing, and allows the single woman to reinvent herself as 'birthmother', presented as one who, albeit under duress via discourses promulgated in Christian maternity homes, 'self-regulates and self-controls her "illegitimate" reproduction via the "rational" decision to give up her child for adoption'. This involves a psychological process of 'pre-natal alienation before the baby's birth' (61).

11. Surrogacy might, however, be figured, as by Jie Yang (2015: 91), as 'a form of the reproductive exploitation of women'. Based on ethnographic work on Changping in China, for example, Yang argues that informal surrogacy is used as a way for men to have more children, so that 'a woman and her womb become instruments of birthing more than simply children – that is, fatherhood, inheritance, self-fulfillment, and filial piety' (93). Surrogacy is read, in this context, as primarily a way to alleviate *male* childlessness and thereby 'renew the possibilities of patrilineal kinship and patriarchal power ... adding flexibility to the reproductive potential of elites' (95). Yang notes that, in Changping, surrogacy also makes hierarchies among women: it is better to have a child than not, but surrogate mothers are devalued once they have performed their duties; as in the Genesis Hagar and Sarah narrative, 'only certain mothers are honoured while others are banished' (108).

Adoptive Identity and Christian Empire

For there is good reason why neither Gothard's nor Milbank's account is adequate. According to one set of arguments, adoption, not birth, is the 'default' for Christian communities. John Dunnill notes that the Christian covenant community which begins to be described in the New Testament texts is no longer marked in exactly the same ways that Israel was. Indeed, it could not be 'naturally' marked at all by identity-markers such as circumcision or marriage only within the community: it exceeded all such bounds. Loyalty to the community was about something other than biological kinship – to the extent that it could lead to enmity between biological relations. Dunnill (2013: 117) says, 'Only much later, in the emergence of a continuing Christian community and the practice of infant baptism, do we see a growing understanding that bodies can be born into the church – that is, born naturally as well as "born from above" (Jn 3:3). Until then, Christian membership and identity rested on a choice, a ritual commitment, made or refused'.

To some extent, suggests Dunnill, this may have been influenced by Roman distinctions between genitor (biological father) and pater (legal, official father). Legal status was more significant than biological connection (101; see also Moss and Baden 2015: 140ff). In some contexts an adopted heir may have been constructed as preferable to a 'natural' one, as the former could be chosen on the basis of good character and other desirable traits in contrast with the biological luck of the draw (Moss and Baden 2015: 146). Roman males could choose to claim or reject the paternity of any child born in their household: in short, 'Roman fatherhood was volitional, legal and social, not biological' (Weiss 2004: 348). It is not surprising, then, that the trope of adoption comes to signify religiously as well as legally: Jesus's 'true' mother and brothers are those who do God's will (and, we might add, it is not insignificant that Jesus was brought up – and presumably, to all intents and purposes, 'adopted' by – a man who was not his biological father; see further Levin 2006). Roman Catholic theologies influenced by the Roman legal conception of adoption, like that of Aquinas, may be interpreted as figuring (actual and spiritual) adoption as in some respects superior to 'natural' birth: 'For Thomas adoptive sonship conjures images of maturity, fulfilment, and rightful inheritance' (Traina 2001: 129). Furthermore, for Dunnill (2013: 121), Abraham's heirs are heirs not of flesh but of faith – and, after Christ, are those rebirthed via the waters of baptism. Their 'former natural status' is immaterial. If, following this logic, family is made by adoption, not birth, then clear binary maleness and femaleness (mapping onto capacity for biologically productive heterosexual relationships), and an elevation of biological parent–child relationships, are less important.

Nonetheless, in all this, there is, as I have hinted, an elephant in the room. There is an emphasis in some strands of the Christian community, and a good and important emphasis on non-kinship relationships. This is all of a piece with the affirmation that in Christ there is no longer Jew and Gentile: Gentiles have been grafted into the 'tree' of salvation, the story of Israel's relationship with its God. The rhetoric runs that this means God is not a tribal God, not a respecter of bounds of race or nationality. All are alike to God, all equal in God's eyes. Anyone may enter into and become part of the church.[12]

But the trouble is that those acting in God's name have frequently not been respecters of race or nationality either. Such distinctions were not enough to prevent those who circled the globe to claim territories in the names of their monarchs and their deity in the fifteenth century and later from going wherever they pleased. The history of imperially inflected missionary activity (which does not, to be sure, account for *all* missionary activity by any means) makes clear that Christianity has often been not only open-armed but actually self-aggrandizing. Christianity has behaved imperially (and imperiously) in its assertions that pre-existing allegiance does not signify – because it can all be subsumed under the new, overarching, potentially all-encompassing Christian identity – which might itself be understood as an ethnicity or race. Christianity's project of 'making all things new' (per Rev. 21.5 and 2 Cor. 5.17) can very easily be appropriated by those who want to say: *Your old identity (language, culture, location) doesn't matter – you're one of us now* (cf. Buell 2005: 165). And this is the case not just for Christianity but, to some extent, the Hebraic tradition which preceded it and coexists with it today. Postcolonial scholars have long highlighted the ambivalence of the story of Ruth, who is congratulated and receives her place in the pantheon of the blessed because she elects to remain with her Israelite mother-in-law rather than returning to her family of origin; makes a second marriage to Boaz, one of the in-group as far as the biblical writers are concerned; and has a child whose own line leads to King David (and, thereafter, to Jesus, the King of Kings). Why, scholars have wondered, is Ruth lauded for her faithfulness and loyalty when it is a non-blood relation, in Naomi, to whom she is most loyal? What about her duty to her original family: to *their* language, *their* culture, *their* religion? Perhaps it is Orpah and not Ruth who should be accounted a postcolonial heroine (Donaldson 2006). The lauding of Ruth is, in this logic, actually a lauding of individualism, of do-it-yourself religious affiliation, of jettisoning existing relationships of affect and denying the web which binds each of us to our origins. It chimes with a modernist, liberalist disparagement of family and community commitments, of structures of affect and bonds of care (and shares, in this sense, something with the tropes mentioned above which hold children to be 'destined' for their adoptive families even while their birth families may be longing to keep them). Is the story of Ruth a rejection-of-difference account which we see echoed through later projects of Christian imperialism? After all, even those Christian streams which appear most inclusive and accommodating might – as Miller Hoffman (2015) has argued with reference to Gal. 3.28 – tend to gloss over the real differences that continue to exist

---

12. For a magisterial discussion of the tensions and points of accord between Jewish and Christian communities in the early days of the Jesus movement and throughout the formation of the New Testament canon, see the third volume of James D. G. Dunn's (2015) *Christianity in the Making* trilogy.

in bodies even in Christ (and it is important that they do, or otherwise distinction risks being lost in assimilation).

I think part of the answer is found in Ex. 3.14, among whose possible translations is 'I am who I will be'. Our families are not only those from which we have come, but also those which we shape and elect. This *can* happen along sinister lines, but it need not. It can be expansive, not just exclusive. Another part of the answer comes from the multivocity of the tradition: Mark G. Brett (2000) and others have noted the resistance to imperialism and to other norms of genealogy and inheritance within the Hebrew Bible which do not necessarily unproblematically wipe away pre-existing allegiances, but reframe and relativize them. The counter-traditions in the texts which disrupt the assumption of divine blessing via male primogeniture destabilize '*any* cultic particularism' (38; my emphasis), and the texts include *both* injunctions to be loyal to family and tribe (such as Gen. 31.3) *and* multiple examples of non-exclusivist proto-Israelite consorting with other nations (e.g. in Gen. 13, 14 and 19; see discussion in Brett 2000: 79–80). And yet another part of the answer is that the colonial legacy might itself be understood, symbolically, as a form of structural sin. As postcolonial scholars like Laura Donaldson have noted effectively, the outworkings of the imperialist mindset continue to be visited on all parties: the former colonizers, the formerly colonized and those born after the fact for whom accidents of geography and culture mean they are also written into and implicated in this story. Bill Gothard's belief that the sins of the fathers are visited on the children and that therefore Christians should not welcome adoptive children into their families lest a curse come upon them is repugnant. But there is one sense in which Gothard is onto something: structural sin's grasp is hard and the bruises it leaves take a long time to heal. A 'curse' comes about not because of adoption and the things which adoptive children may bring to their new families, but because of the net of culpability by which we are all ensnared. The net is sinister, but it is also democratizing in the way that the doctrine of original sin tries to be democratizing: it means that we are all in this together.

One criticism of relativizing biological genealogical relationships is, as we have seen, that doing so elides and undermines our animality, our frequent sense of connection to those we recognize as 'ours'. Do un/familiar reworkings of our theologies and our families also in fact risk undercutting our animal natures and constituting a denial of our embodied connections?

Relativizing Genealogy, Maintaining Animality

Many people experience a not-wholly articulable desire to have their own biological children, or feel a primal kind of joy in recognizing a facial feature or expression in a new child ('She gets her chin from you. … That's Uncle Joe's frown if ever I saw it!' – and, yes, if we must, 'Her hands were an exact replica of her grandfather's'). We are animals, with a sense of connection to our own bodies. We prize bodiliness; we have regard for it. It is unsurprising that we similarly value physical connectedness to our children, a recognition that (often) they come from the same biological stock as we do. Incarnation matters: this link to and regard for our animality is not a bad impulse. Furthermore, as Don S. Browning (2005: 57) notes, there has been a stream in Christian theology – as seen in several nineteenth-century popes, in certain neo-Thomists such as Lisa Sowle Cahill and Stephen Pope, and in Thomas Aquinas himself – characterized by 'an implicit, and sometimes quite explicit, theory of kin altruism' whereby 'it was commonly assumed that "natural" parents were more deeply invested in their children and, on average, more consistent sources of care and nurture than all substitutes'. For Aquinas, parents' love for children was rooted in *both* the children's status as part of the parents, *and* in the children's status as children of God (Browning 2005: 65; see *Summa Theologiae* vol 2 part 2 q 26 aa 3, 8, 9). Browning draws on work by criminologists, evolutionary biologists and psychologists who claim that kin altruism is actually the underpinning of the more developed moral sensibility that follows it: as I hinted in the last chapter, we may, first, prefer the needs of others who are still recognizably like us over our own; to prefer the needs of wholesale strangers is, perhaps, a later moral stage for which kin altruism is a proving ground. However, insists Browning (2005: 59), kin altruism is a finite good; it does not render non-kinship pattern of care and parenting immoral or inevitably inferior. It can manifest as nepotism or tribalism (61). Frequently, it never does develop into a more disinterested preference for the good of the other. It is for this reason that I am far more circumspect than Browning is about appealing to kin altruism as a good, and a justification for honouring what he terms 'intact' biological families (Browning et al. 1997, at 71). Browning (2003: 76–80) himself is well aware that biological parents, especially fathers, do not *always* take their responsibilities seriously, so that any advantage they confer on children over non-biological parents and carers may *only* be a tendency.

So I suggest we can endorse animality without apotheosizing biological relationships. Our primary identities, before those of race or nationality or family, are as children of God, made in the image of God. For David Kelsey, our primary identity is simply the fact of our grounding in something beyond ourselves, in God; this Kelsey (2009) terms 'eccentric existence', and it is the starting point for his theological anthropology. If Kelsey is right, then the logical concomitant is that what is true of us 'in God' – as children of God whose fundamental identity is being grounded beyond ourselves – is truer than what is true of us in other aspects of our identities. Now, this might sound rather compartmentalizing: after all, I cannot escape my biography or my physical locatedness, and to suggest that I must do so in order to live into my God-given identity seems to risk disparaging materiality and the local. I am not suggesting that our bodies and physical identities are not also, and always already, 'in God'. However, our fundamental identity as grounded in God means that our relationships in love have an integrity similarly located in this primary truth, and which is only peripherally concerned with the subsidiaries. We must not disparage the truth of our animality, our biological connection and regard for specificity and recognition – but nor must we allow it to become ultimate.

For if we come to believe that our important locatedness of ethnicity, gender, sex and the rest is so crucial that there is nothing more basic about us as a human among humans, created by and grounded in God, then the risk is that we fail to recognize and respect other humans as our equals simply by virtue of their being human and regardless of what else may be said about them. Likewise, our relationships of care and regard for other humans should not boil down to our biological relationship to them, even if such recognition has its own evolutionary purpose, and even if we continue to be delighted by seeing flashes of a brother in the face of a niece.

As I hinted earlier, the over-relativization of biological relationship may itself undermine and marginalize animality. This is particularly important to interrogate where it leads – as in some religious, scientific and social discourses – to portrayals of (in particular) women who strongly desire the experiences of pregnancy and birthing as irrational, base and driven senselessly wild by their hormones (and as being so much in thrall to them that 'logical' pacifications will not do). This not only pathologizes and marginalizes the significance of such biological urges in women – it also tends to deny the reality of the strong desire for biological parenthood experienced by many men (including same-sex gay couples). It is for this reason that I can only go so far with Michael Banner's (2014: 58) highly persuasive account of the need to relativize, via attention to relationships of 'spiritual kinship' such as those which may be initiated between godparents and godchildren, the significance of what he terms the 'desperation of childlessness'. I remain unpersuaded that the answer to the 'problem' of such animal desire is the provision of a moral-theological 'counter-narration' which merely challenges such 'desperation' (213) without, I suspect, engaging adequately with the specificity of the pain and sense of frustration of animality experienced by many involuntarily childless people. To merely insist that not being able to conceive and/or father and/or carry and/or birth a child when one wishes to is not *really* a problem because theology has already provided a 'better' answer seems to me to be pastorally inadequate, and to risk short-circuiting the process of grief for infertility which is rarely straightforward, linear or unmuddled. Adding in a sense of guilt because hope and trust for non-biological kinship relationships was somehow – for a time or forever – *not enough*, hardly engages satisfactorily with the reality of the effects of unwanted childlessness.[13]

To be fair to Banner (2014: 63), he notes himself that the focus of his discussion is chiefly assisted reproductive technologies and some of the rites and rituals surrounding present-day practices of birth (and especially 'technologized' hospital-based birth) specifically, whereas 'a fuller discussion would have to consider the desire for parenthood in a wider context that would include, for example, changing patterns of sexual relationship and marriage' – as I have tried to do in this volume. It seems to me that it is only in insisting on a prioritization of attention to the

---

13. I am grateful to Julie Gittoes for conversations which prompted my reflections in this direction.

reality and non-pathology of the animality and concreteness underlying many conceptualizations of parenthood and family that we take seriously how far as well as being creatures who shape and are shaped by culture we are also affected by more-than-human common creaturely urges to see our children born and survive.

So how do we deal with this tension, this sense in which we are all irreducibly and undeniably products of our legacies personal and social, but at the same time not wholly bound by or condemned to them because of God's relativization of existing systems and structures? How might we draw on tropes of natality and generativity to tread the tightrope I noted above: the emphasis on the levelling universal commonality of birth on the one hand, and the refusal to erase context or specificity of situation on the other? Here is one possible answer.

A Set of Special (and Un/familiar) Cases

If we do not want to erase the importance of biological connection (first because to do so would seem to repudiate animality and material specificity; second because of the mysterious joy of recognition of a new child as somehow 'one of us'), then we might want to say that adoption is a special case. Adoption is what happens, what needs to happen, when existing relationships of familial care have become unavailable, or proven inadequate or too difficult (e.g. a child survives a car crash in which both parents are killed, and there are no other relations; or a fourteen-year-old girl discovers only after seven months that her thirteen-year-old boyfriend has made her pregnant, and neither is ready to begin to be anything other than children themselves; or a woman cannot bear to bring up the child conceived via rape that she also could not bear to terminate). Adoption in these circumstances does not threaten the fact that, had things been different, it might have been better if the first child's parents had survived to raise her to adulthood; or if the second child had been born to parents in a position to support him in every way necessary; or if the third child had been conceived willingly. This is not the same argument that Milbank makes: in the cases I am setting out here, if adoption is 'second best', it is not because the eventual parent–child relationship is non-biological, but because in each case the circumstances that made the adoption necessary were undesirable in their own right. Adoption is not mere 'mimicry' of biological parenthood (even if it has often been constructed in this way),[14] but nor should biological families be demonized in cases where adoption has been a better option (Post 2005: 183–4). Adoption is a distinct and particular thing in its

---

14. Stephen G. Post (2005: 183) ascribes the practice of 'matching' adoptive parents to children who look as though they could plausibly be their biological offspring to this tendency. However, I think this is to ignore the imperative to make disclosure or otherwise of their adoptive status the child's own decision as they grow up – something more difficult or even impossible when, for example, the child is obviously of a different racial background from their parents.

own right. 'Adoption does not need mimicry. Instead, it should be exalted for the salutary love that it manifests. Adoption ... puts the almighty gene in its place' (184). Furthermore, it is clear that adoption in the biblical narratives is not always presented as a 'plan B': as model for divine–human relationship, 'adoption is not concessionary' (Moss and Baden 2015: 149).

Adoption, then, is a necessary special case. But what if there were a *lot* of special cases? What if the special cases included not just those that most evidently *seem* exceptional, but also those which generally seem completely *unexceptional* – which seem somehow neutral, unmarked or 'innocent'? Same-sex parenting is a special case. Fine, but so is heterosexual parenting; so is single parenting; so is step-parenting; so is surrogacy; so is parenting where one or both parents transitions gender. Adoption by any or all of these parents is a special case: more than that, a whole raft of slightly different special cases. Same-sex marriage is a special case; as is the marriage of transgender people, or intersex people, *or common-or-garden cisgender heterosexual people*. We sometimes like to speak in terms of 'family resemblances' between different phenomena, and I am not trying to suggest that we should not do so: *of course* there is much that adoption by heterosexual parents and adoption by same-sex parents has in common. But the shift I want to make is to say that parenting by married cisgender heterosexual parents of a child they have conceived themselves, biologically, with no extraordinary interventions, *is also a special case*. It is no less so just because it happens to be such a common one. We do not need to impose a systematic all-encompassing story in which there are norms on the one hand and excesses or deficiencies or deviations from those norms on the other. Gay couples, justly, have often not wanted to be considered exceptional or special when it comes to marriage, parenting or lots of other things. In fact, they *are* exceptional and special; but so is every other category of actors.

I am not making quite the same argument that Gerard Loughlin (1996: 308) does when he says, 'There is no one proper sort of family, or rather ... there is, but ... it includes all others. In the light of this proper family all actual families – as we know them in history – are "pretend" families'. Loughlin's claim is that because the ideal family of the Kingdom of Heaven is an eschatological one which is still coming into being, no single family form may be deemed to have yet 'arrived' at it. Provocatively, he suggests, since 'just as the heavenly family dissolves all earthly hierarchies and familial bonds, so postmodernity renders everything and everyone an equal consumer and consumable' (325), what he terms 'promiscuity' might be understood as precisely one instantiation of this new order. Since all in the new community are one another's brothers and sisters, he adds, any sexual relationship might be understood as 'incestuous' (326). Ultimately, Loughlin rejects such libertinism on the grounds that it, too, cannot be understood as fully and properly characterizing the 'one sort of earthly family that repeats the heavenly' (327). But by pushing everything forward to an as-yet-unrealized eschaton, Loughlin risks being circumvented by those who would hold that families as we now know them are fallen and redeemable, rather than still in a process of linear onward motion. When I hold that there are many kinds of special cases, I want to suggest, rather, that what we see in them is *already* an instantiation of various familial forms as *means by which* the eschaton is brought into being.

To construct adoption as being 'just as good' as biological relationship, to say that an adopted child can be made to feel 'just as loved' and 'just as much ours' as a biological child, is still to construct adoption against biological relationship with the latter as unmarked norm. It is to say that adoptive belonging is biological belonging in disguise, not a thing in its own right. But this is to fail to interrogate the contingency, the marked nature, of what appears natural, stable and unremarkable too. When we say that an adoptive child is just like a biological one, we flatten out the real differences between adoption and birth, and this matters *not* because adoption is a stigma to be worn, but because biology and birth also carry their own strangeness and markedness, even if we rarely acknowledge it. Why do we not rather say that a biological relationship is 'just as good' as an adoptive one? In some sense, all children, even those born to and brought up by their biological parents, need to be 'adopted' into their own families. All who marry or parent or mentor or care for or take responsibility for others are, in this sense, special cases – even the ones who have often been deemed somehow theologically 'neutral' or unmarked; about whom no-one says that they are objectively disordered or treating children as a commodity just by virtue of who they are.

Candida Moss and Joel Baden (2015: 10) have noted that, in a US context of private adoptions, where the costs of agency fees, advertising and possibly visits overseas can spiral, the system favours 'conventional families and wealthy couples'. In this sense, then, it might be argued, adoptive families are made to 'imitate' not only biological ones, but a particular bourgeois ideal of what a stable, healthy family looks like. (This may repeat far older concerns to ensure stability and continuity of inheritance and – as in first-century Rome – successions within powerful dynasties (145)). Of course, this is not inevitable: even if the scrutiny attached elsewhere to adoptive parents still far exceeds that attached to parents who have biological children, it is possible to celebrate a broader diversity of situations. Commenting on the mixed, multiplicitous picture of adoption in contemporary Britain – including adoption within families to regularize and systematize legal parental rights; adoption of infants, older children and children with special needs by heterosexual couples, same-sex couples and single people; and the additional factor that more and more adoptions are now 'open' and involve ongoing contact with birth families – Heather Walton (2014: 67–8) suggests that this very 'leakiness' and 'porosity' might itself be theologically significant. If theologies of adoption started from the variegated reality, then, she remarks,

> there would need to be a new acknowledgement of ambivalence in human and divine relations. We would have cause to marvel at the heterogeneity and theological complexity of the ties that bind us. … We would find cause to celebrate in the loving care of the gay couple who adopt the bullied teenager, the blood father who repents of previous neglect and returns in penitence to renew a covenant with his little girl, the mother of a woman who committed suicide rearing her grandchild in grief and grace and hope. So much, I believe, we could

learn of the coming kingdom from experiences such as these. … Christians
might see adoption as a mirror for understanding all familial relations.

Such a reframing would be truly un/familiar.

And there is, indeed, space in the Christian tradition to find narratives of
parenting and family that sit light to biological relationship and do not apotheosize
'natural' families. Moss and Baden (2015) point to the precariousness of the
survival of even biological offspring in the societies contemporary with the New
Testament texts: as well as the odds of dying before birth, there were moments
afterwards at which a midwife might consider a child non-viable, or a father fail
to acknowledge his responsibility for it. Parenthood, they hold, required explicit
'moments of assent' (167). Moss and Baden characterize this as families being
'made, not generated' (167); but we could, rather, simply hold that it complicates the
very notion of generativity. It is a clear reminder that 'natural', biological families
are themselves not unmarked or unencultured. No way of becoming a family is
beyond the reach of social, cultural, economic and legal norms, however much
some commentators might wish that it were so. And this is appropriate: it is in and
through such structures and institutions that we endorse, as societies, notions of
the common good and seek to protect those who are most vulnerable and most
prone to suffering through a lack of appropriate care. If we say that theologies
which recognize this are un/familiar, we mean that they already acknowledge the
complexity and multivocity of relationships and care inside and outside family
structures. After all, Christians worship a God said to act 'against nature' (*para
phusin*) (Rom. 11.24): appeals to what is 'natural' in (biological and social)
reproduction cannot any longer, if they ever could, comprise the untrumpable
winning hand.

Conclusions

Betty Jean Lifton (1975) described adopted children as 'twice born'. In the Christian
tradition, all those who are inheritors of the Kingdom, adopted by God, are also
born again – born from above. If our structures of marriage, parenting and family
may, as I am arguing, be remade and regenerated without losing their essence,
then there is a sense in which, metaphorically, we are all *both* adopted children
and adoptive parents. We are adopted children because we have been claimed by
and initiated into our social and cultural (and theological) stories just as much as
we all were into our families, biological or not. We are children of our time and
context. But we are all makers and generators too: each of us shapes and remakes
and feeds into what marriage and parenting *now* mean: not as immutable inherited
concepts, but as dynamic, shapeable ones. We parent and birth our institutions; we
are guardians of them, not in the sense that we must preserve them in aspic, but
in the sense that we curate them and allow them their agency to interact with each
generation. God came as a child; the relationship between a child and those who
care for it not only initiates the child into a story, but changes the story of those

who attend to it (Soskice 2007: 31). And those of us in positions where we initiate others, as well as being-initiated-into traditions ourselves, will find that we are not always at liberty to control what messages or norms are taken up and handed on by those who come after us – any more than we can entirely control the legacy we inherit from our own forebears (Muers 2008: 135). Our challenge is to negotiate how we welcome and celebrate a child as 'one of us' without simultaneously communicating – explicitly or implicitly – that this other child, this other person, this other thing, is *not* of us, thereby inscribing patterns of exclusion.

Michael Peppard notes that the use of the term 'adoption' in the Pauline epistles is significant given contemporary legal adoption contracts which would have influenced Paul's understanding of the term. Pointing to a Greek adoption contract from antiquity, Peppard (2011: 101) notes that it refers to the adopted child as '"your legitimate and firstborn son, as if begotten to you by your own blood." … Nowhere is it clearer than here … that "firstborn" in Greek often connotes privilege more than primogeniture'. In other words, Paul in Rom. 8.29 does not necessarily understand Jesus as truly begotten but Christians as 'only' adopted children of God; to be firstborn does not necessarily in itself mark one out as superior to adopted children, since adopted children – in this reading – take on exactly the privileges of natural children (102).

Yet, as I have hinted above, there is still a problem attached to arguing that un/familiar institutions are 'just like' or 'just as good as' more familiar ones. As queer commentators have noted (and as I explore further below), expanding legislation to confer marriage rights on same-sex couples does nothing to problematize the institution's chequered history and problematic legacy. Emulating or jumping on board with something, even if the action of doing so changes it to an extent, still confers some kind of privilege on the prototype. Adoption is marked because it casts a light on the success of familial relationships that otherwise often go unremarked: how well-adjusted is this child? How successful have the parents been at making the child feel loved? How well does the child fit into the broader culture and society of the adoptive family? In this way, however, I want to suggest, it should prompt a re-examination of why these questions are so often unvoiced otherwise, in 'ordinary' families. If adoptive families and same-sex couples have to prove themselves 'just as good' as others, there is a problematic reinscription of the normality of the typical: per Sara Ahmed (2006: 174), 'A queer politics is not about laying new tables, whatever their size. After all, to set up new tables would leave the "big table" [the "family table"] in its place'. As I have been arguing, there is no typical. There is, rather, a series of repetitions with difference, which invoke and resist ghosts and memories of their others. Families are unfixed, up for negotiation. Those who live in them will always exceed the role in which they have been cast, so that the very idea of the normal or unmarked family is shown up as fictive. The idea of family is already an inheritance, something that has coloured the concept we inherit and go on to shape (125). Ahmed says,

> Not only do we inherit 'things' down the line of the family … but we also inherit the family as a line that is given. … One's arrival is already narrated as another

line that extends the line of the family tree. When given this line we are asked to follow the line, which we can redescribe as the social 'pressure' for reproduction, which 'presses' the surface of bodies in specific ways. (125)

The family as social inheritance is a fiction, which gathers its own 'thickness' and thereby becomes more than illusory. But because it is also always already a fiction, it is negotiable. We can write our own endings.

But if there is space in the tradition to relativize norms of genealogy, inheritance and blood, what is the significance of the rhetoric of the past several decades surrounding large families for the sake of the Kingdom, which precisely hold that fruitfulness for the (Christian) Kingdom of God must happen in *this* form, in *these* ways? How do the social and political goods underlying the so-called Quiverfull movement and other pro-natalist Christian groups sit alongside the dual strands of querying and endorsement of family across the tradition more broadly? How do discourses of family and belonging in Quiverfull literature challenge and chime with the accounts of generativity, natality and the development of un/familiar institutions that I have been setting out? Are they any better a showcase for pastorally and theologically necessary attention to animality and specificity of location than the approaches we have engaged thus far?

Chapter 6

FULL QUIVERS AND THE DIVERSITIES OF GENERATIVITY

Introduction

In the late 1970s and early 1980s, a new movement began to emerge among Protestant Christians in the United States of America. Proponents of what has collectively come to be known as the Quiverfull movement – though some conservative evangelical pro-natalists eschew this label and distance themselves from it – often appeal to the Hebrew Bible tradition, as exemplified in Ps. 127.3–5, that children are like a warrior's weapons and that divine provision of them both symbolizes and confers blessing. In contrast to observant Roman Catholic and Orthodox Jewish families who had long espoused not limiting family size via artificial contraception, most Protestant couples, during the middle years of the twentieth century, had modest families with two or three children each. But several books emerged through the 1980s and early 1990s that testified to the growing belief among conservative evangelical Protestants that they, too, were to allow God directly to control their family size and were not to use contraceptives or deliberately avoid sexual intercourse during fertile times. These included *The Way Home: Beyond Feminism, Back to Reality* (Pride 1985); *The Bible and Birth Control* (Provan 1989); *A Full Quiver: Family Planning and the Lordship of Christ* (Hess and Hess 1990); and *Letting God Plan Your Family* (Owen 1990). Despite usually coming from small publishing houses and being available only via limited outlets, they captured a mood and became deeply influential among what was then a niche readership. Later, as the movement gained momentum via conferences, specialist newsletters and the internet, these were joined by works such as *Be Fruitful and Multiply* (Campbell 2003); and *Birthing God's Mighty Warriors* (Scott 2004), as well as texts less explicitly associated with Quiverfull but which still counsel an anti-contraception message (e.g. Torode and Torode 2002).[1]

---

1. The Torodes' (2002) book does advocate for natural family planning via methods such as tracking changes to cervical mucus, distinguishing them from some Quiverfull writers who do not legitimate any kind of deliberate intervention to delay or avoid conception. After the publication of the book, the couple 'eventually … disavowed their anti-contraception stance' (DeRogatis 2015: 96), on the grounds that requiring abstinence from sex around ovulation, the time when many women's libido was highest, was unreasonable.

The position of these writers, and adherents to their message, is sometimes described as 'pro-natalist'. But the natalism/natality they promote is far removed, at first sight, from that associated with Arendt and Jantzen.[2] While the Arendt–Jantzen natality account chimes with queer and ecofeminist themes and promotes flourishing in the broadest sense, Quiverfull pro-natalism drills down far more specifically into birth and childbearing as specific phenomena. This is not to say that Quiverfull adherents are unconcerned with broader social-cultural norms, or wholly dismissive of other kinds of generativity, as I will show; nonetheless, their focus on nuclear families (albeit sometimes ones formed or expanded via adoption) and on (in particular) normatively biological motherhood marks them out from the far more dissipated account of natality in the feminists. Jantzen, at least, is far more interested in the concept of children as individuals. This is not to say that Quiverfull adherents see children as somehow interchangeable: indeed, an emphasis on the uniqueness and specificity of persons is part of what underlies their opposition to abortion. Nonetheless, Quiverfull rhetoric is far more about *families* as units: the authority of mothers and fathers to care for and oversee the development of their own children; the relationships between siblings; the need to cultivate habits of unselfishness even where resources are scarce, as in many large families, and so on.

But there are also, intriguingly, respects in which there *is* affinity between Arendtian natality and Quiverfull pro-natalism. In both cases, there is emphasis on being part of a community; of holding resources lightly; of unselfishness and commitment to the common good. This is, however, outworked in very different ways, and at least part of the story for Quiverfull natalists is a suspicion, particularly characteristic of the US context, of government interference in the lives of individual families. So while Quiverfull does endorse ceding individualism for the common good, its 'commons' are more likely to be immediate families or church communities – or, sometimes, the Christian 'nation', which based on the majority of Quiverfull families is strikingly white (DeRogatis 2015: 127) – than society as a whole. Like many US right-wingers, adherents to Quiverfull theology tend to reject anything they consider socialist or communist in flavour (Joyce 2009: 139): part of Quiverfull's characterization of males is that they be good providers who can work to care for their wife and as many children as God sends without relying on social security or charity.

In this chapter I examine some of the key principles of the Quiverfull movement, and conclude that, despite its emphasis on larger-than-average family size, Quiverfull is, in fact, fundamentally about non-biological reproduction: that is, the transmission of norms and culture. As such, despite its stridently pro-natalist rhetoric, it might itself be evidence of the more-than-biological stream across the Christian tradition. Furthermore, those Quiverfull families which practice adoption are an acknowledgement that initiation and cultural transmission matter

---

2. I am grateful to Ruth Mantin for a conversation which helped me to clarify these issues.

as much as, and matter with and alongside, questions of biological heritability and 'natural' family. Then, I go on to engage with critiques of reproductive futurity from scholars such as Lee Edelman, and hold that futurity may be reclaimed and reworked along eschatological lines without either shutting down possibility all told or making unlimited possibility a shibboleth and a good to which our presents must be subsumed.

A Numbers Game?

A characteristic feature of Quiverfull is that its literature and discourse reproduces and reinforces conservative gender roles. Men are to be providers who work outside the home and do not rely on handouts, social security or consumer debt to support their families. Women are to be the nurturers and educators of their children, normally called to be 'keepers at home' (Titus 2.5, AV; the phrase is translated 'good managers of the household' in the NRSV) rather than undertaking paid employment beyond it (though monetized blogs and online ministries, pamphleteering and cottage industries are common ways to stretch the domestic budget). The neoconservatism of the movement is a reaction to the mainstream feminism of the 1970s onwards and its threat to masculinist hegemony. Even if many Quiverfull women feel fulfilled and happy in their designated roles as full-time homemakers, the clear norms of the movement undoubtedly make it harder for women and others who do *not* feel thus fulfilled and do not recognize themselves and their family situations in the idealized picture promoted by the movement.

But the main distinguishing feature of Quiverfull, over and above other subcultures endorsing similar gender roles, is the emphasis on fertility and large families. In the rhetoric of the movement, 'Marriage is to produce children, and make the earth fruitful for God' (Pride 1995: 16). For Nancy Campbell (2012: 3), 'What if you have more children? You can send more enemies to bite the dust. The more children you have around your table, the more prayer goes up to the throne of grace, and the more impact you make upon the world'.

Having large numbers of biological children is a relatively fast route to increasing the overall numbers in one's family if, as is common within the Quiverfull movement, multiple children are born with small gaps (often only a year to eighteen months) between their births. If it is necessary to outweigh through faithful Christian families the numbers of those not obedient to God, then simply having an average one, two or three children per couple will not be enough. Christian families' sizes must increase, and fast. In contexts, like the United States, where most adoptions take place privately and involve many thousands of dollars' worth of agency fees, having biological children wherever possible may prove a cost-effective as well as a rapid way to grow one's family. While childbirth is heavily medicalized and monetized in the United States, there has been some overlap between Quiverfull families and those who live off-grid for other reasons, choosing less-medicalized and sometimes even unattended births

(Joyce 2009: 163–4). This may have multiple motivations, including a desire to be self-sufficient as far as possible and avoid authorities external to the family – but one consequence is that the financial costs of birth are dramatically lessened. As Michael Banner (2014: 68) suggests – though not in specific relation to Quiverfull – a challenge of the hegemony of such medicalization may also be a means to resist 'the imposition of technocratic meaning' on pregnancy and birth. However, I will show later that, far from leaving birth open to a wider range of meanings and some kind of freedom from stifling enculturation, such emphases among pro-natalists actually tend to shut down possibility.

Michelle Duggar, often considered the doyenne of the contemporary conservative Protestant Christian natalist movement, birthed nineteen children between March 1988 and December 2009, including two sets of twins. The longest gap between births was twenty-two months – between her first child Joshua and her second and third twins Jana and John-David – and the shortest twelve months, between her eighteenth and nineteenth children, Jordyn-Grace and Josie (who was born prematurely; had Josie been born at term, the shortest gap would have been thirteen months, between sixth child Jinger and seventh child Joseph). In all, Michelle Duggar has given birth to nineteen children over a span of just under twenty-two years, with an average gap of sixteen months between births.[3]

Harrison and Rowley (2011: 55–6) hold that Quiverfull's focus on reproduction ('unregulated fertility, with conception at the discretion of Jesus') is so compelling that it holds together Christian families with otherwise disparate lifestyles and goals. Indeed, it might be argued that themes common across many Quiverfull books, blogs and other publications – such as household thrift and feeding large numbers of people on a small budget – are pragmatic and responsive, stemming directly from the fact that Quiverfull promotes large families in the first place. In other words, similarities between many proponents' lifestyles may have arisen from their prior shared commitment not to limit family size.

For many Quiverfull proponents, family size is not to be unlimited for its own sake: it is a means to an end. So those persuaded not to limit family size may already have a shared outlook of another kind, namely, a belief that it is necessary to ensure that Christianity prevails in the ongoing spiritual war taking place unseen (Joyce 2009: 158–60; Denson 2013: 13). Many Quiverfullers understand the Christian faith as being under attack from forces of secularism and from other religions, and represent Christians who do use contraception as 'unwittingly buy[ing] into Satan's plan to minimize and the size and influence of God's army by limiting their family size, preventing all the children with whom God would bless them, if they had left their family planning up to Him' (Denson 2013: 13). In other words, Christians are losing this 'war' because they themselves have deliberately chosen to curtail their numbers (12). This rhetoric is evident in some of the key texts of

---

3. The Duggars featured in *19 Kids and Counting*, a long-running reality TV series on US cable channel TLC, before it was revealed, in 2015, that Joshua Duggar had sexually abused minor children including several of his sisters, and the show was cancelled.

the movement. Nancy Campbell (2003: 81) holds that if Christians do not start having more children, 'Satan will win the war against Christians through attrition'. Hess and Hess (1989: 170) explicitly argue that spiritual warfare underlies God's gift of children to Christians. In some instances, this is explicitly not just a case of Christians battling a Godless society, but of Christianity being pitched against other faiths, usually Islam:

> Because God's people have listened to the deceiving enemy and limited their children, the world is now bereft of millions of godly children who could be filling the nations with His glory. ... It is an undisputed fact that the people who obey God's mandate to be fruitful and multiply are the people who will subdue and take dominion. Before dominion comes multiplication. It is an eternal law. If we as God's people want to multiply God's ways across the world, we must first be fruitful! Currently, the Islamic people are outnumbering western civilizations seven to one! They are on their way to taking dominion, unless we wake up! (Campbell 2007: 14–15)

Kathryn Joyce (2009: 189ff) points to claims about a coming 'demographic winter' for American and European Christians – against a rising tide of 'Arabs' – in much Quiverfull literature. McKeown (2011: 48; 2014: 51) cites further examples of pro-natalist writers' appeals to the need to outnumber Muslims and Hindus in their fecundity.

This kind of attitude could be found in more mainstream Christianities until relatively recently (if focused on ethnicity more than religion, though with an implicit assumption that to be white and European was to be Christian): at the 1908 Lambeth Conference, the Anglican bishops called on 'all Christian people to discountenance the use of all artificial means of restriction as demoralizing to character and hostile to national welfare' (quoted in Shaw 2013: 48). At the same Lambeth Conference, the committee charged with considering population restriction noted, worriedly, that 'in every Western country there has been a decline in the birth-rate; but this decline has been most marked among the English-speaking peoples, once the most fertile of races' (Davidson 1920: 399–400; quoted in Shaw 2013: 48). They added, 'There is the world-danger that the great English-speaking peoples, diminished in number ... should commit the crowning infamy of race-suicide, and so fail to fulfil that high destiny to which in the Providence of God they have been manifestly called' (Davidson 1920: 402). At the 1920 Conference, the bishops reiterated, 'We utter an emphatic warning against the use of unnatural means for the avoidance of conception ... and against the evils with which the extension of such use threatens the race' (44–5; quoted in Shaw 2013: 49). It was not until the 1930 Lambeth Conference that contraceptive use for married couples who had pressing reasons for limiting or avoiding conception was permitted. But this kind of privileging of the reproductive capacity of some group over others is at odds with at least some interpretations of Genesis's injunction to be fruitful and multiply: Mark G. Brett (2000: 27) notes that the commandment is to the *whole* of creation, and notes, 'Not only is there no licence for Israelite separatism in Genesis 1, even the distinctiveness of the human species is undermined when humankind has to share the divine vocation of co-creation with the earth and with other creatures'.

In constructions of religious and cultural warfare over the past few decades, fears about world overpopulation are not a good enough reason to limit family size: first, argue Quiverfull proponents, birth rates in some countries (and, notably, in majority-white and culturally Christian nations) are falling dangerously low, while birth rates among other cultures are soaring. Overall world population is not the only concern: the proportions of Christians are also significant. Second, as Provan (1989) holds, if God believed the world were overpopulated, he would simply not allow any additional people to be born. Third, hold some proponents, overpopulation is not really a pressing problem anyway: 'Contrary to the scare tactics of the would-be population controllers, there is still plenty of room on this earth. ... If you have ever driven from the west coast to the east of America, you will know that most of this great land is still uninhabited' (Campbell 2003: 25–6). Of course, this takes no account of the disproportionate effect that a US-quality lifestyle has on natural resources (McKeown 2011: 191; see also McKeown 2014: 201–7), though some Quiverfullers argue specifically that their lifestyle is not in fact as resource-intensive as might be supposed (because, for example, ten children living in one house do not all require their own individual toys, books, bicycles, new clothes and computers as ten only children living in ten separate homes might do). Nonetheless, many Quiverfull proponents, notes McKeown (2011: 58), simply argue that God told human beings to be fruitful and fill the earth and multiply, and has not subsequently delivered any injunction to the contrary. Some Quiverfull advocates and other natalists hold simply that, since people are made in God's image, the more people there are on earth, the better (146). As McKeown notes, this is in tension with the position of those early Christians (including Augustine) who were more inclined to note the tensions and negativities bound up with embodiment even if they simultaneously wanted to affirm incarnation and materiality as good. Augustine was well aware that even the children of faithful Christian parents are born into sin, and that there is no guarantee that they will be saved, or influence others for better rather than for worse. Furthermore, Augustine (in *De nuptiis et concupiscentia* (*On Marriage and Concupiscence*)) held that, while a good, reproduction was not binding on faithful Christians in the end times: '"This I say, brethren, the time is short." No longer is God's people to be propagated by carnal generation; but, henceforth, it is to be gathered out by spiritual regeneration' (Schaff 2007: 270).

It seems likely that, in the US context, Quiverfull opposition to (or denial of) concerns about overpopulation is also coloured by perceived associations between environmentalism and feminism, especially those influenced by Gaia-type accounts of the earth or universe as an organism often characterized in feminine terms. Quiverfull seeks to 'reclaim' the trope of generativity from its purported feminization, echoing an Aristotelian-type account wherein the power to generate is a fundamentally masculine quality.

Populationist narratives are not, of course, unique to Quiverfull; they echo appeals to warrior-reproduction elsewhere, as in Russia, where parents who have brought up seven or more children are recognized with the state award – complete with military-style medal – called the Order of Parental Glory, in the interests of what President Vladimir Putin (2015) terms 'the most important thing of all – preserving our nation, preserving the people of Russia'; or in present-day Israel-Palestine where both 'Jews and Palestinians are depicted as participating in a "demographic race" to birth their respective nations' (Teman 2010: 286).

The language of choice is treated with suspicion in Quiverfull circles. It is associated with feminism, pro-choice abortion policy and those who shirk their responsibilities by using contraception and becoming 'voluntarily barren' (Harrison and Rowley 2011: 62). This voluntary barrenness is, it seems, to do not just with 'refusing' to be biologically generative, but also with refusing to reinforce the 'Christian nation' ideologically. Harrison and Rowley argue that the Quiverfull movement is not simply a hearkening back to an older way of life, but is, in more complex terms, a rearticulation of (US) citizenship which aims to amplify its influence across the culture via the use of new media technologies. The characterization of Quiverfull women as 'domestic warriors' is not only to do with individual families' homes, but also with domestic political policy and homeland security. Quiverfull mothers nurture and protect not just their own children, but the values of their broader Christian family, and (what they characterize as) the Christian nation (52). As McKeown (2011: 116) remarks, it is not coincidental that the Quiverfull movement's passage of choice, Ps. 127:3–5, has Israelite nationhood at its heart.

Quiverfull and Non-biological Reproduction

Clearly, not all families who identify with Quiverfull and its surrounding culture would articulate their motivations for eschewing contraception as a desire to ensure that the numbers of the faithful dwarf the numbers of others. Indeed, some critics hold that Quiverfull is not about numbers at all: they suggest that clash-of-civilization-type discourses are a red herring, and that, for those in the movement, rejecting birth control is merely about handing over responsibility for family planning – as for all other areas of life – to God. If the movement were about maximizing numbers pure and simple, we might expect explicit arguments like, young people should marry as soon as possible after puberty. In fact, however, as McKeown (2011: 43–4) notes from his survey of natalist writings from 1985 to 2011,

> None of my sources advocates a pure natalism that aims to maximize fertility. …
> For example, none (unlike in early Judaism) requires spouses with an infertile partner to divorce and remarry. None condemns breastfeeding (which suppresses fertility) and some commend it. None calls for the legal minimum age at marriage to be lowered, and some set a higher minimum. None prohibits

singleness. Many reject IVF and other fertility treatments. None advises that a fetus predicted to be unlikely to survive should be aborted quickly to make room for a fresh pregnancy. … Some favour home births, and a few disdain interventions by gynaecologists … which may slightly increase natal mortality and so reduce fertility. Clearly other agendas also move these writers.

Although Martin Luther – an acknowledged influence on some Quiverfull writers – advocated early marriage and believed that humans' need to reproduce was as natural and unavoidable as the need to use the toilet, he held that women should marry at eighteen *not* in order to have as many children as possible, but rather because this was the age at which they were likely to be overtaken by sexual urges which would not otherwise have a legitimate outlet (74). Quiverfull families do not tend publicly to seek fertility treatments to increase the number of children they have (though some couples have sought reversal surgeries for sterilizations undertaken before they were converted to the movement (Long 2003; Campbell 2001)). Denson (2013: 6) comments, 'The Quiverfull mindset is that God determines the number of children a couple should have, which is not always a large number (or any at all). … Quiverfull families come in all sizes'.

Notions of authority and influence within the movement are often more nuanced than a simple emphasis on numbers would suggest. Home educating one's children is, notably, a central part of the movement for most families: in this tradition, entrusting children's care and education to childcare centres, nurseries and state schools will lead to a lack of control over what messages they learn:

> A nation is as strong as its families. Families are God's plan for living. Committed families are God's plan for a prosperous nation. … The devil would rather have children raised in day care centers than in the home. This way he can sow seeds of deception in their minds from a young age. The more he can incite mothers to follow their own careers rather than the highest calling God has given to them, the more he can steer the new generation into his deviant thinking. (Campbell 2007: 14)

Just *having* children is not enough: they must be brought up to embrace and reproduce (the right kind of) Christianity (Denson 2013: 15). In a context of spiritual and cultural warfare, numbers are not enough. The children of Quiverfull families have a purpose: 'We need to daily live, understanding that God has a higher purpose than just a nest full of good, obedient children. We are raising offspring to rule and reign' (Lawrence 2005: 5). Even once they reach college age, Quiverfull offspring, especially young women, are often discouraged from leaving home to study at university:

> Liberal professors are infamous for deliberately taking advantage of the impressionable minds of their students to pervert them with ungodly philosophies and justification for sin. Additionally, students on campus are exposed to lifestyles that stand in direct contradiction to biblical standards.

Living in a college dorm is often too overwhelming for a young person to continue pursuing a godly lifestyle after continual exposure to corrupt influences from their peers. (Cohen 2009: 12)

Conceptions of non-biological reproduction are clearly present within the movement, even if they are not articulated as such.

However, it is indisputable that, in more explicitly Quiverfull circles, and in high-profile families associated with movements such as Bill Gothard's ATI, the numbers of children per couple are usually higher than average. Nancy Campbell (2005: 15) may say that 'when you surrender your fertility to the Lord, you can be happy knowing you have the children God has planned for you to have, whether it be two or ten' – but in just one issue of her magazine *Above Rubies*, of the thirteen families profiled, the mean average number of children was eight – strikingly higher than the US average of 2 children and the UK average of 1.7 children per family. In all these cases, including those where there were already fourteen or sixteen children, the youngest was of infant or toddler age and there was no sense that the family was now complete. Indeed, notes McKeown (2011: 45) of his survey of natalist writings, 'each of the writers claiming to be neutral with regard to family size, elsewhere in their writing also deploys natalist arguments in favour of large numbers of children'. Despite the counter-claim from some natalists that their lifestyle is about obedience and not numbers, there is still an expectation that the family God chooses to give you will likely be larger than the one which you would have planned for yourself: in the writings McKeown surveyed, authors usually advocate six, seven or eight children as an acceptable typical family size (46); Campbell (2003: 48), more prescriptive than some natalist writers, explicitly states that 'God is not satisfied with average fruitfulness' (qtd in McKeown 2011: 46).

This is just one of the ways in which the Protestant Quiverfull narrative differs from the mainstream Roman Catholic position. In 2015, for example, Pope Francis explicitly stated to journalists that it was not necessary for Catholics 'to be like rabbits' (in Associated Press 2015), and that, while openness to life remained an important principle particularly in opposition to what he termed 'neo-Malthusianism' (in O'Connell 2015), there were licit ways for Catholic to limit their family size and that, in some cases (citing the example of a woman pregnant for the eighth time after seven Caesarean sections), not to do so would be an irresponsibility. At the same press conference, the pope denounced what he termed 'ideological colonization', an apparent reference to practices where aid organizations will only give assistance on condition that particular (Western-associated) norms are upheld (in Associated Press 2015). At the Synod on the Family in 2014, Roman Catholic bishops from Africa had decried the practice of some organizations to give aid only if condoms were distributed, or only in contexts where there was not anti-LGBT legislation in place. The pope likened such practices to the activities of the Hitler Youth, and said, 'Every people has its own culture. But when conditions are imposed by the colonizing empires they seek to make peoples forget their own identity' (in O'Connell 2015). However, unlike Quiverfull adherents, whose rhetoric is frequently triumphalist and supersessionist, the pope did not frame this as a need for one ideology to win out over others: rather, he said, globalization should not mean that different cultures lost the differences and particularities of their identities.

Quiverfull logic is often bound up with appeals to 'nature' and suggestions that large families are more natural and healthier for all concerned. (This is of a piece with the sometimes romanticized off-the-grid, back-to-the-land pioneer spirit of the movement, which means that Quiverfull families often find themselves in bed – so to speak – with the anti-authoritarian, counter-cultural movement of the far left which frequently spurns vaccination, medicalized birth and state involvement with families for quite other reasons.) Some Quiverfull writers, for example, note the health problems which, they argue, having too few children may cause. An issue of *Above Rubies* from 2007 features a story about a woman with endometriosis who went on to have eight children. At a check-up after the birth of her eighth child, she said,

> I was shown photographs of my 'clean pelvis'. My womb, ovaries and tubes were completely void of any evidence that I ever had this 'career woman's disease.' ... I realize now that [1 Timothy 2:15's claim that 'Women will be saved in childbearing'] means that God will preserve my body from abnormalities that are a direct result of not embracing children during my childbearing years. (Simmons 2007: 8)[4]

Many natalists seem to identify a moral–causal connection between childbearing and good health. McKeown (2011: 62) notes of the natalist discourses he surveyed that they contained frequent claims that early and repeated pregnancy dramatically decreased women's risk of breast cancer, that hormonal contraception caused heart attacks and that vasectomy was the root cause of many male diseases. It is, of course, wilfully ahistoricist to claim that people did not attempt to limit family size prior to the development of modern contraceptives. Appeals to a more 'natural' way of life are often, as we have seen, oddly like those made by the counter-cultural hippies with whom Quiverfullers might be supposed to have so little, politically

---

4. There is much discussion among biblical scholars of the verse about being saved in childbearing. Anna Rebecca Solevåg (2013: 87) notes that some read the term as pointing to the hope that women will be saved during childbearing: that is, kept from harm throughout the risky physical process (cf. Keener 1992: 118–20). She also notes the argument of Bruce Winter, who suggests that women may be being exhorted to take the safer physical path of continuing their pregnancies, rather than the more dangerous one of seeking abortions (Solevåg 2013: 88; Winter 2003: 110–11). There is also, chiming more closely with the natalist or Quiverfull disposition, the reading in which women are told to have children in order to save the community (in a context where sexual renunciation was also being preached, per 1 Tim. 4:3, threatening the continuation of the community) (Solevåg 2013: 89).

and religiously, in common. Both Quiverfullers and left-wing off-the-gridders may eschew medical interventions in birth in favour of midwifery, and for what look like similar reasons. Where appeals to 'nature' and 'health' are made not with an eye to ecological sustainability, but to a blinkered, idealized version of history, however, I suspect that they tend to be just another kind of originism.

It is perhaps unsurprising that, in a context which places so much emphasis on the role of women as mothers and the centrality of family life, infertility and sub-fertility are so often figured as particularly negative: according to foundational Quiverfull writer Charles Provan (1989: 9–10), 'God views childlessness or less children as a negative occurrence, something which he uses as a punishment. ... In our culture, barrenness is "no big deal" and people are always attempting to tell sterile couples that "everything is all right". But everything is not all right!'. Provan appeals to passages such as Hos. 9.10–17, wherein the people of Ephraim are characterized as losing their glory in connection with their lack of conception, pregnancy and birth. In 9:14, Hosea curses Ephraim with a miscarrying womb and dry breast. Among Quiverfull families, miscarriage is also sometimes figured as punishment, as when one woman attributes her own loss to the fact that she was not sufficiently grateful for a sixth pregnancy at the age of forty-two: 'I realized that God had taken back what He had so graciously given us as a precious gift' (Duffer 2008: 8).[5]

Nonetheless, even if Quiverfull is unusually concerned with endorsing and articulating the centrality of biological reproduction, biological reproduction is clearly not the only type of generativity in which it is actually invested. Quiverfull families are certainly likely to have higher-than-average numbers of biological children, but biological children are not the only way in which these families seek to grow and spread their influence. One needs large numbers of children to win the culture wars, but these children may join families via adoption as well as via birth. Many Quiverfull families have also adopted children, usually internationally.[6]

5. While Quiverfull rhetoric in this area may be extreme, it is not unique: Candida Moss and Joel Baden (2015: 14–15) note associations even in more mainstream texts between infertility and flawed character.

6. In 2005, Nancy Campbell began encouraging readers of *Above Rubies* to consider adopting children from Liberia, at the time a country which had been through two civil wars in the last fifteen years and in which there was widespread poverty and instability. Kathryn Joyce (2013a) notes, 'Campbell urged readers to contact three Christian groups – Acres of Hope, Children Concerned, and West African Children Support Network (WACSN) – that could arrange adoptions from Liberian orphanages. At the time, none of these groups was accredited in the United States as an adoption agency, yet they all placed Liberian children with American families for a fraction of the $20,000 to $35,000 that international adoptions typically cost'. Campbell and her husband Colin adopted four Liberian orphans, and her daughter and son-in-law Serene and Sam Allison six. Many other families followed suit. However, the high number of and rapid turnaround on Liberian adoptions that arose from

The Problem with Reproductive Futurism

Both in Quiverfull texts, which do major on actual numbers of children born, and in those which focus more on the significance of the transmission of education, culture and values, there is a strong sense that children are the 'warriors' who will secure the future of Christian culture and civilization. But this 'reproductive futurism' actually shuts down possibility, by delineating in advance the lines along which the transmission of culture may legitimately take place. There is no space here for surprise, or for the goods of the future to be anything other than what the minds of the present can already conceive them to be. If, as I have been arguing, generativity is about discontinuity and difference as well as continuity and progression, then such natalist Quiverfull philosophies are actually anti-generative. They conceptualize children as first and foremost children of their own tribes and families of rearing, for even if they are still putatively gifts of God, for pro-natalists they are gifts which come already heavily laden with a very specific set of meanings.

How, then, might theologies of generativity, which do give such space for veritable newness, play out? What of the critiques of theorists like Lee Edelman who reject futurity as a good at all?

In Rachel Muers's (2008) book on theology for future generations – which focuses particularly on the issues of climate change and ecological justice – she holds that the pregnant, maternal body is an especially significant cipher for considering responsibility to future generations. The undeniable femaleness of pregnancy is, for Muers, a salient reminder that new bodies, new people, do not come from nowhere – and that there is therefore no objective, neutral 'view from nowhere' either (127). Muers's insistence on the embodiedness of personhood is well made, but I am less persuaded than she is about the necessity of associating generation so strongly with only female and pregnant bodies. Muers characterizes the shared responsibility for our human and broader creaturely futures as a maternal one. She herself acknowledges some of the problems embedded in this imagery – such as the self-effacement and self-wounding associated with giving oneself for others, which becomes particularly problematic when womanhood is figured as necessarily existence-for-others. This is demonstrated, for example, in Janice Raymond's (1994: 236) critique of altruistic surrogacy (i.e. surrogacy

---

the *Above Rubies* campaign provoked criticism: 'Given the conditions [in Liberia], the prospect of a $6,000 adoption fee was enough to attract some shady operators. Adoptions that took a year to process in other countries could happen in weeks or days in Liberia, and bribery was rampant. Liberian parents began complaining that adoption had been misrepresented to them as some sort of temporary education arrangement. ... The struggling Liberian government was able neither to keep tabs on children leaving the country nor to distinguish licensed adoption agencies from groups that merely had nonprofit status' (Joyce 2013a). As a result, international adoptions from Liberia were suspended in 2009. More recently, and with tighter restrictions, they have begun again. See also Joyce 2013b.

not done for economic recompense) as repeating tropes of female bodies as necessarily giving:

> The cultural norm of the altruistic woman who is infinitely giving and eternally accessible derives from a social context in which women give and are given away, and from a moral tradition that celebrates women's duty to meet and satisfy the needs of others. The cultural expectation of altruism has fallen most heavily on pregnant women, so that one could say they are imaged as the archetypal altruists.

I would add to these types of criticisms the problem of over-particularization and over-delineation of the *types* (including the genders) of bodies that can carry the symbolism of generation. Now, one might counter that an acknowledgement of the specific generative capacity of the female body is a welcome riposte to the theologies, informed by Aristotelian cosmology and proto-science, which assumed true generativity to be a uniquely masculine quality, with females simply ground in which male seeds could grow.[7] Furthermore, Muers (2008: 150) makes clear that what she wants to do is simply to 'see the work of particular mothers as a focus for what is going on all the time in the lives of communities and societies – the formation of the "coming generation".' But nonetheless, a re-patterning of bodily generativity along lines too closely tied to pregnancy (as we see in much more extreme form in Quiverfull texts) closes down rather than enhances the number of ways in which a body may generate. The question is whether it is possible to foreground materiality and bodily specificity without essentializing.

In his book *No Future*, Lee Edelman (2004: 2) sets up a searing critique of the 'reproductive futurism' he believes is implicit in US culture. The mythic figure of the child – but not necessarily real, actual children – is invoked to justify a range of political and social agendas:

> The fantasy subtending the image of the Child invariably shapes the logi within which the political itself must be thought. That logic compels us, to the extent that we would register as politically responsible, to submit to the framing of political debates – and, indeed, of the political field – as defined by the terms of … reproductive futurism: terms that impose an ideological limit on political discourse as such, preserving in the process the absolute privilege of heteronormativity by rendering unthinkable, by casting outside the political

---

7. Aristotle (in *De generatione animalium* (*On the Generation of Animals*) 1.20) claimed, 'What the male contributes to generation is the form and the efficient cause, while the female contributes the material. … For there must needs be that which generates and that from which it generates; even if these be one, still they must be distinct in form and their essence must be different. … If, then, the male stands for the effective and active, and the female for the passive, it follows that what the female would contribute to the semen of the male would not be semen but material for the semen to work upon' (Barnes 1984: 1132).

domain, the possibility of a queer resistance to this organizing principle of communal relations.

After all, what right-thinking person could deny the importance of building strong families and protecting innocents?

Edelman's book is subtitled 'Queer Theory and the Death Drive', and it has been ardently discussed among queer theorists and LGBT people because of Edelman's controversial suggestion that queer people should embrace rather than resist their cultural associations with death. This may seem deeply counter-intuitive: after all, someone might note, surely we are (at least in the West) past the days when non-heterosexual sexuality was inexorably associated with HIV-AIDS, and when (in particular) gay men were assumed to be harbingers of death. Many LGBT activists fought long and hard to make clear that they, too, could raise and parent children, could build healthy societies, could marry and participate in making a more just future.

But Edelman wants to say that *futurity itself* is a dubious good if it means reinforcing societal tropes of normativity and political quietism. Too often, actual presents have been sacrificed for the sake of mythic futures, and figures of innocents such as children have been invoked to justify maintaining the way things are. In the Quiverfull arena, we see evidence of this in appeals to 'saving' unborn children from abortion – and not even just foetuses, but also the yet-to-be-conceived. More overtly, Quiverfull and natalist discourses frequently appeal to the good of building families in which Christian children may flourish. Humans are tribal creatures: the fictive child whom they seek to protect is almost always a child of their own clan, such that they may hurt and extinguish the children of others 'in the name of their children's future safety or well-being, in the name of making the world fit for *their* children' (Muers 2008: 3). Mark D. Jordan (2011), in his book *Recruiting Young Love*, shows that Christian rhetoric against homosexuality since the 1950s has often assumed that gay adult males in particular are predatory on younger people whom they attempt to 'turn' or 'recruit' to their lifestyle, since they do not have (biological) children of their own through whom to reproduce their culture. In Christian anti-gay rhetoric, young people are at risk both ideologically through 'spiritual recruitment' and physically through 'bodily infection' (144). Combatting such aggressive 'gayness' is therefore necessary 'for the sake of the children' (i.e. 'our' children, 'innocent' children, the children of heterosexual people, who are assumed to be heterosexual themselves if they can be said to have a sexuality at all). Jordan persuasively shows how this kind of rhetoric simultaneously paints only heterosexuality as normal and natural, and highlights its instability (130) (since any young person – especially any young man – is apparently vulnerable to being led astray by gay men and their wiles).

But gender and sexuality, suggests Edelman, are not neat or intelligible or on a clear forward trajectory: queer people should continue to resist and subvert normativity, not show how they, too, can operate within its bounds. Marriage and the nuclear family have been damaging for everyone, not just queer people: the last thing queer people should be doing is seeking to be included within it. If queer people are in some sense exiles from and subalterns of heteronormativity, then this is a perversely powerful position to be in: it means queer people may continue to show up heteronormativity's oddnesses and injustices. This is more difficult to do once they are 'in the fold'. Seeking 'equality' within a broken and unjust system will never trouble it sufficiently. Rather, queer people should continue to stand outside mainstream society and to disrupt it, rejecting accounts of futurity and hope since these tend to reinscribe conservative social and political mores. In a later book, Edelman describes his 'suspicion of rhetorics that privilege viability or survival' (Berlant and Edelman 2014: 7).

I go a long way with Edelman here. He is right to draw attention to those mythic innocents, and the damage that their invocation does to real and extant people here and now by shutting down possibilities in the present. I am also sympathetic to his suspicion of over-triumphalism and rhetorical 'survivorhood', which sometimes teeter on the edge of blaming victims, and those who remain more broken by life's egregious obscenities of pain, for being somehow insufficiently resilient. But I disagree with him that hope must therefore be jettisoned. I do not think that queer participation in institutions such as marriage and parenting inevitably means that the queer 'edge', the capacity to question and resist, is lost. Rather, the queering takes place from inside. The queering of these institutions means that they are no longer (if they ever were) reproduced as exclusively oppressive or damaging. In this way, hope is reclaimed as hope for the 'children' who *already* exist, including those of us long past childhood in chronological terms who may have been hurt, and continue to be hurt, by the injustices of the status quo. When queer people participate in marriage and parenting, marriage and parenting are not merely reproduced in exactly the same way such that queerness is assimilated or absorbed, becoming invisible. Queer participation in marriage and childrearing does not simply reproduce identical norms of marriage and childrearing, any more than people who have biological children are producing mere clones of themselves. Children are new people: even when they are raised by their biological parents, they are far more than the sum of their biology. We cannot say who and what they are going to be just because we know where they have come from. As in Jantzen's and Arendt's account, they are natals, new beginners, inculcating new possibility. Indeed, it is when this otherness is denied or flattened down that tensions between children's own worlds and the worlds of adults who seek to be able to conceptualize them are most likely to clash: natals are, we might say, *queer*, in the sense of resisting neat definition and recalcitrantly bursting bounds. They patently and palpably do not always behave as their adults would like them to; they have hazy motives and inconvenient desires; they frequently challenge the notion of an original innocence: and it is the anxiety this queerness provokes (reminding adults of the motives and desires that they would prefer to believe they have under control in themselves), suggests Kathryn Bond Stockton (2009: 126), which leads to an adult project of attempting to erase risk from children's lives. While this is ostensibly to safeguard children themselves, it also has the effect of wresting child lives back into adults' control – or so adults try to convince themselves.

Likewise, queer participation in marriage and parenting does indeed change them. We may not yet know exactly how. In this sense, John Milbank (2012) is right in his rhetorical claim that, in England and Wales since the passage of the Marriage (Same Sex Couples) Act 2013, *all* marriage is now 'gay marriage': there is no longer an institution exclusively open to heterosexual people.[8] Similar logic is found in the Church of England's response to the UK government's 2012 consultation on same-sex marriage: 'Our concern is for the way the meaning of marriage will change for everyone, gay or straight, if the proposals are enacted' (Church of England 2012: 3).[9] The institution we have now in England and Wales, after the 2013 law, is, indeed, not quite the same one we had before (and the same goes for other jurisdictions worldwide where same-sex marriage is now legal). But this is not a disaster. It is, rather, a good thing, if it means that marriage is now marginally less exclusive, and marginally less associated with ownership, legitimacy and an overemphasis on procreation than before. Furthermore, there is also a sense in which Milbank and the anonymous writers of the Church of England submission are wrong; as Lieven Boeve (2015) notes, interruption of a category does not mean that the thing interrupted disappears. As I have hinted in my own work on intersex (Cornwall 2010, esp. 190–3), the acknowledgement of types of physical sex which do not meet established definitions of male and female constitutes an *interruption* of binary sex, but does not mean that maleness

8. Milbank's comments were made in 2012 before the legislation was actually passed. He noted, *'The intended change in the definition of marriage would mean that marriage as traditionally defined no longer exists.* Thus heterosexual people would no longer have the right to enter into an institution understood to be only possible for heterosexuals, as doubly recognising both the unique social significance of male/female relationship and the importance of the conjugal act which leads naturally to the procreation of children who are then reared by their biological parents. In effect, if marriage is now understood as a lifelong sexual contract between any two adult human persons with no specification of gender, then the allowance of gay marriage renders *all* marriages "gay marriages"' (original emphasis).

9. Later, the document elaborates: 'The effect of the proposals would be that everyone who wished to marry – irrespective of the form or ceremony by which their marriage was solemnized – would be required to enter into the same new, statutory institution of "marriage." That institution would be one which was defined as the voluntary union for life of any two persons. English law would, as a result, cease to provide or recognise an institution that represented the traditional understanding of marriage as the voluntary union for life of one man with one woman. ... The established institution of marriage, as currently defined and recognised in English law, would in effect, have been abolished and replaced by a new statutory concept which the Church – and many outside the Church – would struggle to recognise as amounting to marriage at all. A man and a woman who wished to enter into the traditional institution of marriage would no longer have the opportunity to do so' (Church of England 2012: 9). As per Milbank, this is the 'all marriage is now gay marriage' argument, and it is unapologetic about claiming heterosexual privilege to define and police the bounds of marriage.

and femaleness themselves cease to exist. Rather, it is their significance – and capacity to signify – that changes. Likewise, I am suggesting, Boeve's account of interruption might also speak powerfully into the story of marriage that, in light of the recognition of same-sex marriage, it is now possible for theologians to tell. Boeve (2015) says,

> Interruption signifies an intrusion that does not destroy the narrative but problematizes its advance. It disturbs the anticipated sequence of sentences following one after the other, and disarms the security mechanisms that protect against disruption. … Interruptions cause the narrative to collide with its own borders. They do not annihilate the narrative; rather they draw attention to its narrative character and force an opening towards the other within the narrative.

Reframing Reproductive Futurism

For Edelman, part of the suspicion of futurity is the conviction that there are no happy endings, no time in which everything has been resolved and those parts of life inimical to human flourishing are 'over' – so that 'only the repetitive working through of what still doesn't work in the end – or works only until the radically non-relational erupts from it once more – constitutes the condition in which something like flourishing could ever happen' (in Berlant and Edelman 2014: 11). In theological terms, this might be figured as something like eschatological tension – but minus belief in a future inbreaking of divine order to interrupt and redeem the powers of the present age. For Edelman, there always will be trauma, non-meaning, negativity; to suppose otherwise is to invest in something beyond the bounds of life as we experience it.

But it is for this reason that, in Christian conceptions of hope, another world must be possible. Tim Dean (2008: 134) criticizes Edelman for channelling Christianity in *No Future*'s appeal to what Dean terms 'self-destructive pathology'; yet this account of Christianity does no justice to the possibility of redemption in and through lived life. This is perhaps most effectively and consistently explicated in the work of Jürgen Moltmann, for whom eschatology has been the key across his long career to unlocking the meanings and purposes of humans' relationships to God, the world and one another. In Moltmann's (1996: 118) account, it is precisely because life *remains* traumatic, grindingly painful and obscenely unjust that God cannot allow injustice to be the final word, and there must be a space in eternity – that is, beyond our deaths – for justice to be done. For Moltmann, it is not that the already-work of the Christ-event has erased or eliminated suffering and injustice; rather, it has interrupted the necessary associations between death, obliteration and fear (66). Death is the power of separation: in time as the stream of transience, materially as the disintegration of the person's living *Gestalt* or configuration and socially as isolation and loneliness. The raising to eternal life, conversely, is the power to unite – in time, as the gathering of all temporal moments into the eternal present; materially, as healing for life's configuration in its wholeness; and socially, as a gathering into a new community in the eternal love. The communal aspect is particularly significant, not only in terms of social exclusion, but also in terms of our own relationships with those who preceded us and will follow us: part of the reason why modern people find death so frightening, holds Moltmann, is because of their lack of a sense of the presence of their dead ancestors, and a loss of faith in 'life after death' via the continuing lives of their own children. The dead are cast off, and those alive – for the moment – must press on without them (51). Moltmann means particularly to characterize a narcissistic impulse. It is when people can acknowledge that they are more than individuals that they can live with the knowledge of their own eventual deaths.[10] It is for this reason that Moltmann can figure a real possibility of life transformed this side of the eschaton, even while aspiring to a future hope. Unlike Edelman, Moltmann wants to say that there *is* a real possibility for things to be other than they have been: not in complete discontinuity with life-as-we-have-known-it, but in a transfigured version of life in which the shape of identity, *Gestalt*, is retained and taken forward in transformation.

For another problem with Edelman's account is that it sounds strikingly like one informed by privilege and safety. It is easy enough to say that futurity is naïve and damaging when every day is not a struggle to survive. Investment in a possible future – or even an *im*possible future – is sometimes necessary for psychological survival, and when one scrapes one's existence from the detritus of a rubbish heap, or sees one's entire family wiped out by preventable diseases, or loses one's home and possessions by flood or earthquake, then belief in a different future (this-worldly or otherwise) may well be all that prevents one from such nihilism that continuing with life is not an option. Similarly, while the queer destruction of borders and boundaries may be attractive to privileged Westerners playing at gender deviance, hybrid or 'fuzzy' identities are less of an unambiguous good in contexts where – because of ethnicity, colonization, poverty, gender identity or sexuality – one's subjectivity and right to continue existing are already under threat (Cornwall 2011: 106, 109–10; Anzaldúa 1991: 250). In Judith Butler's (2004: 29, 31) terms, 'Possibility is not a luxury; it is as crucial as bread. … The thought of a possible life is only an indulgence for those who already know themselves to be possible. For those who are still looking to become possible, possibility is a necessity'. Now, Edelman might retort that 'psychological well-being' is itself a bourgeois construction informed by Western capitalist norms of health and productivity and is something that queer people might justly and justifiably resist (and see, further, Bray (2015) for a more compelling crip-

10. Elsewhere I have borrowed Elizabeth Freeman's (2010: xxii) image of 'sociability … with the dead' to describe what is going on when forebears – be they biological ancestors, cultural and moral mentors or voices from the communion of saints – continue to be 'present' in ongoing discussions. I have suggested that, in a theological context, this will include giving the dignity of holding accountable those who preceded us in the tradition for injustices done in their names (Cornwall 2015).

theory-inflected argument which holds that appeals to the productivity of the multitude, while seemingly a democratizing move, actually reinscribe norms of utilitarian neoliberal violence on persons); but I venture to suggest that Edelman's perspective is itself informed by a relatively cushioned existence. This is ironic given that Edelman precisely does want to take account of the inexplicable persistence of life in the face of the unintelligible.

I do not know how Edelman would respond to Moltmann's account. My suspicion is that Edelman would not be persuaded that a transfigured life really has much to do with quotidian life in its grind and struggles. The great risk of Edelman's account, in my view, is that its tendency to anti-futurism can lead to political quietism. From my reading of Edelman's conversations with Lauren Berlant, this is also where he and she part ways (Berlant and Edelman 2014). There is a certain irony here given that Edelman's motivation – or part of it – is precisely to avoid the human sacrifice of some individuals to the juggernaut of 'possibility' which, as we have seen, often manifests in the privileging of mythic, immaculate 'innocents' rather than actual persons (19; Edelman 2004).[11] Edelman owns that political struggle and striving to create new worlds will continue even among anti-futurists: but he remains suspicious of the way politics structures and characterizes itself as *the* vehicle of 'resistance and dissent' (Berlant and Edelman 2014: 122). Nonetheless, for Edelman there is, eventually, a glimmer of a persisting selfhood beyond the undoingness of negativity: 'Fighting our own misrecognitions matters, even if misrecognition as such remains, in the end, inevitable. Such resistance defines the work of thought as a movement, not an end, as an endless self-undoing whose negativity brings us to life' (115).

Self-undoing sounds remarkably like self-emptying, and we might recognize in it many of the same problems and potentials that kenotic theologies have sometimes been held to bring with them: promoting doormat-ism and exploitation; repeating tropes of subordination and subsidiarity for women in particular; tending to privilege masculinist accounts of pride and sin, thereby further eliding the distinctive subjecthood of women. Nonetheless, I also read here an endorsement of non-ultimacy, non-triumphalism and open-ended provisionality with which many a queer theologian (and many a mystic and apophaticist) would find affinity.

Indeed, one recent account which attempts to construct a theological ecclesiology informed by rejections of inclusivity and futurity is that of Linn Marie Tonstad. What Tonstad (2015: 260ff) terms her 'apocalyptic ecclesiology' is one in which the good of 'continuity' (between the risen Christ and the historical person of Jesus; between the transmission of the faith by the church and the conservative modes of reproduction that church authorities have sanctioned) is disrupted.

---

11. Berlant glosses Edelman's explanation thus: 'Your argument against the optimism in futurity was that it enables the straight-identified world to disavow the unbearable fact that it will never coincide with itself and never really reproduce itself, except insofar as it projects out fantasies of repair through the subordination of disturbing enemies, like queers' (in Berlant and Edelman 2014: 116).

As Tonstad notes in conversation with Kent Brintnall (2011), Christianity which constructs itself as being about generation and transmission will be one which is overly triumphalist, overly invested in its own integrity and the maintenance of its own boundaries (Tonstad 2015: 261). Key, in Brintnall's account, is not welcoming more people inside the elastic-but-tangible bounds of the community, but rather ensuring that the community comes to understand itself as appropriately shattered, fractured and boundless (262). Tonstad will not go along with Brintnall wholesale, for she suspects that he conceives of resurrection (as the key identifying and organizing principle of the new community) as more masculinist, more triumphalist than it needs to be. Rather, resurrection coupled with ascension – a clear rejection of undisrupted futurism – can mean 'hope for the return of Christ's absent body, not the securitization of the self and its projects' (263). Despite some of her misgivings about Edelman, Tonstad can hold that such destabilization of subjectivity is precisely, and appropriately, anti-futurist, and that theology must therefore 'refuse both its own and society's … reproductive urges, for the church properly symbolizes the negation of the stability and viability of the symbolic order' (269). Importantly, however, this does not entail a complete collapsing of boundaries between self and other (whether human–human, or human–divine) (272), for such collapsing does precisely what I have noted earlier in this book: it makes Christianity no respecter of the integrity of persons and their histories, rather absorbing them into a boundless morass that all too often skews towards the imperial and assimilationist. Provocatively, Tonstad goes beyond figuring Christianity as anti-futurist, and suggests that apocalyptic ecclesiology might be understood as actively *abortive*. She says,

> This form of ecclesiology figures forth the abortion of the current order of continuity and repetition, and ultimately the abortion of the church. Abortion here indicates a fundamental refusal of the logic of reproduction in both its biological and socio-symbolic senses. This is Christianity's death drive, the excess accessed only by refusing identity's positivity and representation's stability. … The relation of the church to time then becomes one of nonreproduction. (273)

And, despite its provocation, such an appeal is precisely in continuity with Barth's (1968) reminder that theology which purports to be final or ultimate has made itself an idol.

For queer theologians, then, there is – if rarely as eloquently as in Tonstad – at least a suspicious attitude towards the apotheosized (and over-literalized) Christian endorsement of family. Making children repositories for the hopes and aspirations of a community, a nation or a people of faith does just what Edelman fears, painting them as necessarily hetero-asexual[12] carriers of the purity and

---

12. Futurists, as Mark D. Jordan (2011) hints, assume children to be simultaneously asexual and 'naturally' proto-heterosexual. What they are not, definitely not, by nature, is homosexual: their 'emptiness' or 'sponginess' renders them vulnerable to being filled with

uprightness of the culture; but it also undermines the agency and personhood of children themselves. As I have been hinting, children are not merely the vessels and objects and containers of their parents' dreams and desires. They are also natals, new starters, with all the potential to resist and subvert and break down and reject of any other human being. As in Stockton's account, they are queerly recalcitrant, joyously queer. Even the most biddable of children is apt to behave in unexpected ways. This does not, of course, mean that the influence between the generations is insignificant: the moral life of each of us is profoundly affected by the failings and fudges of what we witness growing up. Some writers characterize this as the functional outworking of structural sin; Dorothy Whipple, in her 1943 novel *They Were Sisters*, a harrowing account of the effects of domestic and emotional abuse on an extended family, expresses it through her protagonist Lucy Moore: 'It seems that when we love people and they fall short, we retaliate by falling shorter ourselves. Children are like that. Adults have a fearful responsibility. When they fail to live up to what children expect of them, the children give up themselves. So each generation keeps failing the next' (242).

But the message of *They Were Sisters* is precisely that ties of affection and responsibility do not map solely onto direct biological generation. Indeed, the most functional family unit by the end of the novel comprises Judith Lee, her cousin Sarah Sargeant and their aunt and uncle-by-marriage. Sarah is estranged from both her warring parents and from her younger sister; Judith's sister and brother are on different continents, her father has fled the scene and her mother has drunk herself to death. Only their Aunt Lucy and Uncle William, who have no children of their own, prove suitable as parents.

In further contrast to Edelman, José Esteban Muñoz (2009: 1) believes that there *must* be a possible queer future, figuring queerness as 'the warm illumination of a horizon imbued with potentiality'. Such a future is necessary as a conceptual *other place*, contrasting with the 'quagmire of the present' (1). Without it, we would become condemned by the belief that there is no alternative to the present order: that the way things are is the only way they could be or could ever have been. For Muñoz, whose focus is on poetry, art and performance, the acquisition of such a future is proactive, and requires a processive *creation*, a working-towards. In other words, there is some kind of forward linear (and normative) trajectory here, even among all Muñoz's queer-inflected suspicion of limitation. Indeed, Muñoz appeals to the future in distinctively fixed terms (albeit oxymoronically) as 'concrete possibility' (1).

the agendas of the gay community, who are trying to 'turn' children to their 'lifestyle'. As Stockton (2009: 158) notes, even if children do not tend to be constructed as 'gay' at the time by adults (though children are happy to bandy the word around between themselves, and have a good idea what they mean by it), professed homosexual adults are frequently asked to give accounts of what it was like to 'grow up gay', as a difference discernible from the presumed proto-heterosexuality of the 'normal' child.

Although he borrows the term 'utopia' for the title of his 2009 book, he notes that this usage is grounded more in Ernst Bloch than in Thomas More: that is, more concrete than abstract, and grounded in 'critical and potentially transformative political imagination' (3) rather than in escapism. Muñoz's futurity concerns 'educated hope' rather than optimism; it is anticipatory (3, 49). Muñoz was not a theologian, but I have suggested elsewhere (Cornwall 2015) that there is something profoundly eschatological about him and about all this. Like the eschatological, for Muñoz (2009: 9) the potential is already present despite not yet having been realized. It can be frustrated; it can be elusive; it can seem naïve or ingenuous. But as Muñoz insists in (at least implied) response to Edelman, an absence of future-oriented hope is stultifying. It prevents activity in the here and now, exactly the opposite of what Edelman intends: 'An antiutopian might understand himself as being critical in rejecting hope, but in the rush to denounce it, he would be missing the point that hope is spawned of a critical investment in utopia, which is nothing like naïve but, instead, profoundly resistant to the stultifying temporal logic of a broken-down present' (12).

So Muñoz's account is not only utopian, but anti-*anti*utopian; not only relational, but anti-*anti*relational (14). It is born of a second naïvety well aware of the problematic natures of utopia and relationship, but which nonetheless seeks to critique their bald deconstructive rejection. If a queer theorist like Muñoz cannot quite be said to have emerged from the 'desert of criticism' (Ricoeur 1967: 349), then he has at least appreciated the recalcitrant, tenacious implications of affective bonds on continuities of existence, and returned to them anew from a place of active decision. Muñoz's language of 'surplus' in relationship – that is, all that transcends common sense and logic but persists anyway – chimes with Joerg Rieger's imagery of surplus in Christological theology: that is, all of that in Christ, in Christ-informed Christianity, which resists being subsumed by or assimilated into the service of empires. The key, and another reason why I characterize Muñoz as an eschatologist is because although he is influenced by Heidegger, he also knows very well that Heidegger is far from an unproblematic intellectual or political sage. But Muñoz (2009) recognizes that transformation happens backwards as well as forwards: the 'reach' of queering can remake and redeem what came before, as well as that which is yet to come. In this way, 'Futurity becomes history's dominant principle. In a similar fashion I think of queerness as a temporal arrangement in which the past is a field of possibility in which subjects can act in the present in the service of a new futurity' (16).

But I do not think this is a case of simple plunder or naïve rehabilitation on Muñoz's part. Rather, it is an acknowledgement that the past is not simply over and done with. It is not beyond the scope of redemption. Just as Muñoz can draw on Heidegger while simultaneously denouncing his Nazism, criticizing and queering him, so theologies of non-biological generativity may be informed by the structures of marriage and parenting of the past while also subverting and resisting them. Muñoz can criticize the 'failure of imagination' (18) in antiutopian and antirelational queer theory; in eschatological terms, I suggest, part of the explanation is that renewed imagination is *imagination towards*, something which acknowledges the possibility of a *telos* or direction without being constrained by knowing in advance exactly what it looks like or how it will most justly be outworked.[13] Because the future to come is comprised of unknowns – including not-yet-natals and not-yet-borns – the responsibility of those of us now *is* to them as well as to ourselves, but not in a way that is always (or often) clear or predictable (which is the problem with Quiverfull-type injunctions about the way a Christian family and a Christian nation must necessarily look). It acknowledges these natals' queerness, their recalcitrant otherness, and rejects the flattening out of childhood by, and into, adulthood as the ideal (cf. Stockton 2009: 11). This, then, is emphatically not the kind of invocation of the mythic future innocent that Edelman so effectively explodes. And just as, via lived eschatology, the new world to come is actually *brought into being*, so invocations of futurity do not put off the present for the sake of the yet-to-come, but acknowledge their inextricable relatedness. Queer is here and yet not here (Muñoz 2009: 21, 49); so is the eschaton.

Here we reach yet another tension. The openness of the queer future necessitates, for Muñoz, humility (28). This humility does not purport to know how the queer future will unfold. It resists being programmatic, precisely because justice-inflected programmes of the past and present have so often entailed a shoring-up of unjust structures (so that marriage is 'redeemed' merely by opening it up to same-sex couples; or capitalism is 'redeemed' solely by arguing that its prosperity will trickle down to those currently at the bottom of the heap). Yet because the queer future is anticipatory of 'an actually existing queer reality' (49) which *already* exists, there is a sense in which this queer future cannot, perhaps, be as fully open as Muñoz would like. Its genealogy is in what already exists: the stained and compromised moral concessions within which we all live. I do not think that Muñoz actually wants to claim that practices of queer performativity already have a perfectly just future sewn up; but perhaps he does not adequately trace the mixed motives and methods of the queer, nor the implications of the decidedly unqueer genesis of the world in which the future inevitably has its roots.

One way through this tension is to recognize, as Lieven Boeve (2015) does, the potential *openness* of theological narratives, those which recognize that 'God does not simply confirm and secure the narrative, but does precisely the opposite. … The God who can only be spoken of in the narrative, continuously interrupts this same narrative. … God does not neutralize difference, but *makes* the difference' (cf. Boeve 2014). Christianity's storied and storytelling nature has often meant, in practice, the baptism of hegemonic grand narratives and the exclusion of counter-

---

13. This sounds strikingly like Balthasar's (1990: 176) account in *Theo-Drama II* in which 'we cannot know in advance what the stage will look like at the end of the play' – but Balthasar undermines the possibility of his own narrative via his constraining insistence on gendered parts. If for Balthasar humans are not fixed in essence, but in a process of becoming, then his theology of gender undercuts the multiplicitous nature of this possibility (Beattie 2006: 90–1).

accounts, but this is not inevitable, and the Christian narrative also witnesses to its own graceful, gifted nature which renders it potentially open and malleable (Boeve 2011: 86ff). Boeve holds, 'If grace is the event of the breaking through of God's love, then theology must critique every immediate closing of the event in closed stories' (93). This does not mean that Christians may not make truth-claims, but rather that they must recognize the contingency of their own location when they do so (100).

Alterity and the Otherness of the Child

As a religion which expounds a belief in bodily resurrection, Christianity breaks down the links between biological reproduction and immortality. Living forever is not about (or not only about) living on through one's biological descendants: generativity is about a broader legacy (in which people and things who are not biologically 'ours' still bear our memory), and a sense that genes are not all we have to pass on. Karl Barth (1961: 268) believed that there was no general obligation on Christians to reproduce biologically, even if (as he held in *Church Dogmatics* III/4) there were times at which it would be appropriate to 'awaken' a people-group in order that 'to avoid arbitrary decay they should make use of … merciful divine permission [to reproduce] and seriously try to maintain the race', and even if he also figures procreation as a sign of God's goodness to humanity in what sometimes feel like dark days, such that the use of contraception is potentially 'a refusal of this divine offer' and not to be undertaken lightly (269–70). He was also well aware that the largest and most recent experiment in selective population-increase in his own day, the Nazi eugenic programme, 'had a definitely heathen and nationalistic character, and … was intimately related to military aims and therefore the projected slaughter of whole masses of people' (269). In Barth's construction, however, the begetting of children was a common-sense way to transmit the covenant God had made with the people of Israel, and the continued fertility of Israel was a sign of God's promise to Abraham. But, nonetheless, held Barth, in Christ, God's own Son, reproduction was relativized: filling the earth was no longer an unconditional command, and biological reproduction was 'now only to be understood as a free and in some sense optional gift' (266). Marriages in this new dispensation need not be biologically reproductive in order to be fruitful; all adults may be 'elders', mentors who 'in regard to all young people have the same task as physical parents have towards their physical offspring' (267–8). Jonathan Tran (2009: 206–7) comments, 'Post Christum natum children no longer serve the purpose of granting meaning nor are parents burdened with creating meaning through having children; most importantly, children are no longer burdened with bringing meaning to their parents. Christ has served all these purposes, having become the meaning of human existence.'

Children, then, holds Tran, are pure otherness, pure alterity, pure gratuitousness; 'pure' in the sense not that they are 'innocents' to be protected at all costs, but in the sense that they are not *for* anything but themselves (192). God's blessings now come about not through children, but through Christ (Barth 1961: 266; Tran 2009: 207). Children are undiluted, non-instrumental gift.

This is slightly tainted by Barth's (1961: 162) theological anthropology of human sex and gender, which insists on order and procession, and rejects (his gloss on) Simone de Beauvoir's suggestion that sexual differentiation is as much cultural as ontological, and is ultimately dispensable. Barth holds that Beauvoir's rejection of an 'eternal feminine' principle is a rejection of true humanity, which figures humans as inherently and irreducibly male or female in nature. For Barth, 'rejecting' sex betrays a pathological human individualism; rather, he insists, 'In obedience to the divine command, the life of man is ordered, related and directed to that of the woman, and that of the woman to that of the man' (163). The construction of children as gratuitous 'free gift' must therefore always be tempered by the realization that, for Barth, freedom is *freedom for*, not *freedom from*; to be free is to be as God most fully intended humans to be, which, for Barth, means clearly and dually male or female. Children are given to become fully differentiated male or female adults. But Barth may be reclaimed, along the lines Tran does, and further. Having children is an act of faith, an act of welcome to members of the tribe who are also mysterious strangers and an act of intention not to domesticate all the strangeness out of these strangers even if, pragmatically, there is also delight into initiating them into the ways of our people.

And this is just, surely, what we are also called to do with God. God, too, is a stranger to be welcomed, made the God of our people, without any sense that in doing so God can be corralled or made the God *only* of our people. Furthermore, there is a sense in which children are also pure alterity in imaging and mediating God to and for those to whom they come. This is part of Heather Walton's (2014) critique of theologies of adoption which figure adoptive parents as echoing the parental love of God to those who have formerly been parentless: adoption theologies, she says, too often figure parents, whether adoptive or biological, as imitating God's fatherly love. But, she says, in the birth of her own daughter after infertility and IVF,

> God came to me as child. As the child I ached for. I desired God deeply and God came to me as child. Nothing was unchanged. Every cell, every charged impulse of my soul and body transformed in that birth. I was broken, and I was healed, and I was remade and for ever transfigured in that encounter. I have known such love as cannot be contained beneath the heavens. And I have held it in my arms. (70)

There is something here akin to Stockton's acknowledgement that, in adult–child relationships, there is more back-and-forth reciprocity than there is downward transmission. Contrary to the account in a theologian like Aquinas, wherein the child is conceptualized as 'incomplete, imperfect, and … still growing into her humanity' (Traina 2001: 130), for Stockton the state of being a child is not simply a staging-post on the way to adulthood: rather, a child is already a complete person. Rather than assuming a child will merely 'grow up' and disappear into being an adult, both adults and children might be constructed as 'growing sideways' (Stockton 2009), so that a child's unknown future need not be something to be feared or corralled. The potential of childhood need not be conceptualized as *lack* in contrast with the actuality and fruition of adult life: rather, childhood may be seen as continuing to exist with, in and alongside adulthood, generative and reciprocal in ways that are emphatically not reproductive (13). Childhood is not, then, what Edelman constructs as a permanent deferral of the future; rather, the child, as queer, as natal, already has agency and influence to generate in the present.

We return here to the odd fact that, in some respects, this sits very comfortably with the Quiverfull logic that says that every child is a blessing unto itself, to be accepted and welcomed just because God has given it, for itself, and regardless of whether an addition to the family seems to make financial, logistical or other sense. And there are also authors popular in the movement who explicitly insist that using one's spouse instrumentally as a means to getting children is also wrong (Torode and Torode 2002: 22). I do not want to overstate this point, and I am not a cheerleader for very many aspects of the Quiverfull movement: after all, philosophies which purport to protect the innocent while summarily ignoring or riding roughshod over the good of those overworked mothers and fathers and closely spaced older siblings who already exist do a great deal of harm. There are further important and glaring questions about how far it is possible to grow up without sustaining immense psychological and spiritual damage as a young gay or gender-variant person in a context where gender and sexuality may only be legitimately expressed along deeply narrow and prescriptive lines. And the apotheosization of fertility and fruitfulness which makes it difficult for young women to see what their purpose is if they are not mothers, or exacerbates their suspicion that infertility and miscarriage represent divine punishment, is also deeply troubling. Here we see a denial of the specificity of animality, and the non-universality of the experiences of fertility and birthing, from another angle.

Conclusion

We saw in the previous chapter that narratives which promote the distancing of oneself from family of origin and culture may be understood ambivalently. Nonetheless, from the point of view of critiquing pro-natalist privileging of Christian 'nations' over others, the biblical texts are not an easy ally. Brett (2000: 137) says, 'Against the ideology of the "holy seed" in Ezra 9:1-2, marriage within the covenant community is not seen as a holy ideal that ensures divine favour; on the contrary, divine blessing flows extravagantly over the covenant's borders. ... The stories concerned with Hagar, Dinah and Tamar ... subtly subvert any version of genealogical exclusivism or moral superiority'.

Christianity – both historically and today – might have had particular investment in the dissemination of biblical traditions which draw into question the centrality or exclusivity of Israel within the narrative of salvation history. This might variously have taken place in order that Christianity could promote itself as morally superior to 'tribalist' Judaism, or because of an uncomfortable relationship between church authority and that of nation-states in the modern era such that Christianity had an investment in relativizing the bounds of nationhood (139–41). Christian investment in incarnation and particularity might seem to point to a privileging of material, concrete locatedness – so to say that Christian identity entirely erases such affective histories would be overstating the case.

Nonetheless, particularity can become a fetish. Quiverfull, which purports to promote and celebrate possibility, actually shuts it down. Possibility means acknowledging excess of that which we can conceive of or actualize in the moment. Quiverfull, which tries to welcome strangers, actually welcomes only what Graham Ward and Luce Irigaray might term 'others of the same' (Ward 1998: 67, after Irigaray 1985: 135), variations on a narrow theme. Here is what Irigaray frames as hom(m)osexual, narcissistic desire; here is a rejection of true otherness because of the extent to which owning it would involve interrogating the otherness and alienation of the self. I return to Irigaray in the next chapter, but for now I suggest that Quiverfull philosophy is an exaggerated version of the logic which says that we can know and control what our futures look like, and which says we know what is healthy and good because it is in continuity with what has taken place in the past, with what has been 'revealed' as in line with God's intent. Part of my own perpetual fascination with large families (and not my fascination alone, given the Duggars' long-running media success) is the never-ending novelty of the combination of parental genes in each child. While some families seem to produce uncannily identical-looking stair-step children biennially, in others no two children are particularly alike, yet it is easy to see in each a resemblance to one or both parents. This is alluring, and resonates with the curiosity that many people have about quite how their own genes might combine with their partner's, and how diverse this might be in different offspring. While Jim Bob and Michelle Duggar have had nineteen chances to see the permutations, most people witness no more than two or three in their own children: there are therefore a lot more might-have-been wonderings. But even the Duggars do not, will not, cannot, know how *every* possibility might have turned out. And since each child is more than the sum of its parents' parts, to some extent the indulgence of the joy of recognizing the difference-in-the-same is no more than that.

But such 'repetitions with critical difference' (Stuart 2003) are alluring. They appeal to our human propensity to enjoy patterns and systems while also being easily charmed by novelty. As I will show in the next chapter, navigating the interplay of similarity and difference is what lies at the heart of living with and living into our un/familiar theological institutions, and it is when we retreat to appeals to sameness that we shut down the chance to hear and speak anew.

All happy families are alike, claimed Leo Tolstoy in *Anna Karenina*. But the happy families of theological imagination, the happy families which march through the pages of *Above Rubies*, are not in fact the only way for families to be. And it is ironic that the symbolic of family often has little or nothing to do with real families: Jacqui Stewart describes the disjunction between witnessing a stylized, perfunctory foot-washing done as part of a Maundy Thursday liturgy, and witnessing, during the same service, a tired mother repeatedly replacing her toddler's shoes while wrangling her other small children (Stewart 2015: 21). In Quiverfull literature, too, appeals to family and children are often more about family and children in theory than they are about any one *specific* child. They are of a piece with political oppositions to abortion which purport to protect the vulnerable and innocent but which are often signally dismissive of the ways in which many young women who have unplanned pregnancies have themselves been vulnerable and in need of support. Appeals to the mythic Child are, as Edelman has claimed, damaging to existence in the present, and to those who do not 'fit' the picture of what such an 'innocent' is supposed to look like. For Edelman, the correct response of queers is therefore to reject futurity and hope. But Edelman misses the fact that, in some respects, queer cannot help but to be generative. If Noreen Giffney (2008: 68) is right, then it is the existence of queerness that continually prompts heteronormativity to refresh itself, congratulating itself on what it is not. In Giffney's account, queer acts as a scapegoat, thereby unwittingly and willingly – and however much it resists assimilation into a heteronormative narrative – being part of the mechanism via which heteronormativity reproduces itself. Queer is *useful*.

How, then, might our queered, un/familiar institutions come to look? How do we recognize them as in continuity with what has come before, even as we also allow them their space to be and to grow into veritable newness of life?

Chapter 7

Un/familiar Institutions: Repetition and Difference

Jesus answered and said to him: 'Truly, truly I tell you: if anyone is not born again [born from above], it is not possible to enter the Kingdom of God'. Nicodemus said to him: 'How can someone be born when they are old? Surely it is impossible to go into their mother's womb a second time to be born again?'

(Jn 3.3–4, my translation)

Introduction

Anyone who travels regularly, has moved house frequently or for other reasons often finds themselves sleeping in unknown places will recognize the experience of waking in the night and feeling disoriented because the window, bedside table or other features of the room are not where one immediately expects to find them. I had such an experience recently, yet I was in my own bed, the one I had slept in for at least four-fifths of the nights over the previous year. I half-woke, and reached for the glass of water I keep next to me. The plot of at least one novel has rested on the fact that many of us know so well where this *should* be that we can find it in the dark and knock it back before we know what we have done (such that malicious antagonists, at least those who operate in the 1930s, might substitute poisonous substances such as hat paint in order to see us off).[1] I can't quite explain what happened on this night, but I found myself thinking, 'Things are in the wrong place … but this is my own room … so where does my brain think I am instead?' – and then mentally reconstructing the layout of various other bedrooms I had known to try to work out which one I'd been remembering instead. But all this eager thought had happened in the precise same five seconds during which I was flawlessly finding my glass, drinking my water and replacing the glass on the bedside table, all in the pitch blackness. I clearly *did* recognize where I was, and know where to find my drink, even though it seemed to me that I did not. I *thought* I hadn't found it where I expected to – but I had. I *thought* I expected myself to be in another bedroom – but I evidently didn't, given that I was able to drink my

---

1. See Agatha Christie's (1939) *Murder Is Easy*.

water at the same time as noting my internal monologue about the fact I didn't know where I was. So I both did and did not recognize my surroundings.

It seems to me that something of this kind is going on when we encounter phenomena or institutions – such as marriage, such as parenting – that appear to us to be changed. 'This doesn't seem quite right', we might say; 'this doesn't feel to me how I expect it to feel'. Yet we both know and do not know. We recognize these things as both like and unlike their other forms. The resemblances between marriage-as-we-have-known-it and parenting-as-we-have-known-it and their new forms are there. The essence or core of these relationships is not found in the *types* of individuals between whom they occur – except that these individuals are persons. And in their relationships of love they may also recognize as their own, as 'one of us', creatures whose personhood is doubtful or disputed – including those who die before they are born. These new forms of marriage and parenting, and these relationships with persons and disputed persons, are familiar and not familiar at the same time. They are like and unlike other families we have known. We both do and do not know where we stand in relation to them. They are un/familiar.

Orientation is not just 'having our bearings', knowing where we stand in relation to our objects of recognition: it is also turning *towards* certain things, giving our assent to their conceptual organizational power over our lives and their directions (Ahmed 2006: 1). We want to know where we are in relation to things that we understand and recognize (7) in order to work out how to feel at home amid circumstances which may trouble us. But, as Sara Ahmed notes, even getting lost tells us something about our spatial relationship to the things we do know. The space which we inhabit when we are lost is not nowhere (7); rather, it is simply space *unknown to us* – but which may be known to others. Everyone is a stranger somewhere; conversely, everyone has terrain on which they are the expert. Orienting ourselves is, notes Ahmed, about navigating the tension between the familiar and the unfamiliar: we can, as I have argued, find ourselves disoriented even in what should be familiar space. But our feelings of orientation, lostness and the rest are also impacted by how we *choose* to relate to space as known and unknown: do we focus on our feelings of anxiety, or focus instead on possibility and wonder? Do we assume unknown spaces to be oppressive and dangerous, or do we recognize them as *someone's* home turf if not (yet) our own? Thatcher, Browning and others give salient reminders that not *all* forms of families and parenting relationships may prove equally constructive for those who live in them; my project here is to question whether *any* given form may or should be assumed superior by default, and, indeed, how far apparent evidence that some forms of families work best is shored up by social, political and economic endorsements of only conservatizing patterns.

The ways we move in, respond to and order space also influence space itself. Spaces and bodies are mutually influential (Ahmed 2006: 9). Our individual and communal acts shape the space of the social (and the theological), impacting on what comes to be considered normative, natural and even possible. In considering the shifts that take place in human institutions, we might also therefore borrow imagery from epigenetics, the field of genetic science which describes the effects of environmental factors on cells and bodies, and the ways in which particular sets of genes are rendered active or passive in cells via the epigenome's response to environmental signals. The response of the epigenome, a layer of additional information attached to DNA, leads to differentiated cell types: cells 'remember' the information they have picked up earlier in their development via the enzymes which have become attached to them, in response to exposure to hormones and other chemicals. The implications of epigenetic research are increasingly making it more plausible that explanations for complex phenomena such as gender identity and sexual orientation should be sought not in asking whether the key is nature or nurture, but rather how nature and nurture *respectively* and *reciprocally* constitute and influence one another. The human genome is not static, fixed or unproblematically programmatic of the development of an organism: rather, it is part of an environmentally inflected process in which it is also a dynamic participant (Gagnier 2015). Epigeneticists note that environmental influences affect cells to the extent that altered traits are passed down despite the fact that actual DNA does not change: rather, the 'messages' contained in the epigenome continue to exist even in copies of the cells. Furthermore, and crucially, some epigeneticists now believe that these altered traits can be passed down not just between generations of cells in an individual's own body, but also to individuals' own biological offspring. In this way, we might say, sensory, emotional and motor experiences come to be written onto (and into) bodies.

Epigenetics is an emerging field which contains more unanswered questions than most, so I do not want to overstretch this image. Nonetheless, it is conceivable that epigenetics provides another way in to thinking about the mutually constituted nature of human beings and our environments (including our cultural contexts, which include institutions such as parenting and marriage). If we are not simply passive recipients of our genetic inheritances, but rather organisms in which genes shift and adapt in relation to environmental factors; and if human activity influences the chemical environment which in turn influences the human genome; then the human *Sitz im Leben* must inevitably be understood as being flexible and reactive as well as constitutive. Human development is open-ended.

This is important for understanding both the responsibility to and the freedom from our forebears which we enjoy – and which those who come after us will, in turn, have to and from us:

> Each generation, according to Kierkegaard, has the task of putting its most hallowed truths and values in question. Faith is the category through which the passionate individual (or the generation) approaches this task of creating itself anew. If a particular generation passively accepted the efficacy of the beliefs and practices of a previous generation, then it might have objective, disinterested knowledge of facts, but it would not have subjective truth or a passionate engagement with truth. The truths and values of one generation are always open to revision by succeeding generations. (Dooley 2001: 112–13)

Repetition and Difference

So un/familiar institutions, we might say, invoke both repetition and difference in relation to more familiar social and cultural forms. These exist in tension: neither the likeness nor the unlikeness is absolute. It is important that this should be so.

For Jacques Derrida, a word is never heard or read without invoking a trace of its opposite (Derrida 1976). The hint of this counterpart constantly destabilizes the authority of the original concept. Light is only meaningful as light because it is known to be the opposite of darkness, and its existence cannot help but highlight the absence of darkness; but this in turn threatens the status of light, since it always carries a sense that light is not ubiquitous. Derrida (1997: 297–8) remarks,

> The trace is not a presence but is rather the simulacrum of a presence that dislocates, displaces, and refers beyond itself. The trace has, properly speaking, no place, for effacement belongs to the very structure of the trace. ... Effacement establishes the trace in a change of place and makes it disappear in its appearing, makes it issue forth from itself in its very position.

Language gives the impression of being repeatable, and repeatedly efficacious: communication depends on commonality of definition, taking on trust that when one uses a word, one can summon forth the same concept as one did last time (and that one's interlocutor, having encountered it used in the same way, will understand).

Yet identical repetition is impossible; in Derrida's *Psyché*, language's inevitable mediation and unrepeatability is shown up, and Derrida 'draws emphatic attention to a certain forgetting that occurs in language, the forgetting that what is presented is in fact re-presented' (Ward 1995: 195). The Derridean notion of *différance* carries with it a double sense: deferral as well as differentiation. 'The word *différance* ... is suspended between differing and deferring', notes Stephen D. Moore (1994: 21). Ostensibly repeated words and ideas both *differ* from themselves (because the shade of meaning communicated on two separate occasions is never identical and never for exactly the same purpose) and *defer* fixity of meaning (because the 'final' or 'ultimate' meaning can never be reached, since all concepts are mediated by more words). This is a profoundly temporal account, acknowledging concepts' existence-in-time, and means, for Derrida, that we should be suspicious of any kind of originalism. We can never get back to a simple initial fixed meaning in language.

Something similar goes for the repetition-in-difference of religious ritual. The ceremonial celebration of Eucharist, for instance, is part of what defers arrival at the Body of Christ, for the Body is being changed even in the moment of participation: Gerard Loughlin (2003: 24) comments, 'In the liturgical celebration of the Lord's Supper, the Church participates in that creative work in which we are shown what the world could be like, what it will be like, and so, in some sense, is already, in the creation of Christ's bodily communion'. Celebration of and memorial to the Body of Christ is an institution (a genesis) as well as a commemoration. A religious symbol such as the sacrament of Eucharist, the consumption and dissemination of the body of Christ in order to nourish and perpetuate the Body of Christ, represents (re-presents) an event without itself becoming the sole instance of that event; to do the latter would be to negate the uniqueness and specificity of the original event – as well as of every Eucharist event which follows. This is a coincidence of old acts transformed by new realities (Stuart 2003: 108); it is improvisation which itself echoes and distils God's creative activity (Ford 1999: 144). If in the Eucharist we do not acknowledge that God is doing something new each time, we render the capacity of the sacrament to mediate grace static, fixed and incapable of exceeding our expectations.

And, I want to suggest, something similar goes for our relationships with un/familiar institutions too. Just as the Eucharist is therefore a mixture of old and new, so our new concepts of marriage and parenthood are familiar and unfamiliar. We recognize them and do not recognize them. They are related to the old concepts and yet not related. They are born of them and born from elsewhere (like Nicodemus, born again, born from above – γεννηθῇ ἄνωθεν or *gennēthē anōthen* – in Jn 3.3). (We might use the term *renewed* rather than *new* for this account of the fresh creation: it better reflects the term used elsewhere in the New Testament: *kainos*, as opposed to *neos* which does imply novelty. *Kainos*-newness is newness of quality or opportunity, not a complete rupture with past incarnations. *Kainos* is the new wineskins of Mt. 9.17; the new wine of the Kingdom in Mt. 26.29; the new covenant of Lk. 22.20, 1 Cor. 11.25, and Heb. 8–9; the new teaching invoked in Acts 17; the new human of Ep. 2 and 4; and, significantly, in 2 Pet. 3.13, the new heavens and the new earth.) We remake our institutions; they remake us. This is not (or not entirely) the departure Milbank envisages, for it is intimately associated with these institutions' genealogies. Interruption is not rupture; after all, 'what is interrupted does not cease to exist' (Boeve 2015), but also cannot continue on exactly as it did before. The repetition of a term like 'marriage' evokes older forms of the institution; it may also seem to evoke a cosmic norm of what lies behind the institution. However, this will be fictive. Fictive things have their own power and their own afterlives – as we have seen throughout the tradition of the theology of marriage – but the ground is unstable. We could never get back to a pre-existing form of marriage which was present prior to the people who have made it. Theological readings which deny that they are interpretative – which purport to connect directly and immaculately to real things in all their quiddity – simultaneously deny the *moreness* of concepts beyond language, and shut down the possibility of their organic growth. To say 'marriage has ever been thus' denies generativity: our own generativity in our capacity to make and remake concepts, and marriage's own generativity in its capacity to speak back to us, to be responsible. Responsibility requires agency. God is not marriage's bulldog, even if marriage has been that of the church and of various political parties and other social movements.

Why has the church been so keen to define how marriage may and may not licitly be understood (even if it often claims that what it is actually doing is defending an incontrovertible account of marriage which everyone already recognizes)?

Part of the answer is to do with discomfort stemming from the church's lack of recognition of its position on matters of morality and social organization post-Christendom. The church in the West, and notably in Britain, has not yet come to terms with its own marginality, which should render it an ally to other marginal communities and social forms but has not yet fully done so. Far from embracing its oddness – we might say its queerness – the church often continues to behave as though it is a dominant and authoritative conceptual presence, appealing to certainty rather than contingency. It is uncomfortable in recognizing the authority and licitness of structures beyond itself. But, as I have argued elsewhere (Cornwall 2014b), appearing irrelevant and powerless is precisely appropriate for a Christian community which acknowledges the topsy-turvy nature of power, success and influence in the Kingdom of God. Owning that it no longer has the authority, if it ever did, to define norms of marriage and family on behalf of others may be a painful process for the church, but it will be one which enables it to live more fully into its vocation of marginality and threat of extinction. As Gianni Vattimo (2002) has commented, the death of Christendom may precisely be understood as providential, a form of divine kenosis which allows space for disruptions of power and control.

But the church clings to the memory of its own cultural dominance. It others concepts and notions that it deems threatening without recognizing that, in doing so, it makes itself appear defensive and reactionary. Purported otherness, holds Luce Irigaray, is rarely really otherness at all, or we would have no way to understand it within the mental (or, better, psychic) organization of our world of the same. We need to be able to know what we are seeing in order to know what to call it, how to classify it. For Irigaray (1993), this non-otherness of otherness is an explanation for why dominant psychic and conceptual tropes stamp out recalcitrance: the dominant does not really want otherness at all, even when it tries to scapegoat and exclude. Actually, in doing so, it simply writes the other into its own logic, making it something controllable, apprehensible, explicable (97–8). Thus the church seeks to continue to determine what marriages and what family relationships may and may not look like.

Individual subjectivity is never really individual at all, claims Irigaray: as we have seen in Derrida, phenomena carry with them traces of what they have sought to erase, echoes of what they would like to have silenced. 'You/I: we are always several at once. And how could one dominate the other? impose her voice, her tone, her meaning? One cannot be distinguished from the other, which does not mean that they are indistinct' (Irigaray 1985b: 209). In Irigaray's conception, fear of the 'other' seems to be related to a fear of not being able to divide the 'self' from others, of not knowing where 'I' stop and 'you' begin (which is, for Irigaray, a peculiarly *masculine* fear). Again, part of this is to do with the church's struggle for self-understanding in a context where its social and cultural position has shifted relatively rapidly.

Milbank is right to say that we cannot understand marriage here and now without recognizing its genealogy, its connection to marriage of the past. Yet Milbank does not allow marriage of the past its space to be our natal mother, because he does not recognize that it is other than an unchanging, non-dynamic phenomenon. The Cartesian 'I' to which Irigaray reacts believes it gives *itself* existence, that it has control of everything, that it has simplified everything so that there is effectively nothing left to see but itself. However, says Irigaray, this illusion can only be held together as long as corporeality is denied; the subject-self wishes to believe it is self-sufficient, but this is to deny the importance of the natal maternal body to the psyche. Most mothers do not remain attached to their born children umbilically for very long: they usually cut or sever or chew through the cord so that children, in good time, may make their own way in the world. Marriages of the past are part of, but not all of, the natal maternal (institutional) body which informs the present-day theological psyche. Irigaray's (1985a: 234) appeal is to 'fluidity', such that 'the other can come into play in all kinds of ways providing that there is no imposition of rigid forms. ... For that inflexibility will always sever the exchange; fixing and freezing the apartness between the two into a *one*'. Appealing to a divine form of marriage or family prior to the actual marriages and actual families by which we recognize the terms means appealing to goods which have no connection to the histories of creaturely worlds. This is to miss out on recognizing what Muers (2007b: 126) terms the 'reproduction' within the tradition itself: 'the crossing-over, the conflicts and the unexpected interchanges of many traditions'; the theological statements which 'bear the traces of their multiple origins and cannot be resolved back into singular pure foundations'.

As we saw earlier in this book, the church frequently appeals to origins, to first principles and 'orders of creation', to justify and rationalize its own account of familial institutions. As I suggested in Chapter 1, this apotheosization of purported origins might be figured as a form of 'original sin'. But, as I hinted in Chapter 6, we might also be circumspect about 'originism' on other theological and philosophical grounds, such as theology's rightful orientation to eschatological ends. Consider, for example, the eschatological ontologism in scholars such as Wolfhart Pannenberg and John Zizioulas, for both of whom, in their different ways, reality is characterized not by what it has *been* but by what it will *become*. Beginnings are less significant than possibilities. Pannenberg may be more indebted to Hegel's Whiggish construction of history than is entirely comfortable post-Holocaust, post-9/11, post the rise of ISIS/Daesh and their aftermaths; but there is still something alluring about Pannenberg's assertion that things are most truly and veritably what they are inasmuch as they participate in their own futures, in what they are becoming. So the persistence of identity of a concept or institution is inherently eschatologically oriented. What things are is not fully known until the 'end' (and for Pannenberg, as for Hegel, it seems likely that this implies some kind of chronological end or climax; but we need not go all the way down that road with them): a zinnia plant over the whole period of its growth, even before it flowered, might licitly be understood as 'what it revealed itself to be at the end. It would possess its essence through anticipation, though only at the end of the developmental process would one be able to know that this was its essence' (Pannenberg 2001: 105; see also Pannenberg 1969).

Critics of Pannenberg, as of Hegel, might ask what this means for human (and other creaturely) becoming-in-freedom, and about the possible fatalism or antinormativity necessarily afforded to events. (They might also note that appeals to proto-being have been used to justify blanket oppositions to abortion of even the very earliest pre-embryos on the grounds that they are already just as much persons as the persons that they might, if all things were equal, become.) However, Pannenberg's strength here is precisely his resistance of the cult of the 'original': what matters eschatologically is the extent to which a thing contributes to and participates in the coming-into-being of the Kingdom (and, we might say, of God Godself, even if Pannenberg expresses this less frequently or explicitly than someone like the process-inflected Carter Heyward (in Heyward 1982: 172; 1984: 185)). For Zizioulas (2008), similarly in some respects, theology and the world are most properly determined by their ends, not by their beginnings. They are not determined by what they have been, but freed to become what they will be. Protology cannot override eschatology. What comes into being is determined by that towards which it is directed, that which it is becoming, not that which it has been in the past. This might, I suggest, be of importance in theologically reconceiving the extent to which concepts of marriage and parenting must be understood as in historical continuity with their erstwhile forms. If our direction, our orientation, our telos, is rightfully towards redeemed ends, we can perhaps afford to sit more lightly to our purported beginnings.

Nonetheless, unlike zinnia plants, linear chronology has deep roots, and its psychological–epistemological legacy is far-reaching. We are often disturbed by apparent discontinuities and ruptures, especially with regard to phenomena which have seemed particularly valuable or somehow untouchable as they are or were. The church, after all, is not, I think, entirely conscious that it is chasing its own shadow; rather, it usually operates with a conviction, borne of integrity and goodwill, that the family structures it recognizes and sanctions are those which are healthiest and most life-giving for children and for society at large. Its baptism of certain forms of these institutions is not arbitrary, but grounded in the belief that God gives what is best for God's creatures, and that the institutions of marriage and family which (many Christians devoutly believe) God has given therefore cannot be changed without detriment to everyone. Christian suspicions of, in our own age, same-sex marriages, or, in earlier ages, marriages after divorce, are ostensibly grounded not in a reactionary conservatism, but in a wish to promote what best makes for human flourishing. Furthermore, there is a conviction that changes to understandings of marriage and family mean too great a discontinuity with the forms which – the church holds – have proven themselves best able to promote such flourishing. Indeed, comments Catherine Pickstock (2013: 24), in any shift of forms there might come a time when a given iteration of a thing has moved so far from the thing that it is no longer recognizable as a version of it. This might be deemed problematic.

However, importantly, adds Pickstock, *just* as problematic will be an iteration of a thing that attempts so hard not to vary from the professed 'original' that it does not even recognize itself as a copy, but purports to be the original in its own right (25). This latter type of iteration denies that it is a repetition with difference; and it is precisely this which, I suspect, goes on in Christian appeals to marriage as incontrovertible and unchanging. For things to have relationships between one and another, there must be a recognition that they belong to a pattern, but also a recognition that each iteration is its *own* event (as with every new celebration of the Eucharist – institution as well as memorial, where 'remembrance' is both). Borrowing from the phenomenon of physical motion, Pickstock remarks, 'In order to stay the same, everything must move, since everything is in constant motion and adaptation. If it is to move, as a whole, through reality, and so preserve itself, a thing must move itself in order not to be rent away from itself' (30). Her reading of Plato is that it is precisely because *eidos* or form is eternal that we need not appeal to 'an idolatrous and absolutely fixed and unalterable repertoire of human myths, norms and customs' (90). I contend that the latter is exactly what marriages and families have become in much of the theological rhetoric which majors on their immutability. In actual fact, we can see in theologians spanning the range from John Henry Newman to Marcella Althaus-Reid, Benedict XVI to Linn Marie Tonstad, that stasis cannot be considered a desirable or even a default position for Christian theologians.

Furthermore, says Pickstock,

A newly emergent thing is not pre-contained in the past, like a hidden seed which must unfurl. ... The instructions of the seed ... have to be 'read' by the environment, and from this creative reading emerges something unprecedented. Yet, at the same time, this new and unprecedented thing is not something adjoined or appended, as if it were not in any way emergent from the past as its further development or refinement. For, if this were the case, the new thing could obtain no continuity or kinship with the past. (151)

For Pickstock – and for others, like Maurice Wiles, who critiqued the deterministic nature of the seed image before her – this means the necessity of attention to the past in order not to be doomed to repeat it 'in all its thinnest approximation to identity, and so in all its self-distortions' (153). Pickstock is more persuaded than I am that this means a reaching-back to Platonic essence, to an unreachable origin which nonetheless communicates itself to us (158). For it also means an appreciation of the new's newness: this is Pickstock's metaphor of the seed's interactions with its environment in order to produce something more than what was held 'within' it. It is in this sense that I am suggesting marriage, parenting and the rest are more than immaculate, immutable phenomena passed down to us: in fact, they are far more like dynamic, shapeable, interactive worlds.[2]

2. My nieces and nephews and their friends are currently enamoured of the computer game Minecraft. Minecraft is an 'open world' game: in the 'creative' mode, there is almost no limit to the structures and objects that the player can create using the various resources available. Like any computer game, it has its inevitable inbuilt boundaries: players can only

Now, it may seem that I am trying to claim two contradictory things at once. On the one hand, I seem to want to refute *a priori*, transcendent concepts of marriage or parenting which somehow precede and are independent of the human-made incarnations of these things. On the other hand, I seem to want to note that it is precisely in appealing to such 'beyonds' that hegemony may be resisted and human politicking relativized. In actual fact, however, I do not believe that these things are each other's opposites. For it is precisely in the recognition that marriage and parenting are *not* eternal or unchanging in their outworkings that we may also recognize that they chime with aspects of the divine nature while being appropriately, recognizably human-sized. There is space here to celebrate the good in human institutions without glossing over the ways in which traditionally sanctioned forms of marriage and family have *not* been life-giving or promoted human flourishing – and, indeed, have themselves perpetuated violence, exploitation and exclusion. In this way, what I am setting out here chimes with other theologies which have attempted to resist hegemony, notably those which have pointed out the artifice of theologies' totalizing tendencies.[3]

build so high up into the sky, for example, and although there are no firm constraints on where they may travel in the landscape, since each 'block' of landscape is virtually generated only as and when the player 'goes' there, nonetheless, if they venture too distantly into the 'far lands', the physics of the game may stop working properly. However, in a blog post from March 2011, Minecraft's designer Markus Persson (2011) noted that these problems would occur only when a player had travelled an in-game distance 'about 25% of the distance from where you are now to the sun', and that, to his knowledge, no player had yet travelled that far while playing the game 'legitimately' (i.e. without using cheats or hacks to transport themselves to another part of the gamescape without 'walking' there), and likely never would. A game of Minecraft involves interaction between the player and their environment: in every new game, a brand new world is generated by the game's algorithms in response to where the player travels. The player can also build upon, mine into, craft and otherwise adapt the landscape that has been generated for them, thereby altering it and shifting how the algorithm will generate the next part.

3. This is, for example, something like Tim Gorringe's (2004: 118–20) account of theology as anti-hegemonic (see also Gorringe 1999), which is itself echoed in postcolonial appeals – in Joerg Rieger (2007a, 2007b), in Ched Myers (2008) and others – to a theological 'surplus' or 'over-againstness' which will not be delimited by human ideology. Aspects of the Christian tradition exercise resistance to being written too unproblematically into the agendas of those in charge. The scriptural witness is always other than 'the deafening clamours of conflicting ideologies' (Gorringe 2004: 120), and thus testifies to the fact that God also cannot be subsumed to any one human ideology. Similarly, for Kosuke Koyama, theology becomes ideology when it loses the dimension of the strange paradox and makes a claim that it is at the centre, thus pushing aside the living and dynamic God (Koyama 1985: 100). A centre complex makes people incapable of engaging in critical self-examination; ideologized theology is theology in captivity to a centre complex. What can stop theology from falling into ideology? The acknowledgement that God is always already other than,

Born Again/born from Above

Marriage's being 'born from above', then, does not mean that it descends as an immaculate theological object. Rather, it is born and reborn – as are those who make and remake it – in dialogue with its own history. Discussing rebirth as spoken via the mouthpiece of Kierkegaard's Johannes Climacus, Mark Dooley (2001: 76) comments,

> The individual who is reborn, according to Climacus, is not someone who comes into existence for the first time, but someone who has a history, who lives and resides as all individuals do in the concrete milieu of everyday affairs. The difference is, however, that this individual has 'taken up' the past, has come to a more comprehensive understanding of it by having performed a critical diagnosis of his or her relationship to the world in which he or she is embedded. We could say that repetition is rethinking the past from the point of view of the future.

Doing a new thing is therefore not about denying or jettisoning what has come before. It is, rather, about refiguring it in conscious dialogue with what has subsequently come to be. In Kierkegaard's *Repetition* (whose fictional narrator is Constantin Constantius) and *Philosophical Fragments* (voiced by Johannes Climacus), repetition is a kind of recollection, but one which faces forward, not backward, in time (Dooley 2001: 78). Here, repetition is not simply the recovery of something static: it necessitates cognition of the process of 'gradual and painstaking becoming' (80). Truth is therefore not recollected as such – in the sense of being summoned up – but rather discerned, which – for Climacus – happens only when it has been recognized that it was not formerly something which the individual could have grasped (81; Kierkegaard 1985 [1844]: 13–15). Repetition is therefore 'the process of being born to the world as a responsible and vigilant self through the intervention of God' (Dooley 2001: 100). And, crucially, therefore, 'To believe … is to attest to the fact that, as existing individuals, we

and more than, our most beloved theological goods. Jesus is crucified, and God dwells, with the crucified, at the periphery. Theology reflects on a broken Christ, so must itself be understood as fragmentary, provisional, preliminary, penultimate. For Rieger (2007a: 1), 'One of the key purposes of the study of Christian theology in the context of empire has to do with a search for that which cannot be co-opted by empire, and which thus inspires alternatives to empire, based on … a "theological surplus."' Rieger (2007b: 9) identifies this 'theological surplus' as 'related to not fitting in and being in touch with that which hurts'. Jesus, who exceeds the status quo, sees things that cannot be seen from the 'top' of the system. The theological surplus is also, simultaneously, Christological: 'Christ … not only holds up a mirror to the status quo but also creates a Christological surplus that cannot be captured by this reality and thus points beyond it' (10).

are not inextricably bound to the past, that it can be rethought and re-created through originality of action – what we have been calling "repetition"' (102). The past is not immediate to us, not directly graspable by us; moreover, and crucially for Climacus, the past could always have been another way. Just as the choices we make now influence which of a range of possible futures will come into being, so the past is also contingent: things need not have been that way. Things could have been otherwise. They have *come to be*: they were not *always* thus, therefore they are (were) not *necessarily* thus. Says Dooley:

> To be truly responsible, for Kierkegaard, is to affirm the possibility of imagining otherwise, of calling into question what has been traditionally celebrated as truth, reason, ethics, and community with a view to making each of these structures own up to its contingent configuration. To lack the infinite, or the capacity to envision situations otherwise, is to adhere to what [Kierkegaard's pseudonym Anti-Climacus][4] calls a purely 'secular view', one asserting that the established order (which comes into being from a general conflation of the past with a divine plan) is the concrete manifestation of truth. (107)

In Anti-Climacus, Kierkegaard represents a voice which recognizes humans' indubitable influence by other persons and institutions, but refuses to accept that we are therefore imprisoned by them. Anti-Climacus figures humans as able to interact critically with our institutions and social structures, 'to momentarily

---

4. While Johannes Climacus and Anti-Climacus do represent different perspectives for Kierkegaard, they are not as diametrically opposed as their names may suggest. Johannes Climacus, the secularist, is suspicious of so-called objective truths which ride roughshod over the individuals who have no access to channels of welfare (those whom Gayatri Chakravorty Spivak would characterize as subalterns). Anti-Climacus is far more persuaded than Johannes Climacus that truth and goodness come about in direct relation to God, but he, too, is deeply critical of those who would maintain the status quo for their own advantage. Kierkegaard initially warned readers against assuming any of the pseudonyms' perspectives were unproblematically his own, but, comments David Law (2010: 24), 'By speaking so much of himself in the *Point of View* and also apparently attempting to impose an "authoritative" explanation on the aesthetic authorship. … Kierkegaard would seem to be doing precisely what he warns readers against in "A First and Last Exposition," namely, encumbering the reader with his personal actuality and imposing his own view of authorship on the reader'. Law suggests that this is, in part, because of Kierkegaard's apparent growing belief that the true author of his works was God, and that God alone was aware of the significance of the perspectives of the various different voices (32–3). This 'authorial death' may thus be understood as a form of perceived 'martyrdom' on Kierkegaard's part (Hughes 2010: 208). For many Kierkegaard scholars, it remains unclear to what extent Kierkegaard is playing a game with readers in his use and analysis of the multiple authorial viewpoints (Law 2010: 47).

suspend our affiliation with such frameworks so as to render them more applicable to the demands of the age' (11).

Repetition, then, is never absolute. It is always tempered by discontinuity, by difference. It is necessary and appropriate that this should be so. And, indeed, for Marcella Althaus-Reid, such rejection of repetition like-for-like is a key queer theological task, precisely the vocation of a faith in solidarity with the weak and despised. Why? Althaus-Reid (2003: 51) holds, 'In theology, to repeat can be associated with many modern habitual trappings, such as those into which "theologies at the margin" may fall when they become simply attempts to induce oppressed multitudes to invest their identities in the centre-defined theological exercise by a simple economy of inclusion'.[5]

Per Althaus-Reid, queer theology rests in an 'unhabituated grace' (51). Keeping structures and epistemologies effectively the same while simply changing the personnel will not do: so, we might say, introducing same-sex marriage does not, in its own right, do enough to query the logics of ownership and economic control by which – in some accounts – marriage has operated in the past (which is similar to the anti-futurist argument that Edelman wants to make – and, of course, for Edelman (2004: 31), 'the future is mere repetition and is just as lethal as the past'). For this reason, many people, including many gay people, have spoken out against the good of 'extending' marriage to same-sex couples (see the essays collected in Conrad (2010)). The argument is that, where marriage perpetuates exclusion and marginalization (as, for example, in contexts where marriage affords privileged access to healthcare), its expansion to same-sex couples will not change its broader exclusionary patterning.

Indeed, Kathryn Bond Stockton (2014) has incisively demonstrated the potency of the multivocal nature of queer persons' responses to calls for marriage equality. On the one hand, she holds, it is important that queer people continue to resist marriage, to stand outside it: 'Someone's gotta say: "marriage shall not get the credit for our love."' On the other, there might be good reasons for doing constructively deconstructive work from the inside: as she notes, and as I have pronounced throughout this volume, marriage has always been changing – it did not take LGBT people to do it. Nonetheless, she adds,

> Will we change marriage, we queer folk? Will we insert our *beyond* inside it? …
> Of course we'll change marriage. If we're lucky! If the queers I so respect, I so adore, I so celebrate for their new marriages – thank you for marrying, someone had to do it, someone had to grasp the equality we're asking for – if these folks have their marriages upheld, marriage overall has the chance to become more sex variant, more trans-rich, more divorce-friendly, and, dare I say, more replete with kissing.

---

5. I am grateful to Linn Marie Tonstad for drawing this passage to my attention.

But this will not in itself, she suggests, do all the work there is to do: 'Marriage, as you know, is not a good way to get crucial benefits delivered to people; to make lives secure; to break up dyads; to end the grip of racism; and marriage perhaps is not a good way to redistribute wealth' (Stockton 2014). For this reason, she points to the significance of what we might call *action in the meantime*, where the 'time' in question is not prior to, but related in more oblique fashion to, an 'equal future'. Tying calls for equality to calls for rights is, she hints, inadequate: first, because of the raced and gendered inflection that rights discourses have often had (human rights are all very well, but if someone can construct you as less-than-human, your rights suddenly become less incontrovertible than you might have wished (cf. Loughlin 2004: 79; Williams 2009); moreover, if being allowed on board the marriage train merely makes you more like those whom marriage has traditionally privileged, maybe you would rather walk); and second, because rights language is too easily dismissed by detractors as shrill self-aggrandizement on the parts of uppity queers. Why not, suggests Stockton, cede the language of rights, and call for equality *not* from a position of belonging and inclusion, but from a position of continued exile? Why not campaign for marriage equality for all couples *while simultaneously* working to show the potential of the radical justice of other kinds of lives that do not look like traditional marriage? After all, homonormativity – per Lisa Duggan (2002: 190), expanding access to 'a few conservatizing institutions' but without disrupting their exclusivity or propensity to be written into neoliberal agendas – is troubling as heteronormativity is, if not in quite the same ways.

This is a salient juxtaposition of ideas as we consider to what extent it might be possible to re-pattern and remake marriage along truly revolutionary lines. There is one sense in which marriage is, indeed, exclusive: it sets up a relationship where the spouses are covenanted to each other in a way different from that in which they may be involved in pledges with others (e.g., via professional contracts, holy orders or associations such as fraternities). Even in contexts of actual polygynous or polyandrous or theoretical polyamorous marriage, the partners are legally bonded to one another in a way that they are not to outsiders. The question is whether it is such exclusivity in itself which is problematic, or whether it is its concomitants that are problematic. For example, in a context where there are no financial benefits for married partners, there are also no inevitable financial disadvantages for unmarried ones. Where an unmarried partner may be nominated and recognized as next of kin, partners who are not married need not be edged out. Where children born to unmarried spouses are not considered 'illegitimate', there is no particular need to ensure their 'legitimacy'. More slippery are the types of actual or perceived benefit that marriage has had socially: respectability, recognition, the sense of a rite of passage to full adulthood. And more unambiguously troubling are echoes of models of marriage involving woman and children as chattels. How far is it possible, or desirable, to remake marriage without these associations?

It is possible and not possible. These things are part of marriage's history and will remain so. But it is also possible to model other ways.[6]

Openness and Disidentification in Un/familiar Institutions

Rachel Muers (2007b: 127) holds that theology must be eschatological because the 'attempt to control the future of theology' is not a properly theological project. More emphatically, for Moltmann (1967: 25), eschatology is the key in which all theology must be set, for eschatological hope is the only thing which truly 'takes seriously the possibilities with which all reality is fraught'. It refuses to accept the status quo, or to hold that the way we see now is all there is. So might there be, in theological terms, space, openness for a kind of futurity which is not just repetition of what has come before? For Edelman, the very project of futurity is

---

6. For example, we might ask what the principle of consent necessary for marriage to be validly contracted means throughout the whole life of the marital relationship. Marriage requires consent; once the marriage has been legally established, it is assumed that consent has been established too. But in other contexts, consent must continue to be freely given. The recognition in law of the possibility of marital rape, for example, acknowledges that having given consent to marry does not also entail having given consent for every act of sexual intercourse thereafter. I suggest, therefore, that, at such time as the spouses no longer give their consent to the continuation of the marriage, the relationship has already changed – has already, in some sense, ceased to be a marriage. Legally, it is necessary to go through a procedure to have this formally recognized, because of the financial and other implications that marriage has as a legal institution. But what is the case theologically? If the spouses have withdrawn their consent to the marriage after it has been established, in what sense does the marriage continue to exist? If, as for Peter Lombard, the fact of marriage is established by mutual consent to conjugal fellowship as equals, rather than by consummation (marriage entails 'the marital union of man and woman, between legitimate persons, which places a limit upon the individual habit of life' (Peter Lombard, *Book of Sentences*, book IV, distinction 27; qtd in Rosemann 2004: 176); in other words, neither spouse is at liberty to do things incompatible with 'conjugal fellowship'), then continued consent seems relevant – although Lombard assumed that once mutual consent had been given, the bond formed in marriage was permanent and indissoluble. Furthermore, we might add, the spouses' sacramentality – their capacity to mediate grace to one another in and through their marriage – might also end. There are various necessary caveats to my argument. For example, there are complications raised by mental illness and intellectual disability which sets in after the marriage has been embarked upon. Someone may become intellectually incapable of continuing to give active consent to their marriage, but this does not mean that the marriage should be assumed to have ended. In this case, until there is evidence to the contrary, it should be assumed that the individual continues to accede to the arrangement into which they entered freely when they were capable of consenting to do so.

inseparable from the heterosexual (and heteronormative) procreative futurism, but I want to suggest that it is possible to conceive (see how ubiquitous this language of generation is) of an interrupted and i(nte)rruptive future that does not rest in the repetition of the same. In this way, futurity need not be understood as advancement, as linear forward trajectory or as displacement of the vulnerable here and now. Non-identical repetition might be deemed particularly queer when, as so often, it tends to parody (Stuart 2003: 108): parody entails not (only) the perverse tearing down of the precious, but the tearing down of norms of perversion and preciousness too. As Moltmann (1967: 21) reminds us, 'Faith, wherever it develops into hope, causes not rest but unrest, not patience but impatience. ... Those who hope in Christ can no longer put up with reality as it is, but begin to ... contradict it'. There is hope and faith for something more.

This acknowledgement of continuity and discontinuity – the acknowledgement that the kinds of marriage and parenting and family we are coming to know now are both like and unlike those we have known before – might be understood further as a form of catachresis. Catachresis, misuse or misapplication, is, per Stephen D. Moore, following Gayatri Chakravorty Spivak's usage, 'the process by which the colonized strategically appropriate and redeploy specific elements of colonial or imperial culture or ideology. As such, it is a practice of resistance through an act of usurpation' (Moore 2006: 37; cf. Spivak 1991: 70). I also appreciate Halberstam's explanation, possibly borrowed from Tavia Nyong'o: catachresis is when we use an imperfect, inadequate word knowingly but precisely because no better word exists, such that the very act of using it destabilizes both the thing and its others, and thereby itself becomes an act of resistance.[7] 'Heterosexual marriage' and 'same-sex marriage' are both what I am calling special cases, and are, in a sense, both forms of catachresis. One is not inherently 'closer' or 'more faithful' than the other to an 'original form' of marriage. It is, after all, in the usage that a term like 'marriage' is made meaningful at all.

Similarly, the term 'family' exceeds that to which it is often simplified. Could it be that, like 'butch' in Halberstam's (2015) formulation, a term like 'family' 'serves as a placeholder for the unassimilable, for that which remains indefinable or unspeakable within the many identifications that we make and that we claim'? Might it, like 'butch', exist as 'all that cannot be absorbed into systems of signification, legitimation, legibility, recognition and legality' (Halberstam 2015)? Halberstam might refute this, on the grounds that this recalcitrance is *particular* to the threatened and unarticulable history of butch, and that the use of this characterization to refer to something like the family is just a straight cis person's colonization of it. I would be sympathetic to that kind of response; yet I still want to insist precisely that terms like marriage and parenting and family do *not* belong to straight and non-trans people any more than to anyone else, and that there

7. 'The butch is neither cis-gender nor simply transgender, the butch is a bodily catachresis. The Greek word, catachresis, means the rhetorical practice of misnaming something for which there would otherwise be no words' (Halberstam 2015).

is something important in the recognition that they exceed their definitions by church authorities (who, as we have seen, clamour that they are *not* defining what does and does not constitute marriage, but rather that they are merely pointing to something prior to any human definition at all). But I am also not, despite the pastoral and practical importance for many people of legal recognitions of same-sex marriage and the rights of non-biological parents to be recognized as parents, exhorting just unproblematically expanding the bounds of these terms to bring more sheep into the fold: as Halberstam (2015) says, 'We need a reminder that recognition is NOT freedom, that the absorption of the few at the expense of many others is not liberation and that the illegible, the unassimilable, the inconsolable, the illegitimate multitudes still await a coming emancipation'. And, indeed, there are other exclusions that go along with 'arrival' and 'recognition', as when those who have become parents (by adoption or otherwise) believe that they and only they, unlike all non-parents, truly understand the meanings of care and sacrifice, or that they have 'arrived' as legitimate adults and members of society in a way that non-parents have not.

What I want to suggest is, then, closer to what Muñoz (1999: 11–12) terms 'disidentification':

> Disidentification is the third mode of dealing with dominant ideology, one that neither opts to assimilate within such a structure nor strictly opposes it; rather, disidentification is a strategy that works on and against dominant ideology. Instead of buckling under the pressures of dominant ideology (identification, assimilation) or attempting to break free of its inescapable sphere (counteridentification, utopianism), this 'working on and against' is a strategy that tries to transform a cultural logic from within, always laboring to enact permanent structural change while at the same time valuing the importance of local or everyday struggles of resistance.

This is one reason why I do not exhort walking away from marriage as a concept, and am not persuaded that simply refusing everything about the institution is the best form of resistance to its excesses and inadequacies and violations. And it is why I am suggesting that our un/familiar institutions might be understood as just that: familiar and not; part of the family history and not; perhaps, at least in part, redeemable, but without denying, glossing over or apologizing for their bad behaviour.

Interrupted and i(nte)rruptive futures that do not rest in the repetition of the same are, then, profoundly eschatological. They recognize both rupture and connection, ending and endurance. Eschatology is anti-linear: it insists that whatever is to come colours and shapes what already is. It is ahead, but it is not bound by the now and already (Moltmann 1967: 10–26). Eschatologically inflected futurity therefore also need not be understood as advancement, or as a subsuming of the goods of the present to putative goods yet to come.

That said, and however embedded the eschatological is in the relationships of the present world, it also stands over against them. In recognizing multiplicities of marriage, parenting and family, we need the kind of 'impossibility thinking' that Judith Butler (2004: 29) invokes when she speaks of fantasy, saying that its promise is challenging the limits of what can be understood as the real: 'Fantasy is what allows us to imagine ourselves and others otherwise; it establishes the possible in excess of the real; it points elsewhere, and when it is embodied, it brings the elsewhere home'. And this is surely eschatological, in the sense that the eschaton is a future which exists and yet does not exist, which happens towards a given telos but which is also brightly, profoundly open and unfixed. The 'elsewhere' of the eschaton is simultaneously a real 'elsewhere' beyond this realm; an 'elsewhere' and 'otherwise' already nascent *within* this realm; and an 'elsewhere' which *shapes* the here and there of the opening future. The fantastic, in Butler's terms, is not a utopian no-place, but a possibility for the not-yet and the not-ever-before-like-this to shape the what-will-be. The fantastic is not the opposite of the real, but rather its fuzzy edge, its near future, the expanding boundary of reality itself (29). And while we might call 'new' forms of family and marriage and (in Butler's specific example) gender 'new', in actuality we do so only because our lexicon has not before managed to acknowledge that they 'have been in existence for a long time, but they have not been admitted into the terms that govern reality' (31). And so part of the reason why the new recognition of the not-new matters is because it is in and through such recognition that there is a public endorsement of the expansive nature of the real (for we function as social creatures in time, and require recognition by others (cf. Butler 2004: 32)). This is the moment of political recognition of the reality of multiple marriages and families.

What, then, does it mean to be those who find their meaning beyond themselves; whose ultimate reality and most profound truth is situated not in themselves but 'eccentrically' (Kelsey 2009)? To be those who are born from above recurs in the Johannine writings as a metaphor for the believers. They are said to be 'born from God', to be 'children of God'. As Judith Lieu notes, the linguistic construction in John's writings is significant: birth *from* or *out of* God, with the implication of God's active role in generation or begetting, is marked out here from other New Testament instances of God's being described as 'Father' (which might, as Lieu (2008: 119–20) notes and as I discussed in Chapter 5) be taken to allow for adoptive rather than biological relationship; and from Hebrew Bible texts such as Is. 1:2–4 and Jer. 3.14 where the emphasis is on care rather than on 'consanguinity' (Lieu 2008: 121). While in Jn 1.13, 1 Jn 2.29 and elsewhere, the believers are described as having been born from or out of God, this construction is more commonly used to refer to the *mother's* role in generation (Lieu 2008: 120). As Lieu notes, it is not clear in 1 John whether those who are 'born of God' are born of God spontaneously and regardless of their own activity, or whether coming to be 'born of God' is a reward for the obedient (122) – however, she concludes, 'For those uncertain of their status in the face of the expectation of a divine coming … and for whom divine justice might generate the anxiety of shame (2:28), there is a reassurance that being brought into a relationship with God is as irreversible as is birth' (122). This is not about a future hope, or about a change in status; it is 'a declaration of what is irrefutably the case' (123). Those born of God *cannot sin* (1 Jn 3.9), for God's 'seed' (*sperma*) remains in them: whether the term 'seed' here refers to Christ as the 'offspring' of God who abides in the believers, or to something of God's seed implanted directly in the believers themselves is debatable (Lieu 2008: 137–8). But, for Lieu, the significance is, again, in the permanence either way: 'God's relationship to those born from God is not simply one of generation and origin but continues ("indwells" …) to be effective. … Being born from God means to continue to be vivified by God's creative power: such birth cannot be lost or abrogated' (138).

What does all this mean? It means that the believers' futures are always, and irrevocably, to do with an ongoing, abiding divine faithfulness. For the author of 1 John, it is significant that the believers' status as children of God cannot change; however, this does not, I think, mean that there can be no volition on the parts of these 'children' to walk away from what might be deemed their inheritance. Those born of God have, like God their womb and umbilicus, the quality of making new; yet they may choose not to live into this bequest, and God as mother chews through the cord to let them make their own way (but no more refuses ongoing relationship at the children's behest than most human mothers would). Unlike God, as humans we do not *have* to generate. We may choose not to do so. We may choose to limit our interactions with and influence over the natals who are coming and are to come. I have been suggesting throughout this book that, while biological procreation is not everyone's vocation, generativity in its broader sense is a universal calling. Nonetheless, God does not compel us to live into this work.

Conclusion: Ἰδοὺ καινὰ ποιῶ πάντα (Idou kaina poiō panta)

καὶ ἤκουσα φωνῆς μεγάλης ἐκ τοῦ θρόνου λεγούσης· ἰδοὺ ἡ σκηνὴ τοῦ θεοῦ μετὰ τῶν ἀνθρώπων, καὶ σκηνώσει μετ᾽ αὐτῶν, καὶ αὐτοὶ λαοὶ αὐτοῦ ἔσονται, καὶ αὐτὸς ὁ θεὸς μετ᾽ αὐτῶν ἔσται [αὐτῶν θεός], καὶ ἐξαλείψει πᾶν δάκρυον ἐκ τῶν ὀφθαλμῶν αὐτῶν, καὶ ὁ θάνατος οὐκ ἔσται ἔτι οὔτε πένθος οὔτε κραυγὴ οὔτε πόνος οὐκ ἔσται ἔτι, [ὅτι] τὰ πρῶτα ἀπῆλθαν. Καὶ εἶπεν ὁ καθήμενος ἐπὶ τῷ θρόνῳ· ἰδοὺ καινὰ ποιῶ πάντα. (Rev. 21:3–5a, Nestle-Aland 28th edition)

And I heard a great voice from the throne, saying, 'Behold![8] The tent of God is among humans. God will camp with them, and they will be God's people, and God will be with them. And God will blot out every tear from their eyes. Death will not be,[9] nor mourning, nor crying, nor toil; the things of before have gone away'. And the one sitting on the throne said, 'Remember![10] I make everything new. I do everything anew'. (Rev. 21.3–5a, my translation)

---

8. As we look we *hold* the other in our vision as we are *held* in theirs.

9. Death will not *be*: that is, death will not exist; yet in English we often stutter over a construction of this kind, expecting the verb to be transitive, and ask, 'Death will not be *what*?' This butting-up against unexpected contentlessness is, I contend, itself evocative of the putative non-existence of death.

10. The act of looking is also an act of making and remaking, memorial and remembering.

However originist we may purport to be, we cannot get back to a time before we knew: knew concrete marriages, knew concrete families, knew the kinds of things we have learnt to understand by these labels. We may say we recognize marriages as being of a piece (or not) with what God has given. But recognizing is not just apprehending something we already knew: it is also recognizing, thinking again and (by association) knowing anew. It is, in Ahmed's terms, conscious and active orientation to our objects of desire. Reconnaissance, which has the same root as recognition, is often associated with surveying the terrain in the interests of espionage or warfare; but recognizing need not carry such combative implications. If we say that we know what God has given in marriage because it chimes with the prior conception of marriage we somehow knew before we ever knew concrete *marriages*, then we devalue the humanness of this institution. What is human-made need not be understood as merely a pale imitation of what is divinely created. Creaturely generativity itself is in continuity, as well as discontinuity, with the divine quality of generativity. God gives creatures the creativity and freedom to make and remake, build and remodel; this is the making (new), the doing (anew), the *poiesis* which is also poetry, and which therefore has its afterlives, its meanings which float beyond the grasp of authorial intent to make their own ways in the world. Newness is not, as Byatt (1995: 131) understands, a disavowal of all that is past:

> Art is not the recovery of the innocent eye, which is inaccessible. 'Make it new' cannot mean, set it free of all learned frames and names, for paradoxically it is only a precise use of learned comparison and the signs we have made to distinguish things seen or recognised that can give the illusion of newness. … One cannot think at all without a recognition and realignment of ways of thinking and seeing we have learned over time. We all remake the world as we see it, as we look at it. … Even the innocent eye does not simply receive light: it acts and orders. And we always put something of ourselves – however passive we are as observers, however we believe in the impersonality of the poet, into our descriptions of the world, our mapping of our vision.

This is why un/familiar kinds of family and marriage need not be understood as hollow simulacra of their 'original' forms. Neither are they what Baudrillard calls the specific simulacra of the postmodern age, wherein we determine 'reality' only by the phenomena in front of us now. Things are more complex than that. The marriages and families we know and create can never exist in complete distinction from their genealogy, the history of their manifestations in human culture. But I wonder whether the rejection on theological grounds of un/familiar institutions comes, at root, not from a fear that they are *distortions* of the real, rejections of the uniquely God-given, but, rather, from a fear that their very multiplicity and seeming pluripotence exposes the *lack* of an *a priori* version. Baudrillard (1994: 5) posits that iconoclasts repudiate icons not because these 'obfuscate' or 'mask' the true God, but because perhaps they do not:

> One can live with the idea of distorted truth. But [the iconoclasts'] metaphysical despair came from the idea that the image didn't conceal anything at all, and that these images were in essence not images, such as an original model would have made them, but perfect simulacra, forever radiant with their own fascination.

What if there were, indeed, nothing to our familial institutions but what we had made them, for better or (just as often) for worse? What if we could not hand off the blame, or refuse ownership of our own power and that of our ancestors in them? What a dizzying responsibility that would be.

Every act of looking is an act of ordering the world. We organize what is in our frame of vision so as to understand it, to apprehend it – and, therefore, simultaneously to put ourselves in its power and to exercise power over it. We can look to our institutions – to our models of parenting, of family, of marriage – and seek to place ourselves under their power (as we do when we say, 'Marriage just *is* between one man and one woman – it's not for us to redefine it'). Alternatively, we can seek power over them and try to wipe out their inconvenient histories (as we do when we say, 'Marriage was never *really* about property and ownership of chattels – that was an unfortunate distortion, and marriage is actually something egalitarian with which everyone can and should be happily on board'). Or, we can do yet a new thing, and carry them forward in continuity and discontinuity, as we do when we ask: What gives space for growth and life? What gives space to ask why growth and life are goods anyway, and to interrogate whether the growth and life of some necessarily takes place at others' expense? Or when we ask: Who are the ones in this situation who need safety and protection? Must their protection be at the expense of that of others? Which others? Or when we ask: If a key to life-affirming institutions is the promotion of goods such as flourishing and the nurturing of potential, what multiplicitous ways might there be to do that, and how might we endorse institutions and anti-institutions which do that, even if they do not look quite like what we have formerly known? Or when we say: What, if anything, might it be necessary to jettison although we have held it dear, in order to do a new thing – not because it is new, but because it is right? Judith Butler (2004: 35), in discussing the recognition of multiplicitous modes of gender – which means, in practice, the recognition of the *humanity* of those whose gender has formerly been rendered unspeakable – puts it like this:

> How might we encounter the difference that calls our grids of intelligibility into question without trying to foreclose the challenge that the difference delivers? What might it mean to learn to live in the anxiety of that challenge, to feel the surety of one's epistemological and ontological anchor go, but to be willing, in the name of the human, to allow the human to become something other than what it is traditionally assumed to be? This means that we must learn to live and to embrace the destruction and rearticulation of the human in the name of a more capacious and, finally, less violent world, not knowing in advance what precise form our humanness does and will take.

The response of violence is, she notes, the one that 'wants to shore up what it knows, to expunge what threatens it with not-knowing, what forces it to reconsider the presuppositions of its world, their contingency, their malleability' (35). It is ironic indeed that a Christian tradition which has had space to urge apophaticism and not-knowing, which purports to say that God may not be tied down, has so often also sought to demarcate and delineate what may and may be done via 'God-given', 'God-ordained' institutions.

I am emphatically not trying to be ahistoricist. Indeed, I am acutely aware of what Mark D. Jordan (2002: 1–2) notes, namely that there can be no theological talk about marriage and sexuality which does not invoke (silently or otherwise, wittingly or otherwise) a whole library of older talk.[11] And it is in talking to and with our ancestors that we dignify them by insisting on their accountability, by noting that the things they said and did have consequences that continue to the present day. To be sure, their words and speeches and writings have their own afterlives beyond their creators' control, but we can also say to our ancestors: look what happened! Could you have predicted this? How would you have felt if you had? Would you have behaved any differently? If you would not, what is it about being a person of your time that means you would stand by what you did then? What might that tell me about what it is to be a person of my own time and the consequences, foreseen and unforeseen, that will stem from my actions and inactions now? Indeed, it is by insisting on our ancestors' responsibility, and holding them accountable, that we remain in conversation with – keep faith with – those other counter-voices which did critique or resist them at the time but which were libelled in or redacted from the official histories.

Drawing on her experiences growing up in a migrant family, Sara Ahmed (2006: 10) says, 'What I remember … are not so much the giddy experiences of moving and the disorientation of being out of place, but the ways we have of settling: that is, of inhabiting spaces that, in the first instance, are unfamiliar but that we can imagine – sometimes with fear, other times with desire – might come to feel like home'.

Ahmed notes that the process of coming to feel at home is not always clear or evident until after the fact, when we can look back and trace *how* we have arrived

11. 'Every new speech about Christian sexual ethics comes out of a library of older speeches. Before you speak Christian theology, you have already heard it. You have attended to the words of some scripture, of a local community, of authoritative individuals, of a denominational position or tradition. These words will repeat themselves in what you try to say. Indeed, many Christian speakers claim to do nothing more than repeat exactly what they have been taught (a claim that merits another exercise of suspicion). Others unwittingly repeat as their own clips of older speech. Christian speeches about sex are full up with terms, images, arguments, and rules recorded from older speeches. These clips are remixed to produce new speech, which is sometimes music, sometimes cacophony. So speakers must be suspicious about how they are repeating what they have heard' (Jordan 2002: 1–2).

at inhabiting a particular space or outlook. Moreover, orientations to objects and institutions are inherited: we are initiated into ways of seeing, knowing, acting and feeling towards them (86). It seems to me that the process is at least double: we live with the strange for a season, and, often, the very propinquity over time lessens the strangeness. Simultaneously, though, there is value in re-mystification: sometimes we need to be reminded that the things which we take for granted are actually things which should, by rights, disturb and provoke us, because they are violent or unjust. It is this doubling which is, I am suggesting, at the heart of un/familiar theology: living with the strange until it no longer seems strange, and reclaiming the strangeness of the familiar (which might mean the injustices and inadequacies of even faultlessly ideal 'Christian marriages' and 'Christian families'). Crucially, this 'making strange' is not the purview only of professional theologians (as Milbank (1997: 1) seems to hint). Neither is it to be found only, as Milbank also hints (1), in the machinations of the church. It is the vocation of all who wrestle with working out what our authorities and institutions tell us about ourselves and our relationships with God and our world. This means space for excess beyond the bounds of what the church has understood itself to be and the institutional (and familial) forms it has seen fit to sanction.

For Milbank (1997: 130), it is the fact that as humans we cannot entirely control what we make of our social institutions and cultural products that means there is space for God to meet us in them. We cannot entirely possess or control even that which we have created: this is the afterlife, this is the artistic product making its own way in the world. There is much to recommend this position. But my concern here is that, by folding divine revelation up into the uncontrollability of creaturely generativity and creativity, Milbank compromises both divine and creaturely freedom. To be sure, Milbank is not arguing that this is the *only* way God reveals Godself; more troubling, then, is the way in which Milbank's God enters by the back door of creaturely production, such that there is little or no space for creaturely production to be anything other than what was always intended and ordained.

Our relationships to our institutions are more dynamic than that. Orientation to objects, holds Ahmed, is an inheritance. Importantly, for Ahmed (2006: 178), inheritance can be consciously refused: this is, in fact, the nature of queer commitment, namely, the refusal to inherit the forms that have written the un/familiar out of existence. Ahmed articulates the turn to retreating, diminishing objects as profoundly hopeful, since this entails a consciously chosen alternative genealogy which welcomes the refusal of oppressive inheritances as opening up 'the condition of possibility for another way of dwelling in the world' (178). More theologically, as Moltmann (1967: 36) puts it,

> In the medium of hope our theological concepts become not judgements which nail reality down to what it is, but anticipations which show reality its prospects and its future possibilities. Theological concepts do not give a fixed form to reality, but they are expanded by hope and anticipate future being. ... Their knowledge is grounded not in the will to dominate, but in love to the future of

things. ... They are thus concepts which are engaged in a process of movement, and which call forth practical movement and change.

Inheritances are valuable: they remind us of our history, and tie us into a story of belonging and being known. Yet inheritances can also be millstones around our necks, and we can choose to disinherit ourselves. If part of our religious and cultural inheritance is the family, we need to acknowledge the ways in which real families exceed and subvert their culturally idealized forms. Otherwise the familial ceases to be dynamic and becomes merely a static repetition of what (never) was.

Chapter 8

Conclusion

A theme which I hope has been evident throughout this book is that of the close but complex relationship between accounts of continuity and change across discourses surrounding familial institutions. I have aimed to show that a positive imperative to trace the ongoing influence and legacy of the historic Christian tradition in present-day theological and broader discussions of marriage, parenting and family has sometimes skewed into an almost ahistoricist denial of the fact that it is not possible to trace a smooth or unbroken trajectory of these phenomena across time. Nor, I have argued, would it be particularly desirable to do so: the dynamic nature of traditions, and the gift of God which is human generativity as generously interpreted, means that a disavowal of the conscious and unconscious effects (and affects, in terms of emotional ties) of human cultures and efforts would be a costly loss to our breadth of understanding of these modes of relationship.

As I have tried to highlight, some accounts of the coming changes brought by shifts in understandings of marriage – like those of the Church of England – assume that marriage has been stable and certain over history. What such accounts miss is that *marriage has already changed.* It *already* is more than such accounts would have us believe. When, in 2009, Quakers in Britain were deliberating whether to affirm same-sex marriages, part of the context for many of them was the belief that same-sex couples who had pledged to share their lives had *already* been married, even if it was not, at the time, possible to recognize this legally in Britain. As Rachel Muers (2015: 162–3) comments, 'Against the criticisms at the time and since, that celebrating same-sex marriage was an unjustifiable and highly risky social "experiment", the Yearly Meeting affirmed that it was "experimental" – grounded in experience. The implicit response to oft-cited fears about what *might* happen if same-sex couples were to get married was "we already have some idea, because it already happens".

The church more broadly has, by and large, coped with the fact that people divorce and remarry despite the affirmation that marriage is a lifelong commitment; that many couples do not have children through choice or circumstance despite the fact that marriage is affirmed as a location for the procreation of children; and so on. Marriage liturgies have different emphases between denominations, and civil ceremonies have a different focus again; even so, the Church of England

(2012: 1) can insist that there is no distinction between 'religious marriage' and 'civil marriage', but just different ways of entering into the same state. Of course, this makes it all the more odd and anomalous that at the time of writing it is not legally possible for Church of England clergy to contract marriages between same-sex couples, and that Church of England clergy have been disciplined for entering into legal same-sex (civil) marriages themselves.[1] Likewise, as we have seen, the Church of England (in common with some other denominations) insists that marriage is not defined by human custom, yet also insists that it, as a body, has authority to pronounce on what does and does not entail a marriage licit in the sight of God. The majority of Christians no longer believe that it is a sin to marry the sibling of one's deceased spouse, nor that marriage is primarily a contract between males which transfers ownership of and authority over the bride from her father to her husband. Even if official Roman Catholic teaching outlaws the use of contraception, or remarriage after divorce, practice among many thousands of ordinary Catholics points to a diversity of relationships to the authorized line. Marriage is continuing to change, as it always has changed. This is not a new phenomenon.

Nor should any change be assumed to be a change for the worse. There is good warrant in the tradition for holding that there is a possibility of continual progression towards becoming more like God – per the Orthodox traditions, *theosis* or divinization. Gregory of Nyssa describes this as *epektasis*, a sense of continual progress which does not compromise humanity's goodness but is rather the mechanism by which it develops. Just as humans were created by God with

---

1. Furthermore, since the passage of the Marriage (Same Sex Couples) Act 2013, an additional difficulty has arisen for the Church of England. The Church of England had conceded that it was licit for its clergy to enter into civil partnerships, since these did not carry with them the assumption of sexual activity. Since 2014, however, it has been possible legally to convert existing civil partnerships into marriages. In legal terms, the marriage is deemed to have begun not from the time of *conversion* to marriage from civil partnership, but from the time of the *initial* civil partnership; the marriage certificate is backdated to the date of entry into the civil partnership. The Church of England thus finds itself in a position of having clergy who are not only in same-sex marriages (although the church has not sanctioned clerical entry into such arrangements), but who have, in legal terms, been in same-sex marriages ever since 2005. Detractors of legal conversion might say that holding a marriage to have existed since before it was legally possible for it to have done so is a form of newspeak. On the other hand, however, this legal conception perhaps better reflects what Adrian Thatcher (2002) has appealed to as the gradual 'becoming' of a marriage relationship, which, he has suggested in other circumstances, should be deemed to have begun not at the moment of a wedding service, or at the time of first sexual intercourse, but at some earlier, unspecified point in the couple's relationship. Either way, the Church of England's ongoing disciplinary distinction between civil partnership and marriage – with the concomitant assumption that only one of these entails sexual activity – is likely to become increasingly moot.

a 'germ' of potentiality which was 'sown with it at the very start of its existence, and that is unfolded and manifested by a natural sequence as it proceeds to its perfect state' (*On the Making of Man* 29.3, see Schaff 1892: 420), so we might understand our institutions as developing likewise. In this way, we might figure developments in our models of marriage and family not inherently as distortions of or divergences from the divinely ordained blueprint, but as developments which are of a piece with these institutions' being – per Gregory, with the germ 'not employing anything external to itself as a stepping-stone to perfection, but itself advancing its own self in due course to the perfect state' (ibid.).

I noted with reference to Pannenberg's zinnia plant that seeds are not mere blueprints: they develop and grow in tension and, we might say, epigenetic conversation with their environments. But these environments are *also* developing dynamically. We can hold that same-sex marriage is an appropriate development of marriage without thereby holding too firmly to any degree of originism – for, according to the logic of Gregory and Jantzen and Muñoz and Moltmann and those we might term the 'becomers', it is the future we should be interested and invested in, rather than giving in to the version of original sin that is the sin of the apotheosization of origins. (This account of original sin as the sin of originism is not one that I have encountered elsewhere, and I hope that it will generate further conversation and reflection.) One form of Christian narrative about human beings says that humans are born from above; we are born again; we are about new beginnings which are also deeply connected to our genealogy: a genealogy not only of blood but also of Spirit, so that our ancestors are all who have come before us, and our descendants are all who come after us, not because they are our biological lineage but because they share our human and more-than-human world. All who are born from above are born from the womb of the Father (a phrase which recurs across theologies of the first millennium of Christianity);[2] yet all were also born here, now, below, in irreducible animality.

Earlier I criticized John Milbank for seeming to appeal to a 'prior' version of marriage which descends from on high and up to which humans have failed to live. Milbank well knows that, in Gregory, *epektasis* means dynamic movement, growth and change. Indeed, as Morwenna Ludlow (2007: 254) notes, in Milbank's reading of Gregory, 'Virtue requires a constant "moving out" from passivity to activity *and* the idea that there is a "transgenerational" movement as each generation imitates its own models'. As Milbank (1998: 96) also knows, in Gregory

2. See, for example, the confession of faith from the Eleventh Council of Toledo in 675, in Neuner and Dupuis (1982: 103); Augustine's exposition on Ps. 110, in Schaff (1886: 543); the Syriac Orthodox baptismal liturgy often attributed to Serverus and discussed in Brock (2008: 135); and see, further, discussion in Spinks (2006: 18, 84–8), who points to various depictions of the womb belonging to the Father and to the Spirit in early baptism liturgy; and Collins (2010), who notes further discussions of the womb image in Ps. 110 in Hilary of Poitiers's *De Trinitate* 6.16, Athanasius's fourth discourse *Against the Arians* 27 and Basil of Caesarea's *Against Eunomius* 353.

there is merit in active appropriation, which is itself a revelation of the 'fecundity' of the thing appropriated. So, we might say, pressing Milbank, it is exactly in use and active curation that the fullness of things (fullness not in the sense of pluperfect completion, but of multiplicitous abundance and recalcitrant overflow) comes to be manifest. It is, perhaps, surprising that Milbank elsewhere resists the implication of this dynamism for patterns of relationship and relationality. But Milbank wants to say that, just as receptivity is action, so that a gift cannot be deemed to have been given unless it has also been received (complicated by the fact that, in his account, humans exist *as* gift, such that our whole existence is a tacit acceptance of the gift and we have no real opportunity to reject it), action is receptivity (95) – we receive something *handed down*. He sees in Gregory, despite the latter's exhortation not to 'seek truth in inherited opinions' (96), not a retreat inward to solipsistic individuation, but a quiet and centred orbiting of '*a different, and more abiding doxa*' (96, original emphasis). So the question for us now, in our un/familiar accounts of familiar institutions, is *what it is that abides*.

For where Milbank and his allies do have it right is that there is, perhaps, something to be resisted about appeals to progress for the sake of progress. John Wyndham's post-apocalyptic novel *The Chrysalids* is a salient reminder that master-races attempting to build master-worlds too often ride roughshod over those who have to be figured as subhuman collateral damage along the way. (This kind of reservation is also what underlies Edelman's *No Future*.) Yet *The Chrysalids* also makes clear that attempts to freeze worlds exactly as they are – or, rather, as rhetoric insists they were at some idealized point in a distant past – bespeaks a kind of arrogance when appeals to such past worlds are also appeals to a God (and purporting to be able, uniquely, to speak for such a God) who had reached the apogee of creativity in pronouncing them – and only them – holy. An outlaw character in the novel, resistant to the ruling authorities' attempts to maintain 'purity' by eradicating any human, animal or plant 'deviation', says,

> They weren't God's last word like they thought: God doesn't have any last word. If He did He'd be dead. But He isn't dead; and He changes and grows, like everything else that's alive. So when they were doing their best to get everything fixed and tidy on some kind of eternal lines they'd thought up for themselves, He sent along Tribulation to bust it up and remind 'em that life is change. (Wyndham 1955: 153)

In the end, for Wyndham, it is those who insist on resisting evolution and adaptation who seal their own fates (182).

We need not appeal to a retributivist God who sends down fire on human arrogance in order to take Wyndham's point. For God cannot help but to generate, any more than the sun as we have known it throughout human existence can help but to radiate. Humans, who image God, are also predisposed to be generative and to exercise dynamism in our social worlds (even if this is a vocation we may refuse). Augustine held that only God could veritably create (i.e. from nothing), and that human beings merely reshaped existing matter. Procreative generation was a slightly different affair, since this involved the transformation of one set of (existing) matter into another – though still from something rather than nothing. I have tried to show throughout this book, however, that the distinction between *creatio ex nihilo* and generativity as broadly understood is less clear-cut than it may seem, for as creatures of culture we are not condemned merely to take on the mantle we have received. The 'newness' of our adaptations, regenerations and reconceptions really is novel: we have freedom and ability to resist the cult of the simulacrum. Generativity from existing matter need not be understood as a shortcoming: rather, it is appropriately creaturely. Furthermore, as I have shown, even while being creaturely, it is also not so different from divine process as we might at first assume. God also chooses to create and recreate in this way, from existing matter, placing agential capacity in the hands of humans (and other creatures) and ceding control over both processes and outcomes. What is happening in the present generation – those living and theologizing now – is an active 'transgenerational' conversation (a conversation between generations, as well as a meta-conversation about what it is that constitutes generation – that is, about what it means to generate and about what it is that is being generated) in which there is negotiation about what marriage, parenting and family will mean, will be, will stand for in our collective futures (futures which look increasingly granular and increasingly beyond the grasp of Christendom).

Can the same be said for changing familial structures in general as I have been arguing for marriage? After all, some new family forms seem to represent (and require) the wholesale abandonment of marriage, not the recognition of newer and more adequate forms of it. But here is where discussion of qualities and characteristics is so crucial: marriage is, always has been, multiple and recalcitrant. It is a legal contract; it is an extralegal recognition of standing within the community; it is a testimony to a partnership before God; it is not monolithic. If there are family forms emerging and already in existence which reject marriage on the grounds that it is inescapably sexist, patriarchal, economically suspect and prone to exploitation, then this will be because marriage's detractors recognize different goods which they deem incompatible with marriage as we have known it. But if marriage as we have known it is not the only way for marriage to be – *and* if the goods which its supporters recognize as being upheld in, through and by marriage are not solely coincident with marriage itself, but may also be found in other kinds of arrangements – then we need not, perhaps, quibble too much about semantics. There will continue to be those for whom it is important to avow that their relationship is *not* a 'marriage in all but name', as a mode of political resistance to marriage's genealogy and legacy of violence and exploitation. But we, and they, may nonetheless be able to identify continuity – even if of a limited kind – between the goods they promote and the goods which it is possible to understand as existing within more traditional marital arrangements. This will, however, take humility on the parts of those who have sought to uphold 'Christian marriage' and 'traditional family values', to recognize that theirs are not the only circumstances in which human flourishing may be nurtured – and that appeals to 'flourishing' itself may be understood as attempts to gloss over questionable modes of futurity and alliances with political hegemony. As I showed in Chapter 3, attention to the generosity, expansiveness and critical consideration of the detail of ongoing consent and consultation which many polyamorous relationships exhibit may be a significant catalyst for monogamous marriage's own ongoing self-reflexivity and reform, and this will necessitate further reflections on the parts of constructive and moral theologians for whom marriage continues to be upheld as a uniquely (or at least peculiarly) sanctifying human good.

If relational and familial structures of affect have been relativized, and if even the most apparently 'natural' relationships of sex, marriage and parenthood require rereading in light of our new tradition, then where does this leave all of us in our ongoing commitments? The Christian tradition has known many who have shirked their commitments – often to wives, often to children, sometimes to colleagues and others – for the sake of the perceived 'greater good' of their work. For some Christians this has been a conscious ceding of patterns of family and commitment which pale into insignificance beside the good of service to the divine. In discussion of the thirteenth-century Umbrian mystic St Angela of Foligno, for example, Carole Hill (2015: 16) notes how shocking to today's readers is 'Angela's constant prayer that her family, including her many children, should all die to release her to singular commitment to God, mirroring dramatically Christ's gospel injunction to leave behind father, mother, and family ties, to follow him alone'. As more than one of my colleagues has noted, there would be an instructive – if depressing – project to be had from analysing the acknowledgements sections of academic theological books and noting how many tacitly say something along the lines of, 'I would like to thank my long-suffering spouse and neglected children for having allowed me to behave so badly and cede all but the most rudimentary family responsibilities in order to further my career by jetting off to conferences and/or hiding in my study in order to write this book'. We could point to many other examples.

But what really interests me here is how Hill continues: 'Angela was engaged in an exercise in *imitatio Christi*. When they all did expire in rapid succession she was, naturally, grief-stricken' (16). As Lauren Berlant, Robyn Wiegman, José Esteban Muñoz and others have noted of Edelman and his ilk, we frequently do not find our affective relationships as easy to jettison as all that. And nor, perhaps, should we: as humans we have an instinct to pursue relationality even when logically our continued persistence with given persons or things might be bad for us. We seem predisposed to try to fix and augment, to patch up and make do; and it is precisely in doing so that we communicate our belief in new possibilities and a future not already contained in the present.

That said, *The Chrysalids* is also a reminder that what looks like progress is very rarely an unambiguous good. It is important to note, when imagining un/familiar futures, particularly around expansions of marriage more fully to embrace same-sex relationships within the church as well as beyond it, that it would be tempting to tell a tale which went something along the lines of what Timothy R. Koch (2001: 14) calls the 'I can fit the glass slipper, too!' narrative, whereby LGBT-identified people feel compelled to insist that they are just like cisgender heterosexuals; that they were always present, if hidden, in the tradition; that they are just as capable of fidelity and responsibility, just as disposed to want marriage and parenthood as straight people are – if not *more* so! For some queer people, this is indubitably the case. But, as has been well attested elsewhere, marriage equality may be a poisoned chalice if it means queer relationships are drawn into the mainstream; as Geoffrey Rees (2011: 66) argues, 'It is not possible … to seek to enrol homosexuality within the ranks of innocence and marriage without also conscripting some figure to embody visibly the remainder of sin, which helps chart the fuzzy boundary on the other side of which homosexuality becomes queer'. Similarly, holds Mark Jordan (2013: 158), there is a tendency even among liberal Christians to 'allow' same-sex couples only the most conservative model of marriage there is, the logic being, 'If straight couples have to pay the price of sexual exclusivity in order to get married … shouldn't gay couples have to pay too? Indeed, shouldn't gay couples have to pay a steeper price, since their sexual desire looks to be particularly undisciplined?' Furthermore, Katherine Franke (2015: 206) makes the point that 'expanding' marriage to encompass same-sex couples may also, unwittingly, reinscribe and exacerbate institutionalized and racialized discourses of marriage's 'decency', and thereby further exclude couples still deemed non-normative; legal acknowledgement of one's rights is a double-edged sword, and 'gaining marriage rights can come at the price of stigmatizing other groups and ways of life on marriage's outside'. And there is also and always, crucially, a danger in reinscribing the idea that heterosexual institutions are the unmarked neuter against which others must measure themselves – and against holding un/familiar institutions to an impossible idealized standard up to which even the unmarked neuters cannot expect to live. It is a little like the way some children of immigrant parents describe being held to much higher standards of behaviour and academic industry than their non-immigrant peers in order not to bring shame on the family – and in order to prove that they are just as good as other families via having to appear rather better. Such insistent success has its negative side, and risks veering into a kind of wilfully oblivious triumphalism whereby the actual messiness and imperfection of all structures of family, parenthood and the rest cannot be acknowledged.

I suggested in Chapter 7 that coming to terms with its own lack of cultural dominance and authority is a necessary and important move for the church, and might be an aspect of its vocation to solidarity with marginal and oppressed people. I stand by this; but it is also true that such conscious ceding of power and control carries its own kind of potential. In *The Queer Art of Failure*, J. Halberstam (2011: 120) insists, 'There is something powerful in being wrong, in losing, in failing. … All our failures combined might just be enough, if we practice them well, to bring down the winner'. For Halberstam, the point is somewhat like Edelman's: those designated queer (by themselves or others) will never 'win', never be accepted, by aping straight society, and would do better to embrace this 'failure' and thereby do a veritably new thing. The church might, likewise, do well to recognize the freedom that comes with dissociation from cultural dominance. Furthermore, un/familiar institutions themselves, and those who practice them, must have the freedom to get it wrong. Same-sex marriages will sometimes break down – just as many heterosexual ones do. Children of adoptive parents will sometimes go off the rails – just as children raised by their biological parents often do. Queer families will sometimes harbour abuse and emotionally oppressive relationships – just as other families can. If we do not make our peace with this fact (not that abuse happens per se – this should always be something against which we rail – but that it *can* happen in non-traditional kinds of families just as in traditional ones), if we continue to tell only the stories which tell an impossibly sunny, utopian story about the potential of new models of family and marriage, then we do not respect them at all, but make them something unreal and immaculate. Un/familiar institutions and the people in them need the freedom and the right to be wrong.

All Christians are in a constant process of *regeneration*, of being transformed into the likeness of God. Generation in itself is not the end of the story (and the Christians of the first few centuries did not quite succeed in reconciling their endorsement of bodily resurrection with their suspicion of specifically 'sexual' body parts, or conceptualizing a place for sexuality beyond the reproductive, as Taylor G. Petrey (2016) argues). But it is a part of the story, such that material embodied existence is not to be denied, glossed over or dismissed as so mired in sin as to be only a bad news story. Here I have tried to show that it is the apotheosization of only some family forms that is problematic, limiting as it does divine and creaturely capacities to do a new thing.

There are, of course, further questions raised which I have not been able to answer here, and further ramifications arising from these discussions. These include how, if at all, less conventional modes of marital and familial relationships might come to be formally recognized and celebrated by churches (given that – for example – even certain kinds of currently legal relationship are not recognized as theologically licit by some denominations, such as remarriages after divorce by the Roman Catholic Church, or same-sex marriages by several Anglican churches in provinces where same-sex marriage is legal). They include issues raised by theologians including Adrian Thatcher and Don Browning about the extent to which different modes of family lead to good outcomes for all those involved in them, including children – though I would want to add that the relationships between social acceptance, financial and emotional stability, and well-being are not uncomplicated. And they include the important and more specifically constructive theological question about how far departing from solely two-and-only-two marital covenants represents a loss of cosmic imagery of the relationship between God and creation which is too high a price to pay.

All this said, I hope I have successfully shown that un/familiar theology is a worthwhile mode of theological conversation, precisely because it represents an acknowledgement of, rather than a departure from, the breadth of understandings of family within the Christian tradition.

REFERENCES

Adams, Richard (1973), *Watership Down*, Harmondsworth: Puffin.

Agamben, Giorgio (1998), *Homo Sacer: Sovereign Power and Bare Life*, trans. Daniel Heller-Roazen, Stanford, CA: Stanford University Press.

Ahlgren, Gillian T. W. (2005), 'Julian of Norwich's Theology of Eros's, *Spiritus: A Journal of Christian Spirituality* 5(1): 37–53.

Ahmed, Sara (2006), *Queer Phenomenology: Orientations, Objects, Others*, Durham, NC: Duke University Press.

Althaus-Reid, Marcella (2000), *Indecent Theology: Theological Perversions in Sex, Gender and Politics*, London: Routledge.

Althaus-Reid, Marcella (2003), *The Queer God*, London: Routledge.

Alvarez, Liliana and Klaus Jaffe (2004), 'Narcissism Guides Mate Selection: Humans Mate Assortatively, as Revealed by Facial Resemblance, Following an Algorithm of "Self Seeking Like"', *Evolutionary Psychology* 2004(2): 177–94.

Anzaldúa, Gloria (1991), 'To(o) Queer the Writer: Loca, Escrita y Chicana', in Betsy Warland (ed.), *InVersions: Writing by Dykes, Queers and Lesbians*, 249–63, Vancouver: Press Gang.

Archbishops' Council of the Church of England (1999), *Marriage: A Teaching Document*, London: Church House Publishing, https://www.churchofengland.org/media/45645/marriage.pdf.

Archbishops' Council of the Church of England (2013), *Men and Women in Marriage: A Document from the Faith and Order Commission Published with the Agreement of the House of Bishops of the Church of England and Approved for Study*, London: Church House Publishing.

Arendt, Hannah (1958), *The Human Condition*, Chicago, IL: University of Chicago Press.

Ariès, Philippe (1973), *Centuries of Childhood: A Social History of Family Life*, trans. Robert Baldick, New York, NY: Vintage.

Associated Press (2015), 'Catholics Don't Have to Breed "Like Rabbits," Says Pope Francis', *The Guardian*, 20 January 2015. Available online: http://www.theguardian.com/world/2015/jan/20/catholics-dont-have-to-breed-like-rabbits-says-pope-francis.

Augustine (1984), *The City of God*, London: Penguin.

Augustine (1887), 'De Virginitate', trans. C. L. Cornish, in Philip Schaff (ed.), *Nicene and Post-Nicene Fathers, First Series, Vol. 3*. Buffalo, NY: Christian Literature Publishing Co., 1887; revised and edited for New Advent by Kevin Knight, http://www.newadvent.org/fathers/1310.htm.

Augustine (2007), 'On Marriage and Concupiscence, Book 1', in Philip Schaff (ed.), *Nicene and Post-Nicene Fathers: First Series, Volume V: St Augustine: Anti-Pelagian Writings*, 263–80, New York, NY: Cosimo.

Bailey, Sarah Pulliam (2014), 'Conservative Leader Bill Gothard Resigns Following Abuse Allegations', *The Washington Post*, 7 March 2014. Available online: http://www.washingtonpost.com/national/religion/conservative-leader-bill-gothard-resigns-following-abuse-allegations/2014/03/07/0381aa94-a624-11e3-b865-38b254d92063_story.html.

Balthasar, Hans Urs von (1990), *Theo-Drama: Theological Dramatic Theory, Volume II: The Dramatis Personae: Man in God*, trans. Graham Harrison, San Francisco, CA: Ignatius Press.

Balthasar, Hans Urs von (1992), *Theo-Drama: Theological Dramatic Theory: Volume III: The Dramatis Personae: The Person in Christ*, trans. Graham Harrison, San Francisco, CA: Ignatius Press.

Balthasar, Hans Urs von (1998), *Theo-Drama: Theological Dramatic Theory: Volume V: The Last Act*, trans. Graham Harrison, San Francisco, CA: Ignatius Press.

Banner, Michael (2014), *The Ethics of Everyday Life: Moral Theology, Social Anthropology and the Imagination of the Human*, Oxford: Oxford University Press.

Barnes, Jonathan (ed.) (1984), *The Complete Works of Aristotle: The Revised Oxford Translation, Volume 1*, Princeton, NJ: Princeton University Press.

Barth, Karl (1961), *Church Dogmatics III/4: The Doctrine of Creation*, trans. A. T. Mackay et al., Edinburgh: T&T Clark.

Barth, Karl (1962), 'A Theological Dialogue', *Theology Today* 19(2): 171–7.

Barth, Karl (1968), *The Epistle to the Romans*, trans. Edwyn C. Hoskyns, Oxford: Oxford University Press.

Barton, Stephen (2001), *Life Together: Family, Sexuality and Community in the New Testament and Today*, Edinburgh: T&T Clark.

Baudrillard, Jean (1994[1981]), *Simulacra and Simulation*, trans. Sheila Faria Glaser, Ann Arbor, MI: University of Michigan Press.

Bauerschmidt, John, Zachary Guiliano, Wesley Hill and Jordan Hylden (2015), 'Marriage in Creation and Covenant: A Response to the Task Force on the Study of Marriage'. Available online: http://www.anglicantheologicalreview.org/static/pdf/conversations/MarriageInCreationAndCovenant.pdf.

Baxter, Stephen (2008), *Flood*, London: Gollancz.

Beattie, Tina (2002), *God's Mother, Eve's Advocate: A Marian Narrative of Women's Salvation*, London: Continuum.

Beattie, Tina (2006), *New Catholic Feminism: Theology and Theory*, Abingdon: Routledge.

Beattie, Tina (2013), *Theology After Postmodernity: Divining the Void – A Lacanian Reading of Thomas Aquinas*, Oxford: Oxford University Press.

Belloc, Hilaire (1998[1907]), *Cautionary Tales for Children*, Radford, VA: Wilder Publications.

Benedict XVI (Pope) (2010), *Verbum Domini: Post-Synodal Apostolic Exhortation to the Bishops, Clergy, Consecrated Persons and the Lay Faithful on the Word of God in the Life and Mission of the Church*. Available online: http://w2.vatican.va/content/benedict-xvi/en/apost_exhortations/documents/hf_ben-xvi_exh_20100930_verbum-domini.html.

Bennett, Jana Marguerite (2008), *Water is Thicker Than Blood: An Augustinian Theology of Marriage and Singleness*, New York, NY: Oxford University Press.

Berlant, Lauren and Lee Edelman (2014), *Sex, or the Unbearable*, Durham, NC: Duke University Press.

Betzig, Laura (1995), 'Medieval Monogamy', *Journal of Family History* 20(1): 181–216.

Bianchi, D. W., G. K. Zickwolf, G. J. Weil, S. Sylvester and M. A. DeMaria (1996), 'Male Fetal Progenitor Cells Persist in Maternal Blood for as Long as 27 Years Postpartum', *Proceedings of the National Academy of Sciences of the United States of America* 93: 705–8.

Biss, Mavis Louise (2012), 'Arendt and the Theological Significance of Natality', *Philosophy Compass* 7(11): 762–71.

Boeve, Lieven (2011), 'Naming God in Open Narratives: Theology Between Deconstruction and Hermeneutics', in Joseph Verheyden, Theo L. Hettema and Pieter Vandercasteele (eds), *Paul Ricoeur: Poetics and Religion*, 81–100, Leuven: Peeters.

Boeve, Lieven (2014), *Lyotard and Theology: Beyond the Christian Master Narrative of Love*, London: Bloomsbury T&T Clark.

Boeve, Lieven (2015), 'Interrupting Revelation, Interrupting Church', plenary paper delivered at Society for the Study of Theology annual conference, University of Nottingham, 13 April 2015.

Bohache, Thomas (2006), 'Matthew', in Deryn Guest, Robert E. Goss, Mona West and Thomas Bohache (eds), *The Queer Bible Commentary*, 487–516, London: SCM Press.

Bonny, Johan (2015), 'Synod on The Family: Expectations of a Diocesan Bishop', open letter by the Roman Catholic Bishop of Antwerp, trans. Brian Doyle. Available online: http://www.associationofcatholicpriests.ie/wp-content/uploads/2014/09/synod-on-family-eng.pdf.

Borg, Marcus J. and John Dominic Crossan (2007), *The First Christmas: What the Gospels Really Teach About Jesus's Birth*, New York, NY: HarperCollins.

Borrowdale, Anne (1989), *A Woman's Work: Changing Christian Attitudes*, London: SPCK.

Bourdieu, Pierre (1977), *Outline of a Theory of Practice*, trans. Richard Nice, Cambridge: Cambridge University Press.

Boyle, Marjorie O'Rourke (1998), *Senses of Touch: Human Dignity and Deformity, From Michelangelo to Calvin*, Leiden: Brill.

Bray, Karen (2015), 'The Monstrosity of the Multitude: Unredeeming Radical Theology', *Palgrave Communications* 1, DOI:10.1057/palcomms.2015.30.

Brekus, Catherine A. (2001), 'Children of Wrath, Children of Grace: Jonathan Edwards and the Puritan Culture of Child Rearing', in Marcia JoAnn Bunge (ed.), *The Child in Christian Thought*, 300–28, Grand Rapids, MI: Eerdmans.

Brett, Mark G. (2000), *Genesis: Procreation and the Politics of Identity*, Abingdon: Routledge.

Brintnall, Kent (2011), *Ecce Homo: The Male-Body-in-Pain as Redemptive Figure*, Chicago, IL: University of Chicago Press.

Brittain, Christopher Craig (2014), 'On the Demonisation and Fetishisation of Choice in Christian Sexual Ethics', *Studies in Christian Ethics* 27(2): 144–66.

Brock, Sebastian (2008), *The Holy Spirit in the Syrian Baptismal Tradition*, Piscataway, NJ: Gorgias Press.

Browning, Don S. (2003), *Marriage and Modernization: How Globalization Threatens Marriage and What to Do About It*, Grand Rapids, MI: Eerdmans.

Browning, Don S. (2005), 'Adoption and the Moral Significance of Kin Altruism', in Timothy P. Jackson (ed.), *The Morality of Adoption: Social-Psychological, Theological, and Legal Perspectives*, 52–77, Grand Rapids, MI: Eerdmans.

Browning, Don (2007), *Equality and the Family: A Fundamental, Practical Theology of Children, Mothers, and Fathers in Modern Societies*, Grand Rapids, MI: Eerdmans.

Browning, Don S., Bonnie J. Miller-McLemore, Pamela D. Couture, K. Brynolf Lyon and Robert M. Franklin (1997), *From Culture Wars to Common Ground: Religion and the American Family Debate*, Louisville, KY: Westminster John Knox Press.

Buell, Denise Kimber (2005), *Why This New Race: Ethnic Reasoning in Early Christianity*, New York, NY: Columbia University Press.

Burrus, Virginia (2007), *Saving Shame: Martyrs, Saints, and Other Abject Subjects*, Philadelphia, PA: University of Pennsylvania Press.

Butler, Judith (2004), *Undoing Gender*, New York, NY: Routledge.

Butler, Judith (2005), *Giving an Account of Oneself*, New York, NY: Fordham University Press.

Byatt, A. S. (1995), *Still Life*, London: Vintage.

Cahill, Lisa Sowle (2005a), 'Adoption: A Roman Catholic Perspective', in Timothy P. Jackson (ed.), *The Morality of Adoption: Social-Psychological, Theological, and Legal Perspectives*, 148–71, Grand Rapids, MI: Eerdmans.

Cahill, Lisa Sowle (2005b), *Theological Bioethics: Participation, Justice, and Change*, Washington, DC: Georgetown University Press.

Campbell, Nancy (2001), *A Change of Heart: Stories of Couples Who Have Had Reversals from Vasectomies and Tubal Ligations*, Franklin, TN: Above Rubies.

Campbell, Nancy (2003), *Be Fruitful and Multiply: What the Bible Says About Having Children*, San Antonio, TX: Vision Forum Ministries.

Campbell, Nancy (2005), 'Ready for Adventure?', *Above Rubies* 64: 15.

Campbell, Nancy (2007), 'The Family Charge', *Above Rubies* 71: 14–15.

Campbell, Nancy (2012), 'From Our Home to Yours', *Above Rubies* 84: 2–3.

Carrell, Severin (2015), 'Hundreds Attend Funeral of Unnamed Baby Found Wrapped in Blanket', *The Guardian*, 1 May 2015. Available online: http://www.theguardian.com/uk-news/2015/may/01/mourners-attend-funeral-of-baby-found-wrapped-in-blanket-in-edinburgh.

Carter, Warren (2000), *Matthew and the Margins: A Sociopolitical and Religious Reading*, Maryknoll, NY: Orbis Books.

Central Board of Finance of the Church of England (1995), *Something to Celebrate: Valuing Families in Church and Society*, London: Church House Publishing.

Christie, Agatha (1939), *Murder is Easy*, London: Collins Crime Club.

Church of England (2012), 'A Response to the Government Equalities Office Consultation – "Equal Civil Marriage" – from the Church of England'. Available online: www.churchofengland.org/media/1475149/s-s%20marriage.pdf.

Church Pension Fund (Episcopal Church Standing Committee on Liturgy and Music) (2012), *I Will Bless You and You Will Be a Blessing: Resources for the Witnessing and Blessing of a Lifelong Covenant in a Same-Sex Relationship*, New York, NY: Church Publishing.

Clark, Elizabeth (1997), *St Augustine on Marriage and Sexuality*, Washington, DC: Catholic University of America Press.

Clemson, Frances (2016), 'Taking Time Over Marriage: Tradition, History and Time in Recent Debates', in John Bradbury and Susannah Cornwall (eds), *Thinking Again About Marriage: Key Theological Questions*, 62–81, London: SCM Press.

Cohen, Shawn (2009), 'Time For College! How Can We Afford It?', *Above Rubies* 76: 12.

Coles, Robert (1996), 'Foreword', in John N. Kotre (ed.), *Outliving the Self: Generativity and the Interpretation of Lives*, xi–xiii, New York, NY: W. W. Norton.

Collins, Paul M. (2010), 'Constructing Masculinity: *De Utero Patris* (From the Womb of the Father)', *Journal of Men, Masculinities and Spirituality* 4(2): 82–96.

Congregation for the Doctrine of the Faith (1975), *Persona Humana: Declaration on Certain Questions Concerning Sexual Ethics*. Available online: http://www.vatican.va/roman_curia/congregations/cfaith/documents/rc_con_cfaith_doc_19751229_persona-humana_en.html.

Congregation for the Doctrine of the Faith (2003), *Considerations Regarding Proposals to Give Legal Recognition to Unions Between Homosexual Persons*. Available online: http://www.vatican.va/roman_curia/congregations/cfaith/documents/rc_con_cfaith_doc_20030731_homosexual-unions_en.html.

Conrad, Ryan (ed.) (2010), *Against Equality: Queer Critiques of Gay Marriage*, Lewiston, ME: Against Equality Publishing Collective.

Conway, Colleen (2008), *Behold the Man: Jesus and Greco-Roman Masculinity*, Oxford: Oxford University Press.

Cornwall, Susannah (2010), *Sex and Uncertainty in the Body of Christ: Intersex Conditions and Christian Theology*, London: Routledge.

Cornwall, Susannah (2011), *Controversies in Queer Theology*, London: SCM Press.

Cornwall, Susannah (2014a), 'A Theology of Sexuality', in Susannah Cornwall and Bob Callaghan (eds), *Sexuality: The Inclusive Church Resource*, 55–107, London: Darton, Longman and Todd.

Cornwall, Susannah (2014b), 'The Future of Liberal Theology', *Modern Believing* 55(4): 343–5.

Cornwall, Susannah (2015), '"Something There Is That Doesn't Love a Wall": Queer Theologies and Reparative Readings', *Theology and Sexuality* 21(1): 20–35.

Craft, Anna (2010), 'Possibility Thinking and Fostering Creativity with Wisdom: Opportunities and Constraints in an English Context', in Ronald A. Beghetto and James C. Kaufman (eds), *Nurturing Creativity in the Classroom*, 289–312, Cambridge: Cambridge University Press.

Crisp, Oliver D. (2008), 'On the "Fittingness" of the Virgin Birth', *Heythrop Journal* 49: 197–221.

Danielsen-Morales, Edgard Francisco (2015), 'Re-Writing God as the Holy (Polyamorous) One', presentation delivered at Metropolitan Community Churches virtual symposium, 'Who Are We Really? Re-Engaging Sex and Spirit', 17 October 2015.

Davidson, Randall Thomas (ed.) (1920), *The Six Lambeth Conferences 1867-1920*, London: SPCK.

Dean, Tim (2008), 'An Impossible Embrace: Queerness, Futurity, and the Death Drive', in James Joseph Bono, Tim Dean and Ewa Płonowska Ziarek (eds), *A Time for the Humanities: Futurity and the Limits of Autonomy*, 122–40, New York, NY: Fordham University Press.

DeBruine, L. M. (2002), 'Facial Resemblance Enhances Trust', *Proceedings of the Royal Society London B* 269: 1307–12.

Denson, Juliana (2013), 'Quiverfull: Conservative Christian Women and Empowerment in the Home', *Lux* 2(1): 1–28.

DeRogatis, Amy (2015), *Saving Sex: Sexuality and Salvation in American Evangelicalism*, Oxford: Oxford University Press.

Derrida, Jacques (1976), *Of Grammatology*, trans. Gayatri Chakravorty Spivak, Baltimore, MD: Johns Hopkins University Press.

Derrida, Jacques (1997), 'Differance', in Todd May (ed.), *Twentieth Century Continental Philosophy*, 278–302, Upper Saddle River, NJ: Prentice Hall.

Diprose, Rosalyn and Ewa Płonowska Ziarek (2013), 'Time for Beginners: Natality, Biopolitics, and Political Theology', *philoSOPHIA* 3(2): 107–20.

Donaldson, Laura E. (2006), 'The Sign of Orpah: Reading Ruth Through Native Eyes', in R. S. Sugirtharajah (ed.), *The Postcolonial Biblical Reader*, 159–70, Oxford: Blackwell.

Dooley, Mark (2001), *The Politics of Exodus: Kierkegaard's Ethics of Responsibility*, New York, NY: Fordham University Press.

Duffer, Debbie (2008), 'Nearly Ten Years [sic] Wait!', *Above Rubies* 73: 8.

Duggan, Lisa (2002), 'The New Homonormativity: The Sexual Politics of Neoliberalism', in Russ Castronovo and Dana D. Nelson (eds), *Materializing Democracy: Toward a Revitalized Cultural Politics*, 175–94, Durham, NC: Duke University Press.

Dunn, James D. G. (2015), *Neither Jew Nor Greek: A Contested Identity (Christianity in the Making, vol. 3)*, Grand Rapids, MI: Eerdmans.

Dunnill, John (2013), *Sacrifice and the Body: Biblical Anthropology and Christian Self-Understanding*, Farnham: Ashgate.

Durst, Margarete (2003), 'Birth and Natality in Hannah Arendt', *Analecta Husserliana* 79: 777–97.

Easton, Dossie and Janet W. Hardy (2009), *The Ethical Slut: A Practical Guide to Polyamory, Open Relationships and Other Adventures*, Berkeley, CA: Celestial Arts.

Edelman, Lee (2004), *No Future: Queer Theory and the Death Drive*, Durham, NC: Duke University Press.

Emens, Elizabeth F. (2009), 'Compulsory Monogamy and Polyamorous Existence', in Martha Albertson Fineman, Jack E. Jackson and Adam P. Romero (eds), *Feminist and Queer Legal Theory: Intimate Encounters, Uncomfortable Conversations*, 259–86, Aldershot: Ashgate.

Episcopal Church (USA) Task Force on the Study of Marriage (2015), 'Report to the 78th General Convention'. Available online: http://www.anglicantheologicalreview.org/static/pdf/conversations/TaskForceOnMarriageReport2015.pdf.

Erikson, Erik (1994), *Identity and the Life Cycle*, New York, NY: W. W. Norton and Company.

Farley, Margaret (2006), *Just Love: A Framework for Christian Sexual Ethics*, New York, NY: Continuum.

Ford, David F. (1999), *Self and Salvation: Being Transformed*, Cambridge: Cambridge University Press.

Foucault, Michel (1990), *The History of Sexuality: Volume 1: An Introduction*, trans. Robert Hurley, London: Penguin.

Francis (Pope) (2015a), 'The Family – Male and Female', General Audience, Saint Peter's Square, 15 April 2015. Available online: https://w2.vatican.va/content/francesco/en/audiences/2015/documents/papa-francesco_20150415_udienza-generale.html.

Francis (Pope) (2015b), *Laudato Si'*. Available online: http://w2.vatican.va/content/francesco/en/encyclicals/documents/papa-francesco_20150524_enciclica-laudato-si.html#_ftn28.

Franke, Katherine (2015), *Wedlocked: The Perils of Marriage Equality*, New York, NY: New York University Press.

Freeman, Aaron (2005), 'Planning Ahead Can Make a Difference in the End', *All Things Considered*, National Public Radio (NPR), 1 June 2005. Available online: http://www.npr.org/templates/story/story.php?storyId=4675953.

Freeman, Elizabeth (2010), *Time Binds: Queer Temporalities, Queer Histories*, Durham, NC: Duke University Press.

Fulford, Ben (2016), 'Thinking about Marriage with Scripture', in John Bradbury and Susannah Cornwall (eds), *Thinking Again About Marriage: Key Theological Questions*, 44–61, London: SCM Press.

Gagnier, Regenia (2015), 'Beyond the Nature/Nurture Divide: A Symbiological Approach to Gender, Sexuality, and Writing', keynote lecture delivered at Gender and the Body: Transnational Perspectives study day, University of Exeter, 8 May 2015.

General Synod Marriage Commission (1979), *Marriage and the Church's Task: Report of the General Synod Marriage Commission*, London: CIO Publications.

Giffney, Noreen (2008), 'Queer Apocal(o)ptic/ism: The Death Drive and the Human', in Noreen Giffney and Myra J. Hird (eds), *Queering the Non/Human*, 55–78, Aldershot: Ashgate.

Gorringe, T. J. (1991), *God's Theatre: A Theology of Providence*, London: SCM Press.

Gorringe, T. J. (2004), *Furthering Humanity: A Theology of Culture*, Aldershot: Ashgate.

Gorringe, Timothy (1999), *Karl Barth: Against Hegemony*, Oxford: Oxford University Press.

Goss, Robert E. (2006), 'Luke', in Deryn Guest, Robert E. Goss, Mona West and Thomas Bohache (eds), *The Queer Bible Commentary*, 526–47, London: SCM Press.

Gothard, Bill (1982), *Ten Reasons Why Adopted Children Tend to Have More Conflicts*, Oak Brook, IL: Institute in Basic Youth Conflicts.

Greenberg, Maurice and Roland Littlewood (1995), 'Post-Adoption Incest and Phenotypic Matching: Experience, Personal Meanings and Biosocial Implications', *British Journal of Medical Psychology* 68: 29–44.

Guroian, Vigen (2001), 'The Ecclesial Family: John Chrysostom on Parenthood and Children', in Marcia JoAnn Bunge (ed.), *The Child in Christian Thought*, 61–77, Grand Rapids, MI: Eerdmans.

Haflidson, Ron (2016), 'Outward, Inward, Upward: Why Three Goods of Marriage for Augustine?', *Studies in Christian Ethics* 29(1): 51–68.

Halberstam, J. (2011), *The Queer Art of Failure*, Durham, NC: Duke University Press.

Halberstam, J. (2015), 'From Sister George to Lonesome George? Or, Is The Butch Back?', *Bully Bloggers*, 16 July 2015. Available online: https://bullybloggers.wordpress.com/2015/07/16/from-sister-george-to-lonesome-george-or-is-the-butch-back/.

Halwani, Raja (2003), *Virtuous Liaisons: Care, Love, Sex, and Virtue Ethics*, Chicago, IL: Open Court.

Harrison, Laura and Sarah B. Rowley (2011), 'Babies by the Bundle: Gender, Backlash, and the Quiverfull Movement', *Feminist Formations* 23(1): 47–69.

Hauerwas, Stanley (1981), *A Community of Character: Toward a Constructive Christian Social Ethic*, Notre Dame, IN: University of Notre Dame Press.

Heaney, Seamus (1966), 'Scaffolding', in Seamus Heaney (ed.), *Death of a Naturalist*, 50, London: Faber and Faber.

Heidegger, Martin (2008), *Being and Time*, trans. John Macquarrie and Edward Robinson, London: HarperPerennial.

Herring, Jonathan (2013), *Caring and the Law*, Oxford: Hart.

Herring, Jonathan (2014), 'Making Family Law Less Sexy', unpublished paper presented at Variant Sex and Gender, Religion and Law workshop, University of Exeter, 31 October 2014.

Hess, Rick and Jan Hess (1990), *A Full Quiver: Family Planning and the Lordship of Christ*, Brentwood, TN: Woglemuth and Hyatt.

Heyward, [Isabel] Carter (1982), *The Redemption of God: A Theology of Mutual Relation*, Lanham, MD: University Press of America.

Heyward, Carter (1984), *Our Passion for Justice: Images of Power, Sexuality, and Liberation*, New York, NY: Pilgrim Press.

Higton, Mike (2016), 'Marriage, Gender, and Doctrine', in John Bradbury and Susannah Cornwall (eds), *Thinking Again About Marriage: Key Theological Questions*, 14–28, London: SCM Press.

Higton, Mike and Rachel Muers (2012), *The Text in Play: Experiments in Reading Scripture*, Eugene, OR: Wipf and Stock.

Hill, Carole (2015), 'The Reputation of Angela of Foligno', letter to the Editor, *Church Times* 7925, 6 February 2015: 16.

Hoffman, Miller Jen (2015), 'Healing Queer Bodies and the Body of Christ', panel discussion at Metropolitan Community Churches virtual symposium, 'Who Are We Really? Re-Engaging Sex and Spirit', 17 October 2015.

Hughes, Carl S. (2010), 'Communicating Earnestness: Kierkegaard and Derrida Respond to their (Poorest) Readers', in Robert L. Perkins (ed.), *The Point of View*, 205–37, Macon, GA: Mercer University Press.

Irigaray, Luce (1985a), *Speculum of the Other Woman*, trans. Gillian C. Gill, Ithaca, NY: Cornell University Press.

Irigaray, Luce (1985b), *This Sex Which Is Not One*, trans. Catherine Porter, Ithaca, NY: Cornell University Press.

Irigaray, Luce (1993), *An Ethics of Sexual Difference*, trans. Carolyn Burke and Gillian C. Gill, London: Athlone Press.

Isasi-Díaz, Ada Maria (2003), 'Christ in *Mujerista* Theology', in Tatha Wiley (ed.), *Thinking of Christ: Proclamation, Explanation, Meaning*, 157–76, New York, NY: Continuum.

Jackson, Timothy P. (2007), 'Judge William and Professor Browning: A Kierkegaardian Critique of Equal-Regard Marriage and the Democratic Family', in John Witte Jr., M. Christian Green and Amy Wheeler (eds), *The Equal-Regard Marriage and its Friendly Critics: Don Browning and the Practical Theological Ethics of the Family*, 123–50, Grand Rapids, MI: Eerdmans.

Jantzen, Grace (1998), *Becoming Divine: Towards a Feminist Philosophy of Religion*, Manchester: Manchester University Press.

Jantzen, Grace (2009), *Violence to Eternity (Death and the Displacement of Beauty: Volume 2)*, ed. Jeremy Carrette and Morny Joy, London: Routledge.

Jantzen, Grace (2010), *A Place of Springs (Death and the Displacement of Beauty, Volume 3)*, ed. Jeremy Carrette and Morny Joy, Farnham: Ashgate.

Jennings, Theodore W. (2003), *The Man Jesus Loved: Homoerotic Narratives from the New Testament*, Cleveland, OH: Pilgrim Press.

Jennings, Theodore W. (2013), *An Ethic of Queer Sex: Principles and Improvisations*, Chicago, IL: Exploration Press of Chicago Theological Seminary.

John Paul II (Pope) (1981), Familiaris Consortio: Apostolic Exhortation to the Episcopate, to the Clergy and to the Faithful of the Whole Catholic Church on the Role of the Christian Family in the Modern World, Available online: http://w2.vatican.va/content/john-paul-ii/en/apost_exhortations/documents/hf_jp-ii_exh_19811122_familiaris-consortio.html.

John Paul II (Pope) (1988), Mulieris Dignitatem (On the Dignity and Vocation of Women). Available online: http://www.vatican.va/holy_father/john_paul_ii/apost_letters/documents/hf_jp-ii_apl_15081988_mulieris-dignitatem_en.html.

John Paul II (Pope) (2006), *Man and Woman He Created Them: A Theology of the Body*, trans. Michael Waldstein, Boston, MA: Pauline Books and Media.

Jordan, Mark D. (2002), *The Ethics of Sex*, Oxford: Blackwell.

Jordan, Mark D. (2011), *Recruiting Young Love: How Christians Talk About Homosexuality*, Chicago, IL: University of Chicago Press.

Jordan, Mark D. (2013), *Blessing Same-Sex Unions: The Perils of Queer Romance and the Confusions of Christian Marriage*, Chicago, IL: University of Chicago Press.

Joyce, Kathryn (2009), *Quiverfull: Inside the Christian Patriarchy Movement*, Boston, MA: Beacon Press.

Joyce, Kathryn (2013a), 'Orphan Fever: The Evangelical Movement's Adoption Obsession', *Mother Jones* May/June 2013. Available online: http://www.motherjones.com/politics/2013/04/christian-evangelical-adoption-liberia.

Joyce, Kathryn (2013b), *The Child Catchers: Rescue, Trafficking, and the New Gospel of Adoption*, New York, NY: PublicAffairs.

Julian of Norwich (1978), *Showings*, Mahwah, NJ: Paulist Press.

Kamitsuka, Margaret D. (2007), *Feminist Theology and the Challenge of Difference*, Oxford: Oxford University Press.

Kang, Namsoon (2013), *Cosmopolitan Theology: Reconstituting Planetary Hospitality, Neighbor-Love, and Solidarity in an Uneven World*, St Louis, MO: Chalice Press.

Kärkkäinen, Veli-Matti (2014), *Trinity and Revelation*, Grand Rapids, MI: Eerdmans.

Karras, Ruth Mazo (2014), 'Reproducing Medieval Christianity', in Adrian Thatcher (ed.), *The Oxford Handbook of Theology, Sexuality and Gender*, 271–86, Oxford: Oxford University Press.

Keener, Craig S. (1992), *Paul, Woman and Wives: Marriage and Women's Ministry in the Letters of Paul*, Peabody, MA: Hendrickson.

Keller, Catherine (2006), 'Is That All? Gift and Reciprocity in Milbank's *Being Reconciled*', in Rosemary Radford Ruether and Marion Grau (eds), *Interpreting the Postmodern: Responses to 'Radical Orthodoxy'*, 18–35, New York, NY: T&T Clark International.

Kelsey, David (2009), *Eccentric Existence: A Theological Anthropology* (in two volumes), Louisville, KY: Westminster John Knox Press.

Kierkegaard, Søren (1983), *Fear and Trembling* and *Repetition*, trans. and ed. Howard V. Hong and Edna H. Hong, Princeton, NJ: Princeton University Press.

Kierkegaard, Søren (1985), *Philosophical Fragments* and *Johannes Climacus*, trans. and ed. Howard V. Hong and Edna H. Hong, Princeton, NJ: Princeton University Press.

Kilby, Karen (2012), *Balthasar: A (Very) Critical Introduction*, Grand Rapids, MI: Eerdmans.

Kim, Hosu (2015), 'The Biopolitics of Transnational Adoption in South Korea: Preemption and the Governance of Single Birthmothers', *Body and Society* 21(1): 58–89.

Kirk, H. David (1964), *Shared Fate: A Theory of Adoption and Mental Health*, New York, NY: The Free Press.

Kirk, H. David (1985), *Adoptive Kinship: A Modern Institution in Need of Reform*, Port Angeles, WA: Ben-Simon Publications.

Klesse, Christian (2007), *The Spectre of Promiscuity: Gay Male and Bisexual Non-Monogamies and Polyamories*, Aldershot: Ashgate.

Koch, Timothy R. (2001), 'A Homoerotic Approach to Scripture', *Theology and Sexuality* 7(14): 10–22.

Köstenberger, Andreas J. and David W. Jones (2012), *Marriage and the Family: Biblical Essentials*, Wheaton, IL: Crossway.

Kotre, John N. (1996), *Outliving the Self: Generativity and the Interpretation of Lives*, New York, NY: W. W. Norton.

Koyama, Kosuke (1985), *Mount Fuji and Mount Sinai: A Critique of Idols*, Maryknoll, NY: Orbis Books.

Kundera, Milan (1984), *The Unbearable Lightness of Being*, London: Faber and Faber.

Lambeth Conference (1908), 'Resolution 41'. Available online: http://www.anglicancommunion.org/resources/document-library/lambeth-conference/1908/resolution-41?author=Lambeth+Conference&year=1908.

Lambeth Conference (1988), 'Resolution 26: Church and Polygamy'. Available online: http://www.anglicancommunion.org/resources/document-library/lambeth-conference/1988/resolution-26-church-and-polygamy?subject=Marriage&language=English.

Lancy, David F. (2015), *The Anthropology of Childhood: Cherubs, Chattel, Changelings* (2nd edition), Cambridge: Cambridge University Press.

Law, David R. (2010), 'A Cacophony of Voices: The Multiple Authors and Readers of Kierkegaard's *The Point of View for my Work as an Author*', in Robert L. Perkins (ed.), *The Point of View*, 12–47, Macon, GA: Mercer University Press.

Lawrence, Sheila (2005), 'Let Them Soar!', *Above Rubies* 64: 5.

Levin, Yigal (2006), 'Jesus, "Son of God" and "Son of David": The "Adoption" of Jesus into the Davidic Line', *Journal for the Study of the New Testament* 28: 415–42.

Lieu, Judith (2008), *I, II and III John: A Commentary*, Louisville, KY: Westminster John Knox Press.

Lifton, Betty Jean (1975), *Twice Born: Memoirs of an Adopted Daughter*, New York, NY: McGraw-Hill.

Lincoln, Andrew T. (2013), *Born of a Virgin? Reconceiving Jesus in the Bible, Tradition, and Theology*, London: SPCK.

Liss, Andrea (2009), *Feminist Art and the Maternal*, Minneapolis, MN: University of Minnesota Press.

Llewellyn, Dawn (2016), 'Maternal Silences: Motherhood and Voluntary Childlessness in Contemporary Christianity', *Religion and Gender* 6(1): 64–79.

Long, John L. (2003), *Sterilization Reversal: A Generous Act of Love*, Dayton, OH: One More Soul.

Long, Ronald E. (2005), 'Heavenly Sex: The Moral Authority of an Impossible Dream', *Theology and Sexuality* 11(3): 31–46.

Loughlin, Gerard (1996), 'The Want of Family in Postmodernity', in Stephen C. Barton (ed.), *The Family in Theological Perspective*, 307–28, Edinburgh: T&T Clark.

Loughlin, Gerard (2003), 'Sex After Natural Law', *Studies in Christian Ethics* 16(1): 14–28.

Loughlin, Gerard (2004), 'Gathered at the Altar: Homosexuals and Human Rights', *Theology and Sexuality* 10(2): 73–82.

Lüdemann, Gerd (1998), *Virgin Birth? The Real Story of Mary and Her Son Jesus*, London: SCM Press.

Ludlow, Morwenna (2007), *Gregory of Nyssa, Ancient and (Post)modern*, Oxford: Oxford University Press.

MacDougall, Scott (2015), 'Three Questions for the Authors of "Marriage in Creation and Covenant"'. Available online: http://www.anglicantheologicalreview.org/static/pdf/ conversations/ScottMacDougallResponse.pdf.

Mason, Alistair (1996), 'Victorian Family Values', in Hugh S. Pyper (ed.), *The Christian Family – A Concept in Crisis*, 46–61, Norwich: Canterbury Press.

Mayoue, John C. (2005), 'Legal and Ethical Challenges of Embryonic Adoption', in Timothy P. Jackson (ed.), *The Morality of Adoption: Social-Psychological, Theological, and Legal Perspectives*, 262–82, Grand Rapids, MI: Eerdmans.

McCarthy, David Matzko (2007), 'Fecundity: Sex and Social Reproduction', in Gerard Loughlin (ed.), *Queer Theology: Rethinking the Western Body*, 86–95, Oxford: Blackwell.

McKeown, John (2011), 'US Protestant Natalist Reception of Old Testament "Fruitful Verses": A Critique', PhD thesis, University of Liverpool.

McKeown, John (2014), *God's Babies: Natalism and Biblical Interpretation in Modern America*, Cambridge: Open Book Publishers.

Meilaender, Gilbert (2005), 'Letters to Derek', in Timothy P. Jackson (ed.), *The Morality of Adoption: Social-Psychological, Theological, and Legal Perspectives*, xxiv–xxv, Grand Rapids, MI: Eerdmans.

Milbank, John (1995), 'Can a Gift be Given? Prolegomena to a Future Trinitarian Metaphysic', *Modern Theology* 11(1): 119–61.

Milbank, John (1997), *The Word Made Strange: Theology, Language, Culture*, Oxford: Blackwell.

Milbank, John (1998), 'Gregory of Nyssa: The Force of Identity', in Lewis Ayres and Gareth Jones (eds), *Christian Origins: Theology, Rhetoric, Community*, 94–116, London: Routledge.

Milbank, John (2003), *Being Reconciled: Ontology and Pardon*, New York, NY: Routledge.

Milbank, John (2012), 'Gay Marriage and the Future of Human Sexuality', ABC Religion and Ethics, 13 March 2012. Available online: http://www.abc.net.au/religion/ articles/2012/03/13/3452229.htm.

Milbank, John (2013), 'Do Christians Really Oppose Gay Marriage?', Westminster Faith Debates, Queen Elizabeth II Conference Centre, Westminster, UK, 18 April 2013. Extracts reproduced in Woodhead, Linda (ed.) (2014), *Modern Believing* 55(1): 27–38.

Miles, Rebekah (2007), 'Why We Should Revise Browning's Model of a 60-Hour Workweek for Parents', in John Witte Jr., M. Christian Green and Amy Wheeler (eds), *The Equal-Regard Marriage and its Friendly Critics: Don Browning and the Practical Theological Ethics of the Family*, 151–72, Grand Rapids, MI: Eerdmans.

Miller-McLemore, Bonnie (1994), *Also a Mother: Work and Family as Theological Dilemma*, Nashville, TN: Abingdon Press.

Miller-McLemore, Bonnie J. (2007), 'Generativity, Self-Sacrifice, and the Ethics of Family Life', in John Witte Jr., M. Christian Green and Amy Wheeler (eds), *The Equal-Regard Family and its Friendly Critics: Don Browning and the Practical Theological Ethics of the Family*, 17–41, Grand Rapids, MI: Eerdmans.

Mohler, James A. (1991), *Late Have I Loved You: Augustine on Human and Divine Relationships*, New York, NY: New City Press.

Moltmann, Jürgen (1967), *Theology of Hope*, London: SCM Press.

Moltmann, Jürgen (1996), *The Coming of God: Christian Eschatology*, London: SCM Press.

Monti, Joseph (1995), *Arguing About Sex: The Rhetoric of Christian Sexual Morality*, Albany, NY: SUNY Press.

Moore, Stephen D. (1994), *Poststructuralism and the New Testament: Derrida and Foucault at the Foot of the Cross*, Minneapolis, MN: Fortress Press.

Moore, Stephen D. (2006), *Empire and Apocalypse: Postcolonialism and the New Testament*, Sheffield: Sheffield Phoenix Press.

Moss, Candida and Joel Baden (2015), *Reconceiving Infertility: Biblical Perspectives on Procreation and Childlessness*, Princeton, NJ: Princeton University Press.

Moss, David and Lucy Gardner (1998), 'Difference: The Immaculate Concept? The Laws of Sexual Difference in the Theology of Hans Urs von Balthasar', *Modern Theology* 14: 377–410.

Moxnes, Halvor (2003), *Putting Jesus in his Place: A Radical Vision of Household and Kingdom*, Louisville, KY: Westminster John Knox Press.

Muers, Rachel (2007a), 'A Queer Theology: Hans Urs von Balthasar', in Gerard Loughlin (ed.), *Queer Theology: Rethinking the Western Body*, 200–11, Oxford: Blackwell.

Muers, Rachel (2007b), 'Feminist Theology as Practice of the Future', *Feminist Theology* 16(1): 110–27.

Muers, Rachel (2008), *Living for the Future: Theological Ethics for Coming Generations*, London: T&T Clark.

Muers, Rachel (2015), *Testimony: Quakerism and Theological Ethics*, London: SCM Press.

Muñoz, José Esteban (1999), *Disidentifications: Queers of Color and the Performance of Politics*, Minneapolis, MN: University of Minnesota Press.

Muñoz, José Esteban (2009), *Cruising Utopia: The Then and There of Queer Futurity*, New York, NY: New York University Press.

Myers, Ched (2008), *Binding the Strong Man: A Political Reading of Mark's Story of Jesus (Twentieth Anniversary Edition)*, Maryknoll, NY: Orbis Books.

Najmabadi, Afsaneh (2013), 'Genus of Sex or the Sexing of Jins', *International Journal of Middle East Studies* 45(2): 211–31.

Neuner, Josef and Jacques Dupuis (eds) (1982), *The Christian Faith in the Doctrinal Documents of the Catholic Church*, New York, NY: Alba House.

Nichols, Aidan (2000), *No Bloodless Myth: A Guide Through Balthasar's Dramatics*, Edinburgh: T&T Clark.

Nichols, Aidan (2007), *Redeeming Beauty: Soundings in Sacral Aesthetics*, Aldershot: Ashgate.

Niebuhr, H. Richard (1999), *The Responsible Self: An Essay in Christian Moral Philosophy*, Louisville, KY: Westminster John Knox Press.

Ntagali, Stanley (2015), 'Abp's Statement on Same-Sex Marriage in TEC and USA', Church of Uganda, 7 July 2015. Available online: http://churchofuganda.org/news/abps-statement-on-same-sex-marriage-in-tec-and-usa.

Nydam, Ronald J. (1992), 'Adoption and the Image of God', *Journal of Pastoral Care* 46(3): 247–60.

O'Connell, Gerald (2015), 'Full Transcript of Pope's Press Conference on Flight from Manila', *America: The National Catholic Review*, 19 January 2015. Available online: http://americamagazine.org/content/dispatches/full-transcript-popes-press-conference-flight-manila.

O'Donovan, Oliver (1982), *Transsexualism and Christian Marriage*, Nottingham: Grove Books.

O'Donovan, Oliver (1984), *Begotten or Made?*, Oxford: Clarendon Press.

O'Siadhail, Micheal (2015), *One Crimson Thread*, Hexham: Bloodaxe Books.

Owen, Samuel A. (1990), *Letting God Plan Your Family*, Wheaton, IL: Crossway.

Pannenberg, Wolfhart (1969), *Theology and the Kingdom of God*, Louisville, KY: Westminster John Knox Press.

Pannenberg, Wolfhart (2001), *Metaphysics and the Idea of God*, Grand Rapids, MI: Eerdmans.

Patton-Imani, Sandra (2005), 'Navigating Racial Routes', in Timothy P. Jackson (ed.), *The Morality of Adoption: Social-Psychological, Theological, and Legal Perspectives*, 78–113, Grand Rapids, MI: Eerdmans.

Paul VI (Pope) (1965), *Gaudium et Spes: Pastoral Constitution on the Church in the Modern World*. Available online: http://www.vatican.va/archive/hist_councils/ii_vatican_council/documents/vat-ii_const_19651207_gaudium-et-spes_en.html.

Peppard, Michael (2011), 'Paul and John on Divine Sonship', *Catholic Biblical Quarterly* 73: 92–110.

Persson, Markus (2011), 'Terrain Generation, part 1', *The Word of Notch* blog, 9 March 2011. Available online: http://notch.tumblr.com/post/3746989361/terrain-generation-part-1.

Peters, Ted (1996), *For the Love of Children: Genetic Technology and the Future of the Family*, Louisville, KY: Westminster John Knox Press.

Petrey, Taylor G. (2016), *Resurrecting Parts: Early Christians on Desire, Reproduction, and Sexual Difference*, London: Routledge.

Pickstock, Catherine (2013), *Repetition and Identity*, Oxford: Oxford University Press.

Pius XI (Pope) (1930), *Casti Connubii: Encyclical of Pope Pius XI on Christian Marriage*, 30 December 1930. Available online: http://www.papalencyclicals.net/Pius11/P11CASTI.HTM.

Pontifical Council for Justice and Peace (2004), *Compendium of the Social Doctrine of the Church*. Available online: http://www.vatican.va/roman_curia/pontifical_councils/justpeace/documents/rc_pc_justpeace_doc_20060526_compendio-dott-soc_en.html#SECRETARIAT%20OF%20STATE.

Post, Stephen G. (2005), 'Adoption: A Protestant Agapic Perspective', in Timothy P. Jackson (ed.), *The Morality of Adoption: Social-Psychological, Theological, and Legal Perspectives*, 172–87, Grand Rapids, MI: Eerdmans.

Power, Rachel (2012), *The Divided Heart: Art and Motherhood*, Fitzroy, Australia: Red Dog.

Presser, Stephen B. (2005), 'Law, Christianity, and Adoption', in Timothy P. Jackson (ed.), *The Morality of Adoption: Social-Psychological, Theological, and Legal Perspectives*, 219–45, Grand Rapids, MI: Eerdmans.

Pride, Mary (1985), *The Way Home: Beyond Feminism, Back to Reality*, Wheaton, IL: Good News Publications.

Primates of the Anglican Communion (2016), 'Communiqué from the Primates of the Anglican Communion: Walking Together in the Service of God in the World', 15 January 2016. Available online: http://www.primates2016.org/articles/2016/01/15/communique-primates/

Pritchard, Stephanie and Diana W. Bianchi (2012), 'Fetal Cell Microchimerism in the Maternal Heart: Baby Gives Back', *Circulation Research* 110: 3–5.

Provan, Charles D. (1989), *The Bible and Birth Control*, Monongahela, PA: Zimmer.

Putin, Vladimir (2015), address delivered at Presentation of the Order of Parental Glory, The Kremlin, 1 June 2015. Available online: http://en.kremlin.ru/events/president/news/49613.

Pyper, Hugh S. (2012), *The Unchained Bible: Cultural Appropriations of Biblical Texts*, London: T&T Clark.

Raymond, Janice G. (1994), 'Reproductive Gifts and Gift-Giving: The Altruistic Woman', in Lois K. Daly (ed.), *Feminist Theological Ethics: A Reader*, 233–43, Louisville, KY: Westminster John Knox Press.

Rees, Geoffrey (2011), *The Romance of Innocent Sexuality*, Eugene, OR: Wipf and Stock.

Richie, Cristina (2013), 'Disrupting the Meaning of Marriage? Childfree, Infertile and Gay Unions in Evangelical and Catholic Theologies of Marriage', *Theology and Sexuality* 19(2): 123–42.

Ricoeur, Paul (1967), *The Symbolism of Evil*, Boston, MA: Beacon Press.

Ricoeur, Paul (1992), *Oneself as Another*, Chicago, IL: University of Chicago Press.

Rieger, Joerg (2007a), 'Christian Theology and Empires', in Kwok Pui-lan, Don H. Compier and Joerg Rieger (eds), *Empire and the Christian Tradition: New Readings of Classical Theologians*, 1–13, Minneapolis, MN: Fortress Press.

Rieger, Joerg (2007b), *Christ and Empire: From Paul to Postcolonial Times*, Minneapolis, MN: Fortress Press.

Robinson, Margaret (2009), 'Turning Points in Identity and Theology: Bisexual Women Choosing Between Monogamous and Polyamorous Relationships', PhD thesis, Regis College and Toronto School of Theology.

Rogers, Eugene F. (ed.) (2002), *Theology and Sexuality: Classic and Contemporary Readings*, Oxford: Blackwell.

Rosemann, Philipp W. (2004), *Peter Lombard*, Oxford: Oxford University Press.

Rosenberg, Judith Pierce (1995), *A Question of Balance: Artists and Writers on Motherhood*, Watsonville, CA: Papier-Mache Press.

Roth, Catherine P. and David Anderson (eds) (1986), *St John Chrysostom: On Marriage and Family Life*, Crestwood, NY: St Vladimir's Seminary Press.

Ruether, Rosemary Radford (2000), *Christianity and the Making of the Modern Family: Ruling Ideologies, Diverse Realities*, Boston, MA: Beacon Press.

Sanger, Carol (2012), 'The Birth of Death: Stillborn Birth Certificates and the Problem for Law', *California Law Review* 100(1): 269–312.

Schaff, Philip (ed.) (1886), *Nicene and Post-Nicene Fathers, Series 1, Volume 8: St Augustine: Exposition on the Book of Psalms*, New York, NY: Christian Literature Publishing Co. Available online: http://www.ccel.org/ccel/schaff/npnf108.

Schaff, Philip (ed.) (1887a), *Nicene and Post-Nicene Fathers, Series 1, Volume 3: St Augustine: On the Holy Trinity; Doctrinal Treatises; Moral Treatises*, trans. Peter Holmes and Robert Ernest Wallis, Buffalo, NY: Christian Literature Publishing Co. Available online: http://www.ccel.org/ccel/schaff/npnf103.v.ii.xviii.html.

Schaff, Philip (ed.) (1892), *Nicene and Post-Nicene Fathers, Series 2, Volume 5: Gregory of Nyssa: Dogmatic Treatises, Etc.* Buffalo, NY: Christian Literature Publishing Co. Available online: http://www.ccel.org/ccel/schaff/npnf205.html.

Schaff, Philip (1898), *Nicene and Post-Nicene Fathers, Series 2, Volume 13: Selected Epistles of Gregory the Great, Ephraim Syrus, Aphrahat*, Buffalo, NY: Christian Literature Publishing Co. Available online: http://www.ccel.org/ccel/schaff/npnf213.ii.vii.xxx.html.

Schaff, Philip (ed.) (2007), *Nicene and Post-Nicene Fathers: First Series, Volume V: St Augustine: Anti-Pelagian Writings*, New York, NY: Cosimo.

Schlein, Stephen (ed.) (1987), *Erik H. Erikson: A Way of Looking at Things: Selected Papers from 1930 to 1980*, New York, NY: W. W. Norton and Company.

Scott, James M. (1992), *Adoption as Sons of God: An Exegetical Investigation into the Background of Huiothesia in the Pauline Corpus*, Tübingen: JCB Mohr.

Scott, Rachel (2004), *Birthing God's Mighty Warriors*, Longwood, FL: Xulon Press.

Scully, Jackie Leach (1998), 'When Embodiment Isn't Good', *Theology and Sexuality* 9: 10–28.

Seglow, Jean, Mia Kellmer Pringle and Peter Wedge (1972), *Growing Up Adopted: A Long-Term National Study of Adopted Children and their Families*, Slough: National Foundation for Educational Research in England and Wales.

Selinger, Suzanne (1998), *Charlotte von Kirschbaum and Karl Barth: A Study in Biography and the History of Theology*, University Park, PA: Pennsylvania State University Press.

Shaw, Jane (2013), 'Bonds of Affection? Debates on Sexuality', in Kwok Pui-lan (ed.), *Anglican Women on Church and Mission*, 37–54, London: Canterbury Press Norwich.

Sherwood, Yvonne (2015), 'The "Hagaramic" as a Provocation for Euro-American, "Judeo-Christian" Parochialism: Surrogate, Rogue, Resident Alien, *Foreign Body*', keynote lecture delivered at Religion, Gender and Body Politics: Postcolonial, Postsecular and Queer Perspectives conference, Utrecht University, Netherlands, 12 February 2015.

Simmons, Chace (2007), 'The Rhythm of Womanhood', *Above Rubies* 71: 8.

Smith, David Livingstone (2007), 'Beyond Westermarck: Can Shared Mothering or Maternal Phenotype Matching Account for Incest Avoidance?', *Evolutionary Psychology* 5(1): 202–22.

Snyder, Steven H. and Mary Patricia Byrn (2005), 'The Use of Prebirth Parentage Orders in Surrogacy Proceedings', *Family Law Quarterly* 39(3): 633–62.

Solevåg, Anna Rebecca (2013), *Birthing Salvation: Gender and Class in Early Christian Childbearing Discourse*, Leiden: Brill.

Song, Robert (2014), *Covenant and Calling: Towards a Theology of Same-Sex Relationships*, London: SCM Press.

Soskice, Janet Martin (2007), *The Kindness of God: Metaphor, Gender and Religious Language*, Oxford: Oxford University Press.

Spinks, Bryan D. (2006), *Early and Medieval Rituals and Theologies of Baptism from the New Testament to the Council of Trent*, Aldershot: Ashgate.

Spivak, Gayatri Chakravorty (1991), 'Identity and Alterity: An Interview', *Arena* 97: 65–76.

Stevenson-Moessner, Jeanne (2003), *The Spirit of Adoption: At Home in God's Family*, Louisville, KY: Westminster John Knox Press.

Stevick, Richard A. (2014), *Growing Up Amish: The Rumspringa Years*, Baltimore, MD: Johns Hopkins University Press.

Stewart, Jacqui (2008), 'Embryo, Person and Pregnancy: A New Look at the Beginning of Life', in Bernard Hoose, Julie Clague and Gerard Mannion (eds), *Moral Theology for the Twenty-First Century: Essays in Celebration of Kevin Kelly*, 89–96, London: T&T Clark.

Stewart, Jacqueline (2010), 'Paul Ricoeur and "The Human Person, Adequately Considered"', in J. Verheyden, T. L. Hettema and P. Vandecasteele (eds), *Paul Ricoeur: Poetics and Religion*, 393–404, Leuven: Peeters.

Stewart, Jacqueline (2015), 'Liturgy, Theology, Marriage and the Family', *The Way* 52(4): 21–31.

Stockton, Kathryn Bond (2009), *The Queer Child, or Growing Sideways in the Twentieth Century*, Durham, NC: Duke University Press.

Stockton, Kathryn Bond (2014), 'How I Toast Marriage While Being Against It', speech delivered at University of Utah Pride Week Gayla, October 2014. Transcript available online: https://bullybloggers.wordpress.com/2015/05/30/same-sex-adultery-bigamy-gold-digging-and-divorce-or-what-is-to-be-done-after-marriage-equality/.

Stone, Ken (2005), *Practicing Safer Texts: Food, Sex and Bible in Queer Perspective*, London: T&T Clark.

Stone, Lawrence (1977), *The Family, Sex and Marriage in England 1500-1800*, London: Penguin.

Strohl, Jane E. (2001), 'The Child in Luther's Theology: "For What Purpose Do We Older Folks Exist, Other Than to Care for … the Young?"', in Marcia JoAnn Bunge (ed.), *The Child in Christian Thought*, 134–59, Grand Rapids, MI: Eerdmans.

Stuart, Elizabeth (2003), *Gay and Lesbian Theologies: Repetitions with Critical Difference*, Aldershot: Ashgate

Taylor, John Hammond, (ed. and trans.) (1982), *St Augustine: The Literal Meaning of Genesis*, Vol. II, Books 7–12, New York, NY: Newman Press.

Teman, Elly (2010), *Birthing a Mother: The Surrogate Body and the Pregnant Self*, Berkeley, CA: University of California Press.

Thatcher, Adrian (1999), *Marriage After Modernity*, Sheffield: Sheffield Academic Press.

Thatcher, Adrian (2002), *Living Together and Christian Ethics*, Cambridge: Cambridge University Press.

Thatcher, Adrian (2007), *Theology and Families*, Oxford: Blackwell.

Thatcher, Adrian (2015), 'Families', in Adrian Thatcher (ed.), *The Oxford Handbook of Theology, Sexuality and Gender*, 590–607, Oxford: Oxford University Press.

Torode, Sam and Bethany Torode (2002), *Open Embrace: A Protestant Couple Rethinks Contraception*, Grand Rapids, MI: Eerdmans.

Traina, Cristina L. H. (2001), 'A Person in the Making: Thomas Aquinas on Children and Childhood', in Marcia JoAnn Bunge (ed.), *The Child in Christian Thought*, 103–33, Grand Rapids, MI: Eerdmans.

Tran, Jonathan (2009), 'The Otherness of Children as a Hint of an Outside: Michel Foucault, Richard Yates and Karl Barth on Suburban Life', *Theology and Sexuality* 15(2): 189–209.

Triseliotis, John (1973), *In Search of Origins: The Experiences of Adopted People*, London: Routledge and Kegan Paul.

Trumper, Tim J. R. (2001), 'An Historical Study of the Doctrine of Adoption in the Calvinistic Tradition', PhD thesis, University of Edinburgh.

United Nations Department of Economic and Social Affairs (2013), *World Population Prospects: The 2012 Revision: Key Findings and Advance Tables*, New York, NY: United Nations. Available online: http://esa.un.org/wpp/documentation/pdf/wpp2012_keyfindings.pdf.

Van Aarde, Andries (2001), *Fatherless in Galilee: Jesus as Child of God*, Harrisburg, PA: Trinity Press International.

Vatter, Miguel (2006), 'Natality and Biopolitics in Hannah Arendt', *Revista de Ciencia Política* 26(2): 137–59.

Vattimo, Gianni (2002), *After Christianity*, trans. Luca D'Isanto, New York, NY: Columbia University Press.

Veaux, Franklin and Eve Rickert (2014), *More Than Two: A Practical Guide to Ethical Polyamory*, Portland, OR: Thorntree Press.

Walton, Heather (2014), *Writing Methods in Theological Reflection*, London: SCM Press.

Ward, Frances (2009), 'Why I Still Read John Donne: An Appraisal of Grace Jantzen's *Becoming Divine*', in Elaine L. Graham (ed.), *Grace Jantzen: Redeeming the Present*, 55–68, Farnham: Ashgate.

Ward, Graham (1995), *Barth, Derrida and the Language of Theology*, Cambridge: Cambridge University Press.

Ward, Graham (1998), 'The Erotics of Redemption – After Karl Barth', *Theology and Sexuality* 8: 52–72.

Waters, Brent (2001), *Reproductive Technology: Toward a Theology of Procreative Stewardship*, Cleveland, OH: Pilgrim Press.

Webster, Alison (1995), *Found Wanting? Women, Sexuality and Christianity*, London: Cassell.

Weiss, Jessica (2004), 'Fathering and Fatherhood', in Paula S. Fass (ed.), *Encyclopedia of Children and Childhood in History and Society*, vol. 2, 348–53, New York, NY: Macmillan.

Wells, Samuel (2006), *God's Companions: Reimagining Christian Ethics*, Oxford: Blackwell.

Werpehowski, William (2001), 'Reading Karl Barth on Children', in Marcia JoAnn Bunge (ed.), *The Child in Christian Thought*, 386–405, Grand Rapids, MI: Eerdmans.

Whipple, Dorothy (1943), *They Were Sisters*, London: John Murray and The Book Society.

Willard, Mara (2013), 'Birth as Labor and Natality: Hannah Arendt and the Politics of Maternality', *Theology and Sexuality* 19(3): 227–45.

Williams, Rowan (2002), 'The Body's Grace', in Eugene F. Rogers (ed.), *Theology and Sexuality: Classic and Contemporary Readings*, 309–21, Oxford: Blackwell.

Williams, Rowan (2009), 'Religious Faith and Human Rights', lecture given at London School of Economics, 1 May 2008. Available online: http://www.archbishopofcanterbury. org/articles.php/1161/archbishop-religious-faith-and-human-rights.

Winter, Bruce W. (2003), *Roman Wives, Roman Widows: The Appearance of New Women and the Pauline Communities*, Grand Rapids, MI: Eerdmans.

Witte, John Jr. (2009), *The Sins of the Fathers: The Law and Theology of Illegitimacy*, Cambridge: Cambridge University Press.

Witte, John Jr. (2015), *The Western Case for Monogamy over Polygamy*, Cambridge: Cambridge University Press.

Witte, John Jr., M. Christian Green and Amy Wheeler (eds) (2007), *The Equal-Regard Marriage and its Friendly Critics: Don Browning and the Practical Theological Ethics of the Family*, Grand Rapids, MI: Eerdmans.

Wooden, Cindy (2014), 'Married Couples Prefer Pets to Children Because of "Comfort Culture"', *Catholic Herald*, 2 June 2014. Available online: http://www.catholicherald. co.uk/news/2014/06/02/married-couples-prefer-pets-to-children-because-of-comfort-culture-says-pope-francis/comment-page-7/

Woodhead, Linda (ed.) (2014), *Modern Believing* 55(1), special edition: 'What British People Really Believe'.

Wyndham, John (1955), *The Chrysalids*, London: Penguin.

Yang, Jie (2015), 'Informal Surrogacy in China: Embodiment and Biopower', *Body and Society* 21(1): 90–117.

Zimmerman, Anthony (1959), 'Morality and Problems of Overpopulation', *Proceedings of the Fourteenth Annual Convention of the Catholic Society of America*, 5–27.

Zizioulas, John D. (2008), *Remembering the Future: An Eschatological Ontology*, London: T&T Clark.

Index

CPSIA information can be obtained
at www.ICGtesting.com
Printed in the USA
LVHW050826190419
614807LV00007B/58/P

9 780567 685841